ALL AT SEA

ALL AT SEA

John Cooke

Matador
9 Priory Business Park,
Wistow Road, Kibworth Beauchamp,
Leicestershire. LE8 0RX
Tel: 0116 279 2299
Email: books@troubador.co.uk
Web: www.troubador.co.uk/matador
Twitter: @matadorbooks

ISBN 978 1800460 744

British Library Cataloguing in Publication Data.
A catalogue record for this book is available from the British Library.

Printed and bound in Great Britain by 4edge Limited
Typeset in 11pt Minion Pro by Troubador Publishing Ltd, Leicester, UK

Matador is an imprint of Troubador Publishing Ltd

For Kate, who both lost and found herself on the
precarious path we call life.
And for others on the brink of adulthood, I'd say,
follow your dreams and never stop trying.
Seek, and you will surely find.

ACKNOWLEDGEMENTS

I'd like to thank a few people who have travelled with me on what, I feel, has been a long and arduous voyage. Firstly my wife, Carol, who I love dearly. Her work ethic, fortitude, and two great friends – Percy Verance and Will Power – have undoubtedy rubbed off on me over the years. And so, amongst other things, I am eternally grateful to her for that.

Wrekin Writers, a writing group I enrolled with a few years ago, have given me the confidence to *believe*. And in particular two of their members: firstly, John Dyson, who has literally been another pair of eyes to me. His proof-reading and encouragement have been a constant fillip to my endeavours. Secondly, Simon Whaley, an author in his own *write*. His business acumen and knowledge of the intricacies within the publishing world have been an invaluable resource; something which he has willingly shared with me on more than one occasion. And lastly to Kit Colbeck, wherever he is. The journal he kept of HMS Hermes' 1968–1969 commission has been a rich source of information as we travelled halfway around the world. Thanks to you all; without you I would never have finished this book.

'You wan taxi, Joe…
You wan Seiko…
You wan girl, Joe, young girl…Virgin…'

1960s vendor – Singapore.

PREFACE

The concept of time rarely appears on the radar of young people when they are growing up. It's difficult for anyone to make the right decisions without guidance; but it is especially difficult for young people who have no parents or carers, or anyone else they can trust or believe in. All young people have a God-given right to be loved and nurtured; but many are left disadvantaged in this respect.

It's hard enough for any young person to think things through; but it's far more difficult for those who feel emotionally insecure, or who have been physically abandoned and let down by their nearest and dearest. Yet in spite of the desolation these young people experience, many are still expected to make life-changing decisions during their mid-teens. It's hardly surprising that many such kids don't *give a f---* at that age; never mind thinking about what the future might hold for them. Too many young people are blind to post-school opportunities, and are often left to make decisions that can lead to poor life choices and possible long-term negativity.

All young people need to be wanted and yearn for a sense of belonging, but many of the so-called *disadvantaged* seek consolation elsewhere. Their desire for comfort and reassurance can lead to life within a sub-group; there they not only feel valued but have the freedom to live outside the constraints of family and convention.

Such vulnerable young people often succumb to peer pressure and can be easily coerced into acts of spontaneity which, in themselves, can be another contributory factor to poor decision-making.

Any young person, irrespective of background, can act impulsively and make rash decisions. The fallout is not always immediate; it can take time to manifest itself. For those young people who are alone, with little or no support, it's often too late to settle into another life once they've made that initial lifestyle decision, often a decision that rarely has anything to do with individual needs, aspirations, or talents.

Many young people cannot imagine what life will be like in ten, fifteen, twenty or thirty years' time, as the future is a long way off, a distant, unreal place. When I was seventeen I thought I'd live forever. I couldn't imagine being thirty years old; I thought if I ever got to thirty then the best years of my life were gone. *Finito!* It was then I made a poor decision, a life-changing mistake.

This is my story.

ON THE ROADS

I first met *Rib*, short for Ribble, in Bournemouth. He'd chosen his *road name* after the river that runs through his home town of Preston. I met him under the pier where a dozen or so *beats* congregated towards the end of each day. We'd chat, smoke, and sing, as a few had guitars. And you could always rely on Red Rock to get up, shuffle some sand, and give us his rendition of Little Richard's *Tutti Frutti.*

They were sunny, carefree days where we'd con chicks, who spread themselves out on the manicured lawns of the Pleasure Gardens during their lunch hours. They'd laze there, sitting on coats and jackets, snacking, enjoying the flowers, fresh air and sunshine. We'd smile and say, '*Hi,*' whenever we passed by, and if we received a nice smile, or positive response, we'd ask if we could join them. We'd try to con a sandwich, or a tanner for a cup of tea, and mostly we did alright.

We were seventeen and it was the first time we'd been totally free from parental control; life during that summer was a huge adventure for both of us. Although free, we didn't have much money, but I felt truly blessed when the kind old sun shone down and took the chill from my bones. Each day was filled with anticipation, not knowing who you might meet or what it might bring. Life back then was still a mystery to me, full of untold secrets. I was glad to be alive and took each day as it came.

We'd wander from the pier, through the Pleasure Gardens to French Corner, a popular meeting place, to see who was about. I'd always hope to meet a Swedish chick from the Language School situated on the opposite side of the road; but it never happened. I only ever bumped into other *beats* who were part of the gang who gathered under the pier. It was the only time in my life where I can truly claim I was as free as a bird. Rib and I came and went with our sleeping bags casually slung over our shoulders; they were the only things that weighed us down and they weighed nothing at all.

When it got late and darkness began to creep in we'd wind our way from under the pier, and head westwards along the promenade towards the Chines. We'd pass the sounds of the nearby neon-lit amusement arcade, playing its music of false hope and promises. Then slowly the babble and lights of the town surrendered to silent shadows and darkness as we sauntered along the sea front. The only sound accompaniment was the relentless tide crashing in and sucking its way out again; otherwise peace and tranquillity reigned. By the time we arrived at our sleepy hollow beneath the pines of Alum Chine our shadows had melted into a midnight hue. We'd pause at the entrance and gaze skywards, totally in awe of the star-peppered veil that stretched endlessly over our heads. The silver sprinkling of the cosmos had us mesmerised. Rib always pointed out a terrier-like cluster of stars he called *The Dog*, which I now know to be part of the Orion constellation. Such moments are forever encapsulated in that place and time. We'd stand there enthralled, unable to comprehend the enormity, complexity and beauty of the universe. I felt so small and insignificant in the grander scheme of things: inconsequential, yet paradoxically not out of place. Somehow I felt *I belonged*. I was at one with the world.

There were other nights when we'd sing our way along the prom as we left the day behind. A favourite was our own version of an old Leadbelly song:

Black girl, black girl, tell me no lies,
where did you sleep last night?
In the Chines in the Chines,
where the sun never shines,
We shivered the whole night through...

I never thought I'd get tired of Bournemouth that summer, but I did. Rib and I decided to hitch back along the south coast to Portsmouth. I'd met a girl there before I travelled to Bournemouth when she had given me a haircut at her house. She mentioned I could get a job in the factory where she worked if I wanted one. Rib thought we'd give this a try to earn some money, but when we arrived at her house and knocked on the door we were told she'd left. She'd gone back home to her family in Petersfield.

We slept in a bus shelter that night but decided to hitch back to Southampton in the morning. We knew it was a famous shipping port and were intrigued when we passed through it on our way to Portsmouth. We both wanted to see what it was like as we hadn't been there before. We wanted to visit the docks and have a general mooch around, and thought if the worst came to the worst, then we could always hitch back to Bournemouth.

Our lift back along the coast road to Southampton dropped us off right next to a sign that pointed us towards the docks. I thought fate had conspired to lead us there. It was drizzling, with the wind blowing light rain in off the sea. It was early, but the first light of day was breaking through the clouds in the distance; the last remnants of a murky night were disappearing. We found ourselves standing on Eastern Dock, and we both clambered up onto some railings to scan the view. The rising rays from the golden orb now sparkled across the Solent, as if the surface was teeming with crystal droplets. We stood there in silence, contemplating all that lay before us. It was a new dawn, a new day, a new adventure. We stretched out and up on those railings – like figureheads on the prow of a ship – allowing the dampness to evaporate from our jackets. We held our arms out in the shape of a Y, and let the breeze flow through our hair. We gazed out to sea as far as we could to the horizon, when suddenly a huge passenger liner came into view. It loomed larger and larger, heading straight towards us. I'd seen a picture of the *Queen Mary* once before and thought this could be her, with the three funnels and all her bold black, white and red magnificence. As a young boy I'd always dreamed of going to sea and now both the sea and this liner romanced me away. Rib and I looked at one another in awe; we were hypnotised. The sea had us hooked.

'*We could be coming home on that ship from faraway places – foreign lands...*' I said.

'*We'd have stories to tell, of the adventures we'd had...*' added Rib.

'*With money in our pockets,*' I said.

'*To go back on the roads again,*' said Rib.

We stood there mesmerised, until Rib said, '*Come on, we'll't join Merch.*' And so we set off to find the maritime office. I still think of that huge ship, with its three funnels, as the *Queen Mary*, but I can never be sure. We didn't hang around long enough to see if it was, but I'll always think of her as the *QM*.

*

We sought refuge in a park, which was a stone's throw from the bustle of the port on one side and the city centre on the other. It was a semi-rural sanctuary, an oasis of peace and calm, dissecting two frenetic commercial worlds. The park was filled with old plane trees and long stretches of grass for kids to play on. We were sprawled out, lying full length on some bench seats that surrounded a statue commemorating the achievements of General Gordon. We lay on our backs, fifteen yards apart, using our folded sleeping bags as pillows and gazed skywards. We were silent, and disappointed; we pondered our next move. From where I lay I could see the long necks of dockyard cranes towering above. They stretched high up over the trees, reaching out for puffy-white clouds that billowed across a powder-blue sky. I imagined the cranes were gloating at us, leaning over, saying, *'Look at those fools down there. They think life's easy. Well, it isn't! You have to work at it. Things don't just happen. You have to make them happen.'*

Our plans to join the Merchant Navy had been scuttled. The guy at the shipping office told us we couldn't join *'the Merch'* in Southampton. He said we'd have to go home, Rib to Liverpool (as he was from Preston), and me back to Manchester. This wasn't an option for us; we were having too much of *a gas* on the roads. It was our hassle-free adventure, going out each day to see what we could find. We felt blessed, free to do what we wanted and go where we pleased. I'd never experienced anything like it before. It was the first (and only) time I lived totally carefree. Rib's broad Preston accent suddenly cracked the silence. *'Let's join't Royle,'* he said, half sitting up on one elbow. *'We can still go to sea.'*

'Oh, I dunno,' I said, hesitating. *'I'm not sure. What about the discipline? You have to wear a uniform, you know. And we'll have to get our hair cut.'*

'Yeah, but we'll still go to sea, see foreign places, travel the world…' said Rib.

6

I then thought about money as I had none. Rib had some money in a Post Office savings account and when times got tough, and we became desperate with no chicks to con, he'd go and make a withdrawal. I'd been borrowing off him. Two, five, ten bob, here and there, and it was slowly mounting up. I wondered how I was ever going to repay him.

'I suppose we could go and find out about it... see what's involved,' I conceded. And with that we got to our feet, grabbed our sleeping bags and set off. We headed off down Briton Street, turned into High Street, and on towards Bargate where the Royal Navy recruiting office was. Not long after we had walked in I knew there'd be no escape. The form-filling was endless but they plied us with endless mugs of coffee and biscuits. The recruiting team arranged for us to take IQ tests the next day. The leading hand was stumped with some of the questions and had to ask his superior:

'What do I put here, Chief? It asks for job or profession?'
'What is it you do?' the chief asked us.
'We're hitching,' I replied.
'Well, where do you live?'
'Nowhere.'
'So where did you sleep last night?'
'In a bus shelter. We're sleeping rough.'
'Put them down as vagrants.'

Because we'd slept in a bus shelter and had no fixed abode, they sorted out some accommodation for us. The address they gave us was further on, back up past Bargate. It was an old Georgian double-fronted property, accessed through a heavy iron gate and up some concrete steps. It was impressive. The magnolia façade looked recently painted, and contrasted sharply with the black gloss paint on an old oak door. There was a brass letter box and a matching brass knocker, which we knocked loudly.

The proprietor, Clyde, welcomed us in. Everywhere was warm and carpeted. The place looked immaculate; first impressions outside were matched inside; we were made up. Clyde reinforced the understanding that we could only stay for two nights, as it was a residence reserved for older retired servicemen. And they all looked to be either septuagenarians or octogenarians. He was doing the RN recruitment office a favour by allowing us to stay. For us it was luxurious: warm comfy beds, hot baths and meals. We weren't due at the RN recruiting office until 10.30 the next morning, and so after breakfast we joined the old guys in the drawing room with our mugs of tea.

It was a slow process as most of them had sticks or walking aids, and trooped in one after the other until they found their regular seats. They appeared excited to have youth in their presence and when we were all sitting comfortably, regaled us with stories of their own service experiences. Suddenly Godfrey, an ex-RAF pilot, replete with white handlebar moustache, banged his cane on the floor and shouted:

'Come on, Kiwi! Show them your party trick!'

All the chairs hugged the walls round the room, which meant with our presence there wasn't a vacant seat to be had. When they heard Godfrey it was as if they were responding to an order from a superior officer. The whole room, except Kiwi, started stamping their feet and banging their sticks on the floor.

'*Kiwi! Kiwi!*' they shouted in unison.

Kiwi grasped the brass knob of his stick with both hands and levered himself up into a standing position. He raised his stick aloft as if holding up a trophy and turned full circle, making sure everyone in the room had his full attention. Slowly he made his way to the centre of the room where again he held his cane aloft. I thought for a moment he was about to magic it away, but instead he lowered it and tossed it over to where he'd been sitting.

'*Kiwi! Kiwi!*' The room resounded again. He stood there waiting for silence to be restored. And then, with great deliberation, he stretched out his arms for balance and lifted his right leg up off the ground, so that it was dangling, bent at the knee. He began to count, '*One, two, three…*' until the whole room joined him, counting until he reached "*ten*". Kiwi, a nonagenarian, was the oldest resident, and he had stood on his prosthetic leg for a full ten seconds. Everyone in the room, including Rib and I, clapped, cheered and shouted, '*Hurray! Hurray! Well done, Kiwi!*' who graciously accepted the rapturous applause he received. And without causing offence to anyone, we fell into some side-splitting laughter.

Later that day Rib and I easily passed our entry tests. We were recommended by the recruitment staff to train as radio operators (ROs); this involved nine months occupational training after six weeks of compulsory *square-bashing* and basic seamanship training. We wanted to sail away to sea as soon as possible, and so declined the RO option. We held out for the branch which had the shortest training route inside the RN, which happened to be training to be a steward. And so, without giving it another thought, we enlisted as *flunkies*. I reversed the phone charges to the family I lived with in Manchester. I told them I'd passed the entrance tests for the Royal Navy; everyone sounded made-up for me. They were pleased (and surprised) that I'd made a decision about my future.

Although there were still doubts in my mind about signing on the dotted line, I couldn't help feeling pleased with myself. I knew deep down that I wouldn't be with this family forever but still didn't want to let anyone down. I knew I owed them, and my Great Uncle Harry who'd made the arrangement for me to live with them. I had to try and follow it through. The Armed Forces made sense for everybody concerned; it was a simple solution. I'd have a job, with food and accommodation provided. I'd also be able to pay off my debt to Rib. Yet I continually had nagging doubts as to whether I was doing the right thing, and these doubts remained with me right up until the day I caught the train down to Portsmouth to sign on.

FAMILY

Ever since I started to wear long trousers I'd been asked, *What are you going to do when you leave school?* And the answer was always the same: *I don't know.* Although I'd now committed myself to something, I still wasn't sure whether I was doing the right thing.

My childhood had been an unhappy one, ever since my mother walked out when I was four years old. I cried and cried when she left, but I never saw her again. She left me with my dad, a sergeant in the RAF, who placed me in a home run by nuns. I hated it from the first day when older kids stole all my toys. And then when my dad was supposed to come and visit me, I'd wait for him in a darkened room, but he rarely showed up. Bath times in the home were something else I dreaded, when the Holy Sisters, *Mary Mother of God*, would dump me in a bath full of other bigger kids. They'd make more room for themselves by constantly kicking, elbowing and splashing me. There was nothing I liked about the place. Everything was alien to me and a far cry from the place I'd always known as *home.*

Eventually it became too much, and one day after school I decided to turn in the opposite direction and head back to the RAF base. Unfortunately a girl from the home spotted me taking the wrong turn and shouted that she was going to tell Sister. I took off, running away along the Corstorphine Road as fast as my little legs would carry me, bawling my eyes out as I went. A stranger came out from his front garden and stopped me; then he flagged down a tram and instructed the conductor to drop me off at the terminus at the end of the road. As soon as I took the road towards the airbase a lorry driver picked me up; thankfully he dropped me off at the main gates to RAF Turnhouse. I made my way to the sergeants' mess and found my dad on the phone in the entrance lobby. When he turned and saw me I heard him say, *'Oh, he's here now!'* It was the sister from the home. I was glad he never sent me back there; instead I was sent to a pre-prep boarding school in Hythe on the south coast. I spent several years there as a boarder, living with my gran (dad's widowed mother) during school holidays. I later learned it was my gran who paid the fees. During most of this time my dad served abroad with the RAF; but when I was eleven he asked me if I wanted to live at home again. He'd met a woman he planned to marry, and although I'd just started another boarding school (which I hated), I jumped at the chance to leave and live at home again. I spent a summer holiday with Dad and his new partner and got on really well with her. She bought me my first pair of jeans; they were something I cherished as I'd never had a pair before. And during that holiday I started to call her *Mummy*, which she didn't seem to mind. I spent another term at school before I said goodbye to everyone there, and headed back to live in my new home. I was happy and full of expectation, but when I arrived I discovered the woman he planned to marry had disappeared. Dad hadn't mentioned this to me previously, and he never gave a reason afterwards as to what happened between them. I wasn't brave enough to ask him and I never saw her again. I'd told everyone at school I was leaving to go and live at home with a new mum, and so there was no way I was going to go back and face them all again.

Gran's personal circumstances meant that it was no longer possible for her to look after me, and so it was decided I'd still live with my dad, just the two of us. He was now stationed at a missile base near a village in Northamptonshire and rented a council house, whilst I was enrolled at the local secondary school in a town three miles away. Dad worked split shifts at the airbase, and so I found myself either having to get myself up and catch the bus to school in the morning or come home to an empty house after school. It was a lonely, miserable time, when I learned more about my dad and his drinking. I found out how he could turn on you when he'd had a few, how he could be hyper-critical, sarcastic and nasty; a real *Jekyll and Hyde* character.

And then Dad met another woman, Diane, and brought her back to the house a few times. She was kind and brought me some strawberries and cream when she visited. She'd park her car outside the house and sometimes stay late into the night.

Dad said if anyone in the village asked about her visits I was to say she was my aunt. All the kids in the village knew this was a lie and took the piss out of me; they knew she lived on a farm about ten miles away. One night when I'd gone to bed I was woken up by Dad shouting. I crept out of my bedroom and sat on the top stair of the landing. I could hear Dad shouting at Diane in the front room; making demands in his drunken, vile way. *'Take that off! Take your dress off! Take it off now!'* She was saying, *'No. No. Stop it, Vic. I don't want to.'* He kept on, even though it was obvious she didn't want to get undressed. But Dad wouldn't stop and he got louder and louder. And then when I thought I heard her sobbing it made me cry too. I tip-toed back into my bedroom and lay still in bed, listening, and then I heard a door slam. I felt ashamed and cried some more until I finally fell asleep. I wasn't surprised when I didn't see Diane again. At twelve years old I still had faith in my (hero) dad. I hadn't a clue as to what went on with my mum and Pauline, the woman I thought he was going to marry, or the reasons why they had deserted Dad. His alcoholic illness hadn't registered with me.

It was whilst I was living with Dad that we had a fallout and nearly came to blows. I'm not sure how it started, but he came at me and decked me with a full-on punch to the side of the face. I couldn't fight back, although I'd clenched my fists down by my side. I saw him come for me, and I was ready, but I couldn't throw a punch at him. I just couldn't; all I kept thinking as he advanced was, ' *You're my dad, you're my dad.*' So I just stood there and let him hit me.

At fourteen, with only a year to go before I could legally leave school, the missile base closed down and Dad was posted miles away to an airbase in Yorkshire. He decided I should stay at the secondary school to finish my education, and found me some lodgings in the town near school. The proprietor of the boarding house became my new Aunty Ida. I now lived in a large detached Georgian house that had three floors and numerous bedrooms, most of which were occupied by travelling salesmen during the week. I was given a large ground-floor bedroom and Aunt Ida allowed me to have friends round to play cards or table football. I also had a new Uncle Walter, Aunt Ida's husband, who was a local bookmaker. I learned it was through him that Dad had arranged my lodgings; things about my father were now beginning to click. I was learning more about the type of person he really was.

Aunty Ida received an allowance for my upkeep from the RAF, and began putting money away for me in a Post Office savings account. She bought me a suit and overcoat; clothes, other than school uniforms, that I'd never had before. I got a delivery job in the town and played lots of sports outside of school with my mates. We attended youth clubs in the evenings, and I loved the time I spent there. It was the happiest year of my childhood.

When I reached fifteen, and was still living with Aunt Ida, I had a seamless transition from school into work. I was taken on as a chainboy with a surveyor named Sid, who was a lodger at the boarding house. Sid, it turned out, was up to no good and fiddled our timesheets. He not only made false claims regarding lodging allowance for me and kept the money for himself, but he claimed we worked every weekday from Monday to Friday. The truth was that on both of those days he was travelling up to Scotland and back again; there he spent every weekend luxuriating in the arms of a lady friend. On one of these free days, when he was travelling, I was out playing football with my mates and turned an ankle. It was badly sprained and I couldn't put any weight on it, and so ended up on crutches for a couple of weeks.

During this time, when I was hobbling around, my father turned up unexpectedly, both drunk and broke. He made me withdraw a month's wages from the savings account Aunt Ida had started for me, on the pretext of it being a loan. When she found out money was missing and I explained to her what had happened, she gasped, threw her hands to her mouth, turned crimson and stormed out of the room.

Aunt Ida already knew something of my father's reputation, and of the relationship I'd shared with him when we lived together in the village. She knew about the time when I'd been left on my own for hours without anything to eat. How I'd ventured down to the local pub to see if Dad was there, but no one had seen him; how I'd asked if they had something I could eat. A pork pie, perhaps? Aunt Ida had heard that story.

It wasn't long after my father's ill-fated visit to borrow money from my PO account that Great Uncle Harry, my grandmother's brother, got involved in my affairs. I don't know how he heard of my predicament, but he did. But there were other issues, concerning my welfare, that surfaced simultaneously around this time. Firstly, I now needed another roof over my head, as Aunt Ida and Uncle Walter had decided to sell the boarding house and retire. Secondly, my employer, the fiddling surveyor Sid, had been caught out and the police were scouring the length and breadth of the country for him. He'd been trying to get a new van from the firm, as multiple trips to Scotland had resulted in both excessive mileage and wear and tear. They'd refused to replace his van with a new one and so he set fire to it, claiming it had been an accident.

As for me, I'd never had to make a decision in my life, about what was happening, or what was going to happen to me. Someone else had always taken charge and told me where I was going to live, and who was going to look after me. Adults were in total control of my life; I just waited for things to happen. Any serious career-making decisions about what I wanted to do with my life were equally baffling and mysterious. I might as well have been living in another world. Life was just passing me by without a clue as to what I might do in the future. I lived in a mental fog as far as my future was concerned. It was at this point that Great Uncle Harry (GUH), Henry Cobden Turner, appeared on the scene. He was quite a big wheel in Manchester, and was fully aware that my father was incapable of looking after me. Much later I saw a letter he wrote to my only *bona fide* Aunt (Betty). She was Dad's sister, living in Scotland, and GUH asked if she was in a position to look after me. In it he stated my father was, 'A complete waste of time.' It was no surprise to me that Aunt Betty declined the offer to look after a fifteen-year-old stranger, as she had recently got married. I didn't blame her.

Instead GUH found a Catholic family in Manchester who were willing to take me on. The head of the household was a widow who he'd employed in the past, and so she became my new Aunty Marj. She had three children, and the family lived above a tobacco, confectionery and gift card shop in Moss Side. Chris, the eldest son, was five years older than me and had moved away to study at Cambridge University. Tim, two years younger than me, was the youngest and still at school. And Susie, the daughter, was two years older than me and had enrolled at the Manchester School of Music. It was an academic family and something GUH advocated. One of the first things he mentioned to me just after we first met was, 'Education's the thing, my boy.' But I didn't particularly wish to return to learn back then, as my educational experience at secondary school had hardly blown me away.

Still the question remained as to what I was going to do with my life. And since it was highly unlikely I was going to make it as a footballer, my work experience with the surveyor came to the fore. It was a possible career move as I enjoyed both the outdoors, the fresh air and the freedom it offered. However, there was an academic drawback to this ambition – mathematics. It was my worst subject at school, something I couldn't get to grips with. But I attended Stretford Tech for eighteen months, at GUH's behest, in pursuit of this surveying ambition. Unfortunately I only managed to gain the paltry achievement of two O Levels during my time there: History and Geography.

After summer term I hit the road with Huw, a college friend, and we hitched down south looking for vacation work. Apart from some labouring in private gardens our plans didn't materialise; although we did meet some sweet Norwegian girls and decided to follow them to Bournemouth. When we arrived it turned out they had far greater aspirations than to spend time with two skint hitch-hikers. We were left with little alternative but to seek solace with the resident group of *beats* who hung out there. They'd congregate under the pier each day, and then doss down and sleep in the Chines at night. Huw eventually went back home to Trafford Bar, where he had a job lined up in a bank, whilst I stayed on in Bournemouth and teamed up with Rib. It was some weeks later when we both wandered into the Royal Navy careers centre in Southampton.

HMS ST VINCENT –
R N TRAINING PART 1

When I arrived at HMS St Vincent in Gosport, Hampshire, and went through the arched main gates, I was confronted by an enormous rectangular parade ground. On the opposite side to the main gate was a huge mast and rigging, surrounded by a safety net that stood twenty feet off the ground. The top of the mast towered over the roofs of some three-storey redbrick buildings, which were uniformly spaced out behind the mast. You entered them through a chain of precisely constructed arches that stretched the whole length of the parade ground. I soon discovered these were to be our accommodation blocks, home sweet home for the next six weeks of intensive basic training.

As I stood there waiting to sign on, I wondered if I was man enough to get through RN training? Could I take *whatever it takes?* I thought about my freedom, then the discipline, of being a man and, absurdly, of John Wayne. I really thought about my future, perhaps seriously for the first time. Did I really want to do this? The answer was: I felt it was too late to back down. I had to sign on. I had to give it a go and save face. John Wayne kicked in again with those immortal words: *'A man's gotta do, what a man's gotta do.'* Was it a *macho thing?* I wondered what he'd do in similar circumstances, and thought he'd just get on with it. He'd probably say, *'Get on your hoss!'* Such crazy thoughts filled my head, but I ignored them and blindly went through with the signing on process.

A gust of wind blew my collar-length hair across my face; I stroked it back behind my ears, and remembered I'd mentioned haircuts to Rib back in Southampton. I didn't want a haircut, and I wasn't too enamoured about having a regulation short back and sides. The clacking rhythm of synchronised studded boots on tarmac brought me round. I half expected to see Rib come doubling round the corner, but it wasn't him. I still owed him over £20 and one of the main reasons for signing up was to pay him back. It was a deal we made on the roads, when we hitched around the country together. Rib had been called up before me because I was born abroad and my application took longer to process.

When I left my adopted family for Portsmouth I knew they had expectations of me; as did GUH, who came to the railway station to see me off. I knew I owed him something and didn't want to let him down. My debt to Rib also played on my mind. Whatever I thought about myself, I always thought I was honest and kept my promises. And yet here I was, waiting by the main gates of HMS St Vincent, still with nagging doubts about signing my life away for nine years, not to mention three additional years in reserve. I was only seventeen, and my service time wouldn't start until I reached eighteen, but I kept kidding myself with, *It'll be OK. Everything will work out.* But the reality was that I didn't have a clue what I was letting myself in for.

*

We must have looked a slovenly bunch, or more precisely a motley crew, when we first assembled in front of our training instructor. All of us had been shorn of longer locks, and looked as though a saucer had been placed squarely on top of our heads and everything below that, down to the collar, had been completely shaved off. Our haircuts only exacerbated the size and angles our ears stuck out from our heads.

We were supposed to be standing at ease but few, if any of us, fully comprehended what that meant. Some of us slouched with legs crossed and arms folded; others held kit bags, or had grounded their kit bags and stood with their hands in their pockets. We lined up in two rows as our instructor paced up and down in front of us. I'm sure he didn't know what to make of us, although he must have been through this many times before. Suddenly he stopped and came to attention. He did a right-turn to face us and then carried out the correct stand-at-ease drill.

'*This is the correct way to stand-at-ease*,' he said. '*Now do it!*'

There were some mumblings and shuffling of feet until silence gradually prevailed. Everyone attempted to replicate the stance of our leader.

'*They call me BB*,' he growled. '*That's not Bridget Bardot. It's Bastard Bates. And it's my job to chase you from arsehole to breakfast.*' BB then proceeded along the rows, halting and addressing each of us, correcting our posture as he went.

'*Chin up; shoulders back; chest out; stomach in; head up.*' He went through this routine with all of us.

Soon afterwards we assembled in a long hut to mark out our kit. We were issued with black ink pads and carved wooden blocks with our own initials and surnames on. The task was to press the wooden blocks into the ink pad and then on to our kit. The ideal result was to have your name in the right place, so that when you folded your kit neatly for *muster* your name would be printed at the front. Kit musters occurred regularly during basic training, and they demanded that each piece of kit was stacked neatly on top of another. This left a precise square with your name displayed at the front in a straight line from top to bottom.

Unfortunately Halifax, a pasty-faced skinny youth with bright ginger hair, got it wrong. Somehow he'd managed to stamp his name on the inside of his underpants and on the wrong leg. These pants were the original passion-killers with the texture of muslin, the colour of urine, and a button fly; they hung down to below knee level. In all the time I was in the RN I only saw one person continue to wear them as underpants; everyone else preserved them in their pristine condition for kit-musters. Once Halifax realised his mistake he looked nervously around and slowly raised his hand. You couldn't help but notice how his haircut magnified his large ears, which shot out at right angles from the side his head.

'What is it, lad?' barked BB. Halifax explained his error. 'What's your name?'

'Halifax, sir.'

'Your lugs remind me of a Hackney cab with its doors wide open. What have you got inside 'em? Wax!' Some derisory laughter filled the hut. 'You can't have a hearing problem or you wouldn't be here, so try and bloody well listen. If this wasn't your 'f...ing first day you'd be on a f...ing charge!'

I was just glad it wasn't me who'd made a cock-up. I had no idea about rank at the time and thought BB was an officer, which he was, a petty officer (a PO). He was a non-commissioned officer, the equivalent of a sergeant in the Army or RAF, but I thought he was of a much higher rank at the time. Although not a tall man BB looked impressive. He was tanned, had a chiselled jaw and clean-cut features. His uniform, which consisted of a black tie and blazer, white shirt and white-topped cap with a black peak and gold braided badge at the front, was immaculate. The toe-caps of his boots glistened blackness, and contrasted vividly with the immaculate white gaiters he wore above them. But I'd never heard so much "f...ing and f...ing", especially by someone who I thought was an officer and a gentleman. Yes, we all swore (kids do) but it shocked me. I couldn't believe it, and yet in a matter of days such swearing and cussing passed between us without note.

It didn't take Rib long to track me down, and I managed to pay off some of my debt with left-over cash I had travelled down with. He said he was in a boxing match the following day. It made me quite envious as I'd done some boxing at the pre-prep boarding school I'd been sent to. My arrival at HMS St Vincent meant I was too late to enter myself, but I managed to stand at the ringside and watch Rib perform. The draw for opponents seemed evenly matched as both boxers were more or less of equal height and build.

The bell went and Rib came out slowly, crouching. I shouted to him to get his guard up as it was too low. His gloves were down by his waist band and he looked as though he wasn't sure of what he was supposed to do. The other guy skipped straight out from his corner, and caught Rib unawares with a straight left jab. Rib momentarily stood motionless, as if stunned. And then, in that split second, Rib's opponent followed up with a right hook. It landed somewhere in the vicinity of his chin, but in all honesty it was more of a glancing blow than a clear-cut punch. Unbelievably, Rib's knees buckled and he fell to the canvas. He momentarily knelt there, with both eyes shut, before he keeled over onto one side. He lay on the canvas right by my ringside position, his face pointing towards me, as the referee began his count: '*One, two, three...*' When the ref got to five, six… Rib opened his eyes and saw me. He stared briefly at me and then quite deliberately winked. The ref reached eight, nine, ten, and counted him *out*. Afterwards Rib openly admitted that the first punch had hurt him, and so he decided to go down as soon as his opponent threw a second punch. He said he didn't want to get hurt. I said if I'd known he was going to get knocked out so easily, I'd have put money on the other guy and paid off the rest of my debt to him. Whatever, we had a good laugh about it.

At HMS St Vincent there was another guy in my mess called Hole; we all called him *Plug*. He appeared to have his limitations and struggled to keep his kit in order. Plug was always losing or mislaying things, and was forever having to buy replacement silks, lanyards and caps. He struggled to put a high gloss on the toe-caps of his boots, which were supposed to shine like mirrors. BB said the reflection of your face, shining from the toe-caps of your boots, should be good enough for you to see for shaving. The only way you could get such a high gloss result on the toe-caps of your boots was through persistence, patience and endurance. It took me hours and hours of polishing, rubbing little circles into the leather with a soft cloth, dipped in boot polish and pumice powder. Plug took twice as long as anyone else to achieve this, and only with the assistance from some others in the mess did he succeed.

During these intensive first six weeks of basic training it didn't go unnoticed that Plug received regular food parcels from his mum. He stashed all these goodies away in a standard-issue small brown case, which he kept on top of his locker.

One of the guys, Wilko, a chocolate addict, had been hankering for a while to see what goodies Mum sent Plug; eventually his curiosity got the better of him. When Plug was away tending to his ablutions one evening he wandered over to Plug's bunk with the key to his own brown case, and tried it in Plug's. Eureka! He struck gold. Silence reigned in the mess as everyone tuned into Wilko's move, but as soon as he lifted the lid on Plug's case everyone cheered and hollered; they descended like gulls on a landfill site. By the time I arrived Plug's case had been completely rifled; biscuits, cake and chocolate had vanished. All that remained was a solitary item, an individual fruit pie in its cardboard casing. *Mmm – apple pie,* I thought, *one of my favourites.* It was too good to resist. And so under the dim light of my fading torch, I opened it and hurriedly took a healthy bite. *'Ugh!'* It wasn't apple; it was apricot. I'd always had an aversion to apricots ever since I was served a bowl of them for dessert on one of my school dinners; there, to my horror, I found a nest of maggots squirming in and around the fruit. I'd never tasted an apricot since. I quickly replaced the pie back in its container and returned it to Plug's case. Wilko locked the case again and placed it back on top of Plug's locker. It was as if no one had touched it. Plug returned and, as was his custom, sat down on his bunk and reached for his case. He unlocked it and lifted the lid.

'Oh no!' he cried. *'Someone's taken all my grub! Who's taken it? I don't believe it.'* The sound of sniggering filtered through the mess. Plug then appeared to be appeased: *'Well, at least someone's had the decency to leave me my individual fruit pie; that's something.'* He quickly unpacked it from its box. *'Oh no! Someone's taken a big bite out of it!'* The sniggering erupted into uncontrollable laughter. Poor old Plug.

Rib finished his basic training ahead of me because he signed on a few weeks before me, but I managed to clear my debt to him before he left for Part 2 training. I now didn't owe anybody anything, although I was conscious that GUH and members of my adopted family had expectations of me. The fact that I didn't want to let anyone down weighed heavily on my mind, and I still felt obliged to make a go of it.

At the end of six weeks' intensive training everyone in our class could swim, or stay afloat for three minutes, follow marching orders, tie knots, climb rigging, shoot and perform rifle drill. We learned to look after and present our kit for muster, and keep a high gloss on our boots. We all agreed BB was a sound guy who had earned the respect of the whole class. We were genuinely sorry to say goodbye to him. Before I left HMS St Vincent I asked him if it was possible to switch trades, as I now had reservations about being a steward, never mind serving nine years in the RN. I thought another branch or trade might be more interesting than the life of a steward.

BB off-handedly dismissed my request, and claimed chief stewards were some of the happiest guys he'd ever known on board ship. Perhaps I should have pursued this request further and been more determined, but at the time I didn't know any better. I thought to myself, *Well, carry on. I've survived basic training, and I've tried to swap trades. Give it a bit longer and see what happens.*

PART II TRAINING – WINTER AT HMS PEMBROKE

In the 1960s HMS Pembroke was the hub of training for all things catering. Our billets were rows of long single-storey huts at the far end of the camp, about a mile and a half from the main gates. At around 2100 hours the 'Nine O'Clockers' wagon rolled into trainee town. It was an old open cart that rumbled along on two giant spoked wheels. Two trainee chefs steered it from the front, one on either side, each holding on to a long wooden handle. The cart was crammed with finger rolls, baps, hot dogs and burgers.

The journey was an arduous one because the galley was adjacent to the main gates. The trainees steered the wagon as best they could but sometimes had to hang on for dear life, as it swerved and bounced around, especially when it came across a pot-hole or uneven terrain. Often the *Nine O'Clockers* wagon arrived late, which if you tried to second-guess this delay, by lingering until the last minute in the relative comfort and warmth of your billet, you'd end up stepping outside into the freezing cold to find yourself at the end of a queue a mile long.

The cart escorts were also responsible for doling out these precious victuals, and were scrupulous in obeying orders; these stipulated each trainee should only receive either one hot dog or one burger. There should have been enough *Nine O'Clockers* for every trainee to have a bap or a roll, but these guys couldn't care less if there wasn't enough to go round. It didn't take us long to suss out something was amiss, because the last few trainees would always end up without a morsel. It happened to some of us from our hut a few times, and it didn't go unnoticed that this supper shortfall coincided with one of the regular escorts, a smart-arse Jock, being on duty. Every time it happened was on his watch, and he'd add insult to injury by standing there smirking, and reciting the same old line to those unfortunates at the end of the queue who were left feeling aggrieved and hungry.

'Remember lads. There's only two kinds of people in this world: the quick and the dead!'

The subject of *scran* (or lack of it) became a topic of conversation almost from the day we arrived. Food standards regularly hit the *no star* award, being both bland and tepid. And when on the odd occasion they passed the quality muster, they managed to fail on quantity. As time passed myself and a couple of messmates, Skags and

Doog, had a daily *drip* about our rations. Inevitably, the smart-arse Jock, or the CJ, as we referred to him (Cocky Jock), entered these conversations. By the end of the conversation, if not during the course of it, he was usually referred to as *a wanker*! On that we were all agreed.

Apart from us all being hungry 17-and 18-year-olds, with insatiable appetites, there was another reason for our obsession about the standard of food that was dished up at HMS Pembroke, the so-called HQ of catering training for the entire RN. When you entered the dining area you passed into, and along, a servery, moving left to right and collecting your scran as you went. You then returned to the dining tables through an exit at the far end. All meals were served on manufactured machine-pressed stainless-steel trays, with indents that could accommodate soup, main and dessert. The tepid temperature of the food they served meant that if you had more than one course, then the others would be cold by the time you got to eat them.

Another major problem was the servery ceiling; it was plastered with thousands of cockroaches. These were continually on the move, habitually climbing over one another. Unfortunately they'd failed to master the ability to cling on and so nose-dived, kamikaze-like, straight into the trays that passed below. You could have been George Best, weaving left and right, but you could always guarantee to have a few free extras in your meal. We imagined the galley, situated directly behind the servery, must have been ten times worse. But whenever this was mooted over a meal it was left, unlike the cockroaches, hanging in the air…

Our daily *drips* about victuals not only added to our misery, but gradually sowed the seeds of a master plan: *The Great Nine O'Clockers Robbery*. One night, when previous intelligence informed us that the CJ was on duty, we decided to put our robbery plan into action. We knew the *Nine O'Clockers* wagon would roll along Central Avenue from the main gates and although there was no cover, along this stretch of road, there was some further along when it merged into a narrow lane. This lane led down to our huts and was fenced on both sides. It was not much bigger than a footpath and only just wide enough for the cart to travel down: an ideal place for an ambush. Anyone steering the cart from the rear would find it virtually impossible to squeeze themselves around the sides to the front. The pathway ran for about 500 yards and had a recess halfway along that accessed a storage hut. There was some shrubbery near the recess entrance which offered cover, and so we decided this was where we'd lie in wait for the *Nine O'Clockers* cart.

Under the cover of darkness we left our hut and stepped out into a damp, cold, misty night. Patches of fog became thicker as we left the bright lights of the huts behind. I guessed no one in their right mind would be out tonight and we saw no one. We strode on, purposefully, keeping our heads down, heading towards the amber glow of the narrow pathway. The chilled night air heightened the tension and filled my head with sinister images: the dimly lit alleyway; the damp, empty, narrow path; the freezing, clinging fog. It was murky and complemented my feelings of suspended anticipation. We waited for the familiar sound of heavy studded boots on tarmac.

Before we left our hut we dressed to replicate the *Nine O'Clockers* escorts: boots, gaiters, gloves, sailor's caps and long navy gaberdine coats that trailed below the knee. Under our coats we'd concealed standard-issue gas respirators which we planned to wear as masks. They were the old rubber-faced version, with two huge eye-pieces and a long concertinaed trunk attached to a tin box. When we donned these we resembled green-eyed monsters straight out of a 1950s horror film. As soon as we arrived at the recess we went through our plans.

'*Remember. I'll take the CJ*,' said Skags. Skags wasn't that tall, but his shoulders were as broad as his torso was long. He was solid. His neck, as thick as a silver birch, was the giveaway. I never met anyone who wanted to take him on, particularly if they sensed his rippling physique beneath his shirt. I was glad to have him on our side and relished the thought of him spearheading the ambush.

'*I've got the bag*,' said Doog. '*So as soon as we stop 'em I'll be ready*.'

'*I'll grab as much as I can*,' I said. '*If I get a dozen rolls or baps that'll be OK. Let's get ready*.' We knew we'd hear them approaching, pushing that creaky old cart and clacking along in their boots; we donned our masks in readiness. As they approached our hide-away Skags jumped out and screamed, '*Aaaagh!*' The muffled roar from within his mask sounded more like a bellowing cow in the final throes of labour. As luck would have it the CJ had the handle nearest to us, and Skags knocked his cap off as he threw his arms up when he jumped out. It flew up in the air and rolled back down the path behind him. The CJ immediately deserted his post by letting go of the cart and scampering back after his errant cap.

Skags instinctively grabbed the handle as I pulled my mask out from my chin.

'No one's going to get hurt,' I blurted out to the other escort. 'We just want some grub.' Doog held the bag open and I grabbed some rolls and baps and pushed them in. The hot stuff, heavily wrapped in silver foil, followed. We were soon done. We hurried back to our billets, de-masking as we took a detour around the Nine O'Clockers' queue. Once inside our billet we stuffed ourselves, plying burgers and hot dogs with some red sauce purchased earlier from the NAAFI. There were a few extras for some of our messmates.

Apart from poor victuals there was another major blight on my time at HMS Pembroke, which manifested itself in a creep called Carter. On the night of the robbery evidence suggested that Carter must have been at the end of the Nine O'Clockers queue, because he returned to our hut empty-handed. He appeared puzzled, as if he knew something was amiss. I doubt he noticed that the three of us were absent from the Nine O'Clockers' queue that night, but he returned whilst some of us were still eating. The convivial atmosphere and air of bonhomie inside the mess appeared to reinforce his notion that something wasn't quite right. Although suspicious, Carter wasn't brave enough to challenge anyone directly. Instead, he wandered up and down the mess in a perplexed state. He snooped around, peering into gash cans and spittoons as he went. At one point I saw him bend down and unravel some discarded foil wrappers. He knew something had gone on but couldn't work out what had happened and who had been involved. And no one was going to tell him.

Carter had been selected as our class leader by the time I arrived at HMS Pembroke, and it was rumoured he'd had an infestation of crabs at HMS St Vincent during Part 1 training. It was thought he spread it around his mess through dirty clothes or unwashed bedding; although how he initially became infected remained a mystery. Rumour had it that someone else reported his outbreak of crabs to the sick bay, since Carter ignored his infection and stubbornly refused to seek medical care.

I now lived in the same hut as Carter and could see his personal hygiene left a lot to be desired. He was a pale, sickly-looking guy, who had a myriad of spots and blind boils erupting beneath his skin. His facial blemishes served only to match his greasy complexion and matted hair. Carter had a reluctance to shower and wash, and appeared to wear the same clothes and use the same bedsheets for days on end. Their was an odour about him and I soon found myself avoiding his company whenever I could. My dislike of him and his hygiene habits soon gravitated into a lack of respect for him. I couldn't believe the RN had placed Carter in charge as class leader, let alone allowed him to perform duties within a catering environment. To me it didn't make any sense and only added to my growing disillusionment with the RN and how it operated.

And these feelings towards Carter were compounded when he put me on a charge for disobeying an order. It was when Taf and I were talking quietly after lights out.

We both admitted we'd made mistakes signing on, but realised there was no easy route back into civvy street. We were discussing where we would go if we went absent without leave (AWOL) and what our punishment would be if, and when, we returned back on board. We came to the conclusion that going on the run once, wouldn't cut the mustard as far as getting a discharge from the RN was concerned. At the time our options were to either serve at least six years, when you could then buy yourself out, or serve the full nine years after your eighteenth birthday, which was what we'd initially signed on for.

I was standing by Taf's bunk and we were whispering when Carter ordered us to stop talking and for me to return to my bunk. As we weren't offending anyone we carried on for a while. I think Carter, as class leader, wanted to prove a point and demonstrate his authority, so he put us both on a charge for *disobeying an order*. Taf and I came to an agreement between us; because it was me out of my bunk we agreed to say that I was the only one doing the talking, which meant I'd take the rap for both of us. It seemed pointless for us both to be charged for the same offence. Carter couldn't prove otherwise. And so Taf and I stuck to the same story and the charge against him was dismissed; I was put on *Number Nines* for two weeks.

We both felt the sentence meted out to me was disproportionate to the crime, if you could call it a crime? *Number Nines* meant that I had to continually report to the regulating office, which was next to the main gate a mile and a half away. I had to be there first thing in the morning at 6am, when I was given a menial task for an hour, such as polishing the huge brass bell which was on display there. I'd then return to the trainee camp and carry on normal training duties until lunchtime, when I'd have to report back to the main gate again. This resulted in me losing half an hour of my one-hour lunch break. At the end of the day I'd be given another menial task to do for an hour, before finally at 2100 hours, I'd have to report to the regulators at the main gate again to prove I was still on board and hadn't skipped ashore and taken some leave. Essentially it was hassle; it meant extra work and stoppage of leave. I had little physical time to myself during that fortnight, and I missed out on *Nine O'Clockers* – although Skags, Doog and Taf sacrificed some of their suppers so that I didn't totally miss out. I did a lot of thinking on those journeys to and from the regulating office, where my resentment towards Carter went without saying. But my thinking now embraced the RN and everything it stood for. Those seeds of doubt, about whether it was possible for me to have a worthwhile career in the Royal Navy, had now begun to germinate.

HMS OSPREY

HMS Osprey, precariously perched halfway up Portland Bill, was accessed via a causeway from Weymouth, and was my first draft after Part II training. It was a helicopter base manned by the Fleet Air Arm, who were affectionately known as *Airy Fairies*. As a steward I worked mainly in *the bunrun,* which had stunning views high up over the English Channel and back across the causeway to Weymouth. The sun shone through the giant wardroom windows in the mornings and lit up the whole dining area where we prepared tables for lunch.

After the last of *the pigs* finished their breakfast and left the wardroom the pressure was off; it became a relaxed atmosphere to work in. It was the *Summer of Love* and we were allowed to listen to a transistor radio whilst we worked. Scott McKenzie sang about *San Francisco* and *flowers in your hair,* whilst *The Young Rascals* sang about *Grooving.* We were left to sing along to both records, cavorting around the tables, as we laid cutlery, plates, glasses and folded napkins into mitre shapes. The hippie movement was in full swing and I was envious of the freedom they enjoyed. My memories of dossing down in Bournemouth the previous year were still fresh in my mind. *I wanted to be out there, man, doing my own thing.* I envied those guys who were free: free to grow their hair; to go where they pleased; do what they wanted, and for as long as they wanted.

After training at HMS Pembroke, my first three months at HMS Osprey passed without incident. I performed my duties as well as any of my peers who had finished training at the same time. Technically, during those first three months, you were still classed as a trainee (an assistant steward), which was below the rank of able rate. It was only after this probationary three-month period that you could be made up to able rate (full steward status). This was the first rung on the promotional ladder and was usually a formality; it not only brought status and recognition but additional pay as well. Each branch or trade had their own divisional officer (DO) who was in charge, and it was they who decided when someone was ready to be made up to full steward (able rate) status.

Our DO was a sub-lieutenant named O'Hassell, and it was rumoured he began his naval career on the lower decks, before he progressed up through the ranks to officer status. I thought this was positive, since he should be able to empathise with others who started out at the bottom but who had aspirations to work their way up. I assumed, having not incurred the wrath of any of my superiors during my first three months at Osprey, that I'd be duly be made up to full steward status along with my peers. O'Hassell had different ideas; he turned me down. But he did this in the politest possible way, although for no apparent reason. He said, '*I don't think there is anything specific, Alcock. Nothing I can put my finger on. I just feel you need a bit more time; you need to gain a bit more experience.*' And so he stood me over for another three months, adding, '*Give it another three months, eh? There should be no problem. And we can make you up then, eh?*' I accepted this bollocks and was more determined than ever to see out the next three months as I exited his office. I decided to give it another go, to persevere. After all, another three months wasn't the end of the world. I took O'Hassell at his word and saw no reason why I shouldn't be made up in due course.

I was always keen on sport, particularly ball games, and one afternoon I was playing tennis on a court situated right next to the wardroom. Suddenly O'Hassell appeared out of nowhere in something of a bluster.

'*Alcock!*' he screamed. '*Where's your tennis rig?*'

I doubled over to him, came to attention and saluted.

'*Your whites. Your tennis rig!*' I was wearing a blue football shirt, white shorts and red socks. I looked down at my white pumps.

'*I've got tennis shoes on, sir.*' I looked up and stared straight into his eyes, something I'd heard you weren't supposed to do when addressing an officer. His eyes were bleary; he was swaying, having difficulty standing still, rocking forwards and backwards. He was pissed.

'You need whites, Alcock. Tennis rig is whites.'

'This is my sports kit; it's all I've got, sir.'

'You need whites! Get off the court. Now! You are banned from the tennis court. This is for officers only with the appropriate tennis rig.'

I thought it strange that he hadn't collared Jim, my opponent, who was definitely not wearing anything close to whites; but he'd managed to slip away unnoticed.

I served another three months and had to see O'Hassell for a second time about being made up. After the tennis incident my gut feeling informed me as to what the outcome was likely to be. And I was right. He stood me over again for another three months. I saw this as a slap in the face and felt it was totally unjustified. For some inexplicable reason he'd singled me out. He was my Divisional Officer and I had no one else to turn to; there was nowhere else to go to address my grievance. I was the only one O'Hassell turned down for promotion out of a whole cohort of trainees who had joined Osprey straight from training. And he didn't do it once but twice; and both times I was never offered an explanation behind his decision.

I now questioned the whole *modus operandi* within the RN. I began to mentally catalogue incidents, injustices, discrepancies, regarding ethical and moral behaviour and decisions, especially amongst the hierarchy of the so-called senior service. I admit I allowed my grievance to fester, and convinced myself that a life in the RN was not for me. I thought about this almost on a daily basis: that I'd made a terrible mistake when I signed on.

It was when O'Hassell stood me over for the second time that I decided to take some unplanned leave; this really was my first step, (although I didn't realise it at the time), towards finding a way out of the RN. I headed for Bromley, and some Christians Rib and I had stayed with when we were on the roads a year earlier. I thought they could help me out with food and accommodation again. As it happened I ended up buying a sandwich in Bromley and crashing out in a local park. When I awoke I noticed a large girl sitting on the grass not too far away. She shouted, *'Hello,'* and waved, then asked if I had a light for a cigarette. I went over, gave her a light and sat down beside her. After a few drags she asked *'Are you ticklish?'* and giggled as she said it.

'Not particularly,' I said, *'except on the bottom of my feet.'* And then I caught on. I thought I might be able to con her, recalling those halcyon days back in Bournemouth the year before.

'Are you ticklish?' I asked.

She nodded enthusiastically.

'Whereabouts?'

'Everywhere.' She grinned. I moved closer. It was obvious I was being invited in for a grope. I went to tickle her tummy, but she grabbed my wrist and moved my hand upwards over her ample breasts.

'I like it here best,' she said. I started massaging them but didn't want this to lead anywhere. She wasn't my type and I didn't want to kiss her. I thought, *This isn't me… What am I doing?* I needed to get away, escape, and so

quickly confessed that I was in the RN and needed to give myself up to the authorities. I got to my feet and asked for directions to the nearest police station. I couldn't believe it; she was too good. She then got to her feet and offered to take me to the police station. I said there was no need. I said I could find my way there if she just pointed me in the right direction; but no, she insisted. She said she had to get back home anyway and it was on her way. I tried to get rid of her, but she wasn't having it. I had no option but to let her accompany me to the police station. I stopped outside once we arrived and thought she'd walk on; but no, she just stood there, hanging around, watching me. I half turned, hesitated, and looked at her. I waited for her to move on, but she didn't budge. I thought to myself, *She doesn't believe me?* I now had no option but to step inside; I didn't want to lose face. My first attempt to go AWOL had failed miserably. It had barely lasted two days by the time the police contacted the RN and an escort arrived to take me back to HMS Osprey. I lost a month's pay and a month's leave for my trouble; but I resolved to plan things better next time.

A young Geordie lad arrived at Osprey as an assistant steward before I was drafted to my first proper ship. He was no more than sixteen, having completed his Part 1 training at HMS Ganges, a well-known boys, training establishment near Harwich, Suffolk. First impressions when you met young Geordie (YG) were not favourable; *a braggart* sprang to mind. He had an unfortunate habit of letting his mouth run away with him. And this wasn't the most endearing habit to have amongst some of the more senior *salts*. We were in the men's navy and among us were housed some hardened *three-badge f...-alls* (3 x B FAs). A 3 x Badge FA meant you had three stripes on your arm, but each stripe merely denoted four years' service rather than any sign of promotion. Three stripes on your arm in the other armed services signalled the rank of sergeant, but in the RN it only meant you'd served at least twelve years with no promotion. Usually when communicating with these characters you had to watch what you said; something I learned quickly. The old adage *'Keep your eyes and ears open, and your mouth shut'* stood me in good stead as I ventured through the tempestuous sea of seniority inside the RN. It was something I relied upon when faced with a strange, new or threatening environment. Unfortunately this truism, *'To look, listen, and say nothing,'* hadn't yet registered with YG.

McGuiness, Mac for short, was one such 3 x B FA. He was of average height but had a huge girth, almost as wide as the table he sat at, certainly as wide as a keg of ale. The round table he dominated sat in the centre of the mess and was the venue for card games and *uckers*. It could comfortably seat four, possibly five at a push; but it was always a good idea to keep your cards close to your chest. When Mac wasn't on duty he'd sit there for hours without ever getting up.

Not long after YG joined us he claimed he could jump five feet and asked everyone in the hut if they could jump that high; nobody was interested and most told him to piss off. But YG kept on about his personal athletic feat and wouldn't let it drop. No one took him seriously, but he kept on and on. It was as if he needed to impress to feel accepted by others in the mess. He elaborated, *'Am not talking aboot the Fosbury Flop, ya know; no.'* He actually claimed he could jump sideways over a five-foot-high bar. It was as if this was his only claim to fame; the more he went on about it the more people tended to ignore him. YG appeared to take this response personally, as he became increasingly upset and felt no one believed him. It was also unfortunate that not long afterwards YG overstepped the mark with Big Mac who, at the time, was concentrating on playing his hand during a high-stakes game of three-card Brag. YG's incessant prattle eventually got through to Big Mac, who suddenly slammed his cards down on the table, because he couldn't take anymore of YG's bullshit.

'Right. That's it. You swear you can jump five feet?' YG nodded. *'We'll soon see. Get two brooms and some heavy-duty tape,'* he demanded of those present. The broom handle ends were quickly bound together and placed on the floor. The whole mess came to a stand still. Mac got someone to roughly measure and mark out five one-foot lengths along the handles. When this was done everyone slowly filtered outside and congregated onto a slabbed patio area at the back of the huts. The five-foot markers on the broom handles were lifted vertically and then turned horizontally. It was plain to see YG was nervous. The taped broom handles were held firmly in the horizontal position. Mac had hold of one brush end whilst someone else held the other. YG questioned the accuracy, claiming it looked too high. Mac went through the measuring process again, and then ordered YG to retreat and prepare for his run-

up. The broom handles were again raised horizontally. YG dithered and appeared flustered. He was unsure, until he eventually retreated and prepared for his run-up. Everyone became quiet and focused on YG and his deliberations. When he was ready he took an almighty run and leapt full pelt at the broom handles. He failed miserably, crashing through the middle of them and landing awkwardly onto the concrete slabs. He may have reached three but no more than four feet off the ground. Mac had held on to his brush end as if it had been welded into the palm of his hand. Although the other end was let loose, no one was surprised that big Mac didn't let go of his end. He'd openly admitted he was going to teach YG a lesson and had almost willed YG to take a nasty fall.

Unfortunately Big Mac hadn't quite finished with YG. It wasn't long after the high-jump event, when Big Mac was sitting in his customary seat at the card table, that he offered YG what appeared to be a conciliatory gesture. As YG passed by he commented on Mac's inseparable table companion: a flagon of the best *scrumpy* Weymouth could offer.

'Gan'an. *That looks bloody lovely, Mac.*'

'Fancy some – d'yer?' responded Mac.

'Do I. It was bloody hot in the bunrun today.'

'Well, go and get your mug and you can have a good wet on me.'

YG came back and Mac topped him up. 'Ay – fair play, Mac – and thanks.'

Mac had his own glass and lifted it. 'Down the hatch,' he said, and took a huge gulp.

YG did the same. *'Aaagh!'* he screamed, spitting nearly all of it out across the mess floor. *'It's warm,'* shouted YG.

'Well, it would be,' retorted big Mac. *'It's come from the wrong flagon.'* And with that Mac reached under the table and pulled out another identical flagon and placed it next to the one already there. The bottles and contents looked identical, but the taste was different. I'd always wondered how Mac could sit for hours at the table without getting up to take a leak. And now I knew. He explained he didn't like leaving the table in case anyone tampered with the cards whilst he was away.

Not long afterwards I left Osprey for HMS Victorious, but it had been over a year since I'd stood on the dock at Southampton. I couldn't believe it. I'd expected to go to sea in a matter of weeks; but now it had been more than twelve months and I hadn't even set foot on the gangway of a ship.

HMS VICTORIOUS

When I joined HMS Victorious (known as the *Vic*) I discovered that nearly all of us who'd signed on, and completed training at both Vincent and Pembroke, as well as spending over six months at different shore bases around the UK, were all reunited on board the *Vic*. It was great to see some old mates and comforting to see familiar faces; although the one exception was Carter, who appeared as crabby as ever. The *Vic* was in dry dock undergoing a major refit in Portsmouth when we joined her, and so we lived on HMS Centaur, another aircraft carrier berthed close by, which was where we ate, slept and took care of our ablutions.

The diminished living space on board the Centaur highlighted the luxurious shore-based accommodation we'd been used to. Unfortunately Skags, a mate from

Pembroke, rued his transfer to cramped living conditions. He found himself too close for comfort when he was berthed next to Carter, who was still a stranger to soap and water. Skags also discovered Carter's kit went AWOL as far as *dhobying* was concerned, even though he repeatedly dropped hints to Carter about hygiene. It fell on deaf ears. Skags used to say Carter didn't have to put his socks on because, *'They did it for him – all he had to do was whistle.'*

The fact that the *Vic* was in dry dock meant the whole ship's company, apart from *the pigs,* had to go ashore to take a leak. We worked on the Vic during the day, mainly glifting and gleaning flats, mess decks and painting bulkheads. There were too many of us to be employed on these tasks and so confusion often reigned as to who was assigned to do what. For us it was an ideal opportunity to chew the fat and discover more about the mess mates we didn't know.

Brains, another 3 x B FA, led many of the discussions around this time. He had the three red stripes on his arm, but there was no anchor placed above his stripes, which would have signalled he was a leading hand, a rank above all of us who were now classed as able rates. Brains was something of an orator and claimed, during his long, illustrious and unsuccessful career, that he had once achieved the rank of leading hand, only to have been busted back down to able rate for punching *a pig.* He was a short, brawny guy with tattoos that smothered his forearms, and you wouldn't want to argue with him unless you had to. He regaled us with stories of where he'd been and where we, on the *Vic,* were heading to.

He'd probably sailed the seven seas seven times and his seniority, amongst us rookies, went unhindered. He held centre stage when addressing us. His big thing then was that he was now *a conscientious objector*. He said if war broke out he'd down arms and refuse to fight. Something about this didn't quite ring true; especially when his three stripes meant he must have passed nine years' service and signed on again to serve additional years.

It was common knowledge that Stewards were expendable, similar to infantry in the Army. And so stewards were expected to be in the firing line and it didn't matter to command if they survived or not; they were cannon fodder. Brains argued that it was pure folly, for us at our age, to be killed or maimed fighting for our country. His argument rested on our right to vote. He questioned the validity of being old enough to die during a war yet not being old enough to vote. I thought Brains had a point there, but really I wasn't interested in politics at the time. Undoubtedly Brains had had plenty of time to think things over during his years of service, but regardless of his opinions, and seniority, we journeyed on and grew in confidence through our own experiences. We got to know ourselves and others better, and soon realised that Brains was all mouth and trousers.

During the *Vic's* refit a lot of skiving ensued. It was another way to relieve the monotony and boredom of having too many hands and not enough work. We'd spend the time of day by wandering around the decks, visiting places we had no right to be in. If we were questioned as to why we were in an unfamiliar location, we'd say we were looking for a bucket or a broom, which someone had borrowed but not returned. Obviously the most popular excuse for being absent from your place of duty was to say it was *a call of nature* and that you'd had to go ashore to relieve yourself.

As time passed I became increasingly bored and disillusioned with the whole set-up. It occurred to me that if we, lower rates, had to go ashore to take a piss, then shouldn't everyone on board have to go ashore? Obviously not. Large metal dustbins were placed strategically on each deck for *the pigs* to piss in. And guess who had the task of emptying them? Yes, it was the flunkies who had to empty them. It was an arduous and nerve-racking task which involved humping them up and down ladders, struggling between decks, through hatches, and down gangways to get them ashore. Inevitably piss would splish-splosh and splash over the sides of the bins during these tricky manoeuvres. I don't think a bin was ever emptied without leaving the unfortunate carriers soaked in urine. I copped it once; but only once. I avoided it afterwards by monitoring which bins were virtually full, morning noon and night. If I clocked any bins that were nearly full and would need emptying at the earliest opportunity, I'd employ the disappearing tactic by making sure I went ashore, and stayed in the heads on the jetty long enough to make sure all the relevant bins had been emptied.

Two to three months on and we were living on the Vic, had running water and were almost shipshape; the refit was nearly complete. It wouldn't be long before we'd slip anchor and put to sea. Skags had already had a gutful of

Carter and his unhygienic ways when, inevitably, things came to a head one day. He sought assistance from a few of us to help him deal with this problem. One night, as Carter lay sleeping in his stinking pit, we gathered up every piece of kit he'd been wearing over the past few weeks; his manky socks as stiff as cardboard; the original passion-killers issued at St Vincent that only he now wore, and which no one wished to touch. Everything was shovelled up on the end of a broom, from his working shirt to his white front and bell-bottom trousers, and then dunked into two buckets of cold, soapy water. Carter blissfully slept on, oblivious to the activity going on around him. Inside our mess was a hatch and ladder that led directly down below to showers and wash basins, a place where the buckets containing Carter's kit were left.

When he awoke in the morning and couldn't find his clothes he started to panic. Starkers, he had to grab a clean towel from his locker and wrap it around himself. He hunted high and low for his clothes, until someone mentioned there was a load of gear in the showers down below. He had no alternative but to put on clean kit. Although it didn't immediately cure Carter of his unhygienic habits, it was a start. Skags approached this issue as if it was his Holy Grail; he was determined to educate Carter in the merits of staying clean. At every opportunity he tried to drop hints regarding Carter's BO problems; he even, on occasion, sprayed Carter's bunk with deodorant, or accidentally (on purpose) he left his spray lying around, in the remote hope that Carter would use it. Periodically the bucket exercise would be repeated if Carter's noxious odour again became too much. At other times he'd wait until Carter was away and then strip his bedding and add this to the buckets; everything in the vicinity of Carter's bunk at one time or another was douched. I couldn't swear that Carter ever became convinced about the merits of personal hygiene, but he began to change his clothes more frequently, and his BO became less noticeable.

Just prior to the Vic being commissioned a fire broke out on board. Rumour had it that a CPO arrived back on board late, and the worse for wear. He'd switched a boiler on to make a brew, but immediately crashed out; allegedly it had overheated and caught fire. It was also claimed that he woke up but found the fire extinguisher didn't work; that he rang for help but couldn't escape because the hatch was too hot to open. It was reported that damage from the fire destroyed over a million pounds' worth of cable that served the radar. I'm not really sure what happened, but the government decided to scrap HMS Victorious.

We were all asked to put in requests for a draft to another ship, one of our own choosing. I put in for a small ship; I didn't want another carrier with 2,000 jolly-jack tars running amok in every port we called at. What actually happened was that most of the *Vic's* ship's company (including yours truly) were automatically transferred on to another carrier, HMS Hermes. I wondered why they bothered to ask us in the first place when obviously it was a *fait accompli*.

The commissioning ceremony for the *Vic* still went ahead, but it now became a wake. I took time out to wander around the empty mess decks on my own. Only a few days before the same mess decks were buzzing with activity, full of laughter, bawdy behaviour, card games and *uckers*. The mess cul-de-sacs were now soulless, laid bare, stripped not only of personnel but their belongings. Abandoned lockers were left with doors hanging half open, dark and empty inside; others exposed a glimpse of a torn leg, breast or torso, belonging to a one-time playmate of the month. It was strange, the emptiness, the hollow silence, but it got to me; the sadness of what this huge ship had meant to so many for so long. And now it was a shell, deserted, devoid of life. The bunks, stripped bare of their thin mattresses, pillows and blankets left exposed to lattice webbing, stark and naked, like so many rib cages stripped of flesh. Cold metal frames conspired with gunmetal-grey bulkheads and added a chill to the atmosphere. I shivered, paused and felt the presence of so many who'd passed this way before, all the spirits that had lived, breathed and sailed across vast oceans were now lost and gone forever. As I meandered around, Traffic, the supergroup, filtered through the tannoy system with their recording of *Hole in my Shoe*. And then, as if on cue, as I drifted around this skeleton of a ship, I heard the young girl on the record mention an albatross and wondered if an old sailor had recently killed one.

HMS HERMES –
ON THE RUN

Although I moved from the Vic to HMS Hermes as ship's company, I'd already decided I wasn't going to sail away in her. My plan was to absent myself just before she sailed to the Far East, which would increase my chances of being re-assigned to another ship, hopefully a small one. I couldn't envisage the RN taking the trouble to fly a flunkie out to join a ship that was halfway around the world. And I was sure the Hermes would manage without the services of one disinterested able rate steward.

As the time to sail approached I re-acquainted myself with my trusty old blue sleeping bag – the one I'd used on the roads. And I purchased a decent-sized haversack for a few essentials to take with me on my travels. I decided to make my move after I took some embarkation leave, with my adopted family, just prior to sailing; so instead of returning back on board, to what was known as *the Happy H,* I took a detour and revisited Bournemouth.

It had now been nearly two years since Rib and I had spent that summer dossing there, but it was still a place I loved and felt I had an affinity with. Strangely, one of the first people I bumped into in the Pleasure Gardens was Red Rock. He was still wearing the same old grubby string vest, underneath a shiny, well-worn, pavement-grey suit with frayed cuffs. His pasty face, now with a sprinkling of ginger bumfluff under his chin, looked well scrubbed and contrasted sharply with his greasy, slicked-back ginger hair.

'I wondered what happened to you two guys,' he mused in his phoney American accent. I told him that we'd both joined the RN, that I hated it and was taking time out.

'*Heavy,*' he remarked. I relayed last year to him, when I was at HMS Osprey in Portland and saw him on a local TV news bulletin. He was with a group of hippies outside the Pavilion Pier, arguing the toss with Frankie Vaughan the singer, who was appearing there. Frankie was calling them "*scroungers*" and "*lazy scoundrels,*" who should get a job. Red Rock's reply extolled the virtues of "*peace and love,*" and "*freedom.*" He said Frankie needed to *get* "*hip, man*" and become "*one of the beautiful people.*" Ironically, Frankie didn't look too bad in a tuxedo and bow-tie.

Not long after I saw Red I bumped into Rollo, another *beat* from two years before, who was hanging out on French Corner. He claimed Red Rock was a fraud, and said he'd lived in Bournemouth all his life and never been to the USA. Rib and I had often wondered, during our time in Bournemouth, why Red Rock never slept in the Chines with us. Each evening he'd just melt away, only to reappear in the Pleasure Gardens the next morning. We had often wondered where he went but had never asked him outright. We thought he must have somewhere to sleep with a proper roof over his head and decided he was more of a *raver* than a real *beat*. But we'd always got along with him and accepted him for what he was; although I'm sure he said two years ago that he was from Pittsburgh and not Philadelphia? Maybe Rollo was right.

The next day in the Pleasure Gardens I spotted a pretty girl with long dark hair, sitting alone on the grass reading. She looked perfectly at peace with the world. *A child of the times,* I mused. *All she needs is a flower in her hair.* I was about to move in on her when two young guys asked me if I had a light for a cigarette. I told them to hang on as I had business to attend to (with little Miss Harmony).

'*Hi.*' She smiled when I approached. I asked if I could sit and join her. She stretched out her arm and beckoned, '*Help yourself.*' She smiled again. Now she *did* sound American, so I asked what part of America she was from.

'*Boston.*'

'*Massachusetts,*' I said.

'*You know it?*' she asked.

'*No.*' I knew Boston was in that state; nothing to do with my O Level geography, but more of my interest in faraway places. I asked her what it was like.

'*Cold,*' she said. '*Snow.*' After chatting for a while I asked if she could spare anything for a cup of tea or a bite to eat.

'*Sure,*' she said, and delved into her handbag and pulled out her passport. Inside the front cover she revealed a wad of notes. '*Here. Will that do?*' She held out a shiny green one-pound note. I was speechless. '*Go ahead, take it.*' I hesitated and asked if she was sure. She was fine about it. I thanked her and returned to the two guys who were still there on the path gawping. They couldn't believe it; and neither could I. They'd witnessed my best con ever.

I learned that both of them had left their respective homes in the Midlands without saying a word to anyone. They'd hit on Bournemouth because the younger one, Sean, had an older brother who lived in the suburbs. Later that afternoon Sean went to look him up and that was the last we saw of him. Jace, his friend, didn't fancy joining him and was happy enough to join me and sleep rough. We broke into a sea-front chalet that night, because it was cold, wet and windy. Inside we wedged the door shut and spent a semi-comfortable night on a couple of deck chairs that were housed there.

The next day Jace and I dropped in at the SS (Social Security) and pleaded poverty and homelessness. They said we needed to bring them an address and confirmation from the landlord that we were staying there. We soon found a B&B with vacancies and a friendly landlady who took pity on us; she provided us with a letter to take back. I gave a false name to the SS, but they took us at face value and still funded each of us for three days' board and lodging; there was some extra cash for expenses. They said we'd receive a full week's board and lodging, plus expenses, at the end of the week, after the three days had expired.

We celebrated our first night in lodgings by going to the cinema for free, where we watched *Where Eagles Dare,* starring Richard Burton and Clint Eastwood. In those days you could sneak in without paying if you estimated what time the film finished. On leaving the cinema most of the audience jammed the main aisle that led back to the foyer and main entrance, but many others chose to stream out using the emergency side exit near the front. If you waited by this side door there was always the opportunity to squeeze past those leaving and grab a seat without being noticed. And it wasn't uncommon in those days for audience members to stay in their seats and watch a second showing without having to pay again.

When the SS doled out our full week's allowance, Jace and I decided to move on. I felt sorry for the landlady, who had initially felt sorry for us, but we couldn't let her know our plans. We had to remain anonymous and keep moving. I relayed a story to Jace about a young guy I'd met on a train who had absconded from the Army. He had told me about Newquay, Cornwall, and how cool it was, so we decided that would be our next stop. We hitched as far as Exeter and spent a night of luxury in an AA-listed hotel. The comfy bed, en-suite facilities and full English breakfast satisfied both our stomachs and souls; it wasn't cheap and we found ourselves virtually skint again. SS money doesn't go far!

When we arrived in Newquay we had to seek refuge in a semi-covered bus shelter for a couple of hours. The persistent rainfall, accelerated by strong winds that blew in off the Atlantic, soon dampened our spirits as well as our clothes. We stamped our feet and swung our arms about trying to keep warm, staring at the heavy black clouds that rolled over the hotel rooftops. During this time we debated where we would sleep that night. I wasn't sure where the idea came from (possibly from the Army guy I'd met on the train), but we hit on a bus depot. We thought there must be one here; and if we could find one we'd kip on the top deck of a double-decker. Problem solved.

We had enough cash to get something to eat but waited until dusk before we visited a fish and chip shop to satisfy our needs. The girl in the chippy was a sweet thing and told us where the local bus depot was. When we found it we waited until dark before we crept inside a parked double-decker. We chose one hemmed in by others, as we didn't want to be on board one of the first buses to pull out of the depot the next morning. We clambered onto the top deck and settled down, one of us at each end of the back seat. I gave Jace my jacket as I had my sleeping bag, and we dosed off until we were rudely awakened. A guy in uniform, probably security employed by the bus company and accompanied by a policeman, shook me awake first. When they tried to awake Jace he reacted, swearing profanities, as well as questioning the parentage of both of these guys on patrol. The policeman took exception to this outburst and struck him over the head with his torch. More cussing ensued until the copper threatened to arrest him. Eventually Jace fully woke up and quietened down, but we were soon turfed off the bus and out of the depot.

It was about one-thirty in the morning and we had nowhere to go. Newquay was a dark, empty, desolate place at that time in the morning; the pitter-patter of rainfall was the only sign of life. We didn't see a soul as we wandered along the top road until we came across a dimly lit public convenience. Inside were four empty traps and, as the sole occupants, we settled in the first two and left the doors open. It was shelter from the rain, but you'd be hard pressed to say it was anything beyond that. There was an inescapable heavy smell of liquid disinfectant, which after a while burned your nostrils and stung your eyes. I looked around at the uneven concrete floor, where little purple puddles gathered in nooks and crannies. Sleep was virtually impossible as the smell was too nauseating. I thought it healthier not to unroll my sleeping bag but to use it as a cushion, wedging it between my back and the cistern. I spent the rest of the night shivering, yawning and praying for the first light of dawn to arrive. It was the worst night I'd ever spent sleeping rough.

Our funds were now desperately low. Jace decided to contact his mum reversing the charges, and ask her to wire some money to the local PO. When he returned from his call he was downbeat. His mum had had some sort of breakdown; she'd been sick with worry about him ever since he'd left home. He said he'd promised to return, and confirmed I'd be OK as his mum was going to send him money for train fare. He'd asked for more than he needed and so reassured me again that I'd be alright.

We survived that day by revisiting the chippy. The pretty girl was serving again and I'd liked to have got to know her better. She smiled when we entered but flashed her eyes towards the guy doing the frying. I interpreted the signal as, *I can't be too friendly.* I guessed it was her dad, and it was apparent that me and Jace fell way short his expectations with regards to anyone having designs on his daughter. We scraped enough money together for two portions of chips through illicit means; we'd nicked some empty Coke and lemonade bottles from behind The Sailor's pub and then returned them to a nearby shop. In those days you could get a refund on empty pop bottles. The chips were enough to sustain us until Jace collected the money his mum planned to wire through.

During our time together Jace and I had a brief fallout; yet we managed to reconcile our differences with a firm handshake. Jason had also attended private school, and this rekindled memories of my earlier days in pre-prep boarding school, where a subliminal culture existed: *to be a good sport, to observe fair play,* and in my particular school the motto was, *manners maketh man.* It followed then that a mutual trust and respect existed between us; and when we finally said farewell Jace was as good as his word. He gave me a couple of quid before we shook hands and went our separate ways.

I immediately hit the road back to Bournemouth and managed to get a ride as far as Dartmoor. Unfortunately, I was dropped off in the darkest of hours on a lifeless, wet, cold and misty night. The whole terrain was deserted, soulless. I knew as soon as we stopped I wouldn't be travelling any further that night. No one was about to stop and offer me another lift.

'Look,' said my driver as he dropped me off, *'there's a local cricket pavilion just off the main road, to the right. It has a covered porch, a wooden bench. It's sheltered.'*

I thanked him and took off down the road. The clinging mist was now a thick fog, and once the rear lights of his car had faded and disappeared (from no more than twenty yards away) a solitary stillness remained in the cold night air. I felt lonely. The buzzing sound of overhead electricity cables eclipsed the scuffing of my footsteps; they were my sole, or do I mean *soul,* companions. As I trudged along the dark, dank, deserted road, I tried to recall when I'd last seen anybody, other than the guy who'd dropped me off. I actually couldn't recall when it was. The eerie, chilled stillness of my surroundings started to play tricks with my mind.

I thought more about Dartmoor; everything I'd ever seen or read about the place appeared to be true. The mist and fog, the moors, the loneliness and isolation. And of course there was the prison. I wondered, had anyone escaped recently? I remembered Foxy Fowler as a boy. *Was he still about, lurking in the shadows or the hedgerows?* I half expected to hear the Hounds of the Baskervilles baying for blood! I looked around, strained my eyes, searched for anything that moved or was lying close by. I checked behind me, to see if anyone was following or creeping up on me. I was thankful when I came across the turning that I hoped would lead to my cricket ground sanctuary for the night. And yet for all the dark thoughts I had about Dartmoor that night, I still rank the worst night I ever spent on the roads was the one I'd just spent in the toilets at Newquay.

I woke up to a bright, windy but dry day, and soon managed to hitch a couple rides back into Bournemouth. Again I immediately bumped into Red Rock, who told me they had been advertising for deckhands on the fishing trawlers in Lowestoft. Since going on the run money had been a perennial problem for me. I knew, somehow, I had to find a job. The problem with finding work in the UK was that it was almost impossible without a National Insurance record. I knew employers would require some evidence of this; it was something I couldn't provide. I thought I'd take my chance though, with the trawlers, and headed for Lowestoft. I needed to have a good reason why I hadn't got an NI number.

On the way there I stopped off in Pompey, hoping to contact some of my messmates on board the *Happy H* to see if they could help me out. I was pretty certain she hadn't sailed away yet, and so decided to discreetly hang around the dockyard gates near to Aggie Weston's. I decided if I could catch one of my mates coming ashore, I'd ask them if they could organise a whip round to help me on my way. Luckily I caught Wills, who was a good mate from my *St Vincent* training days. He said he'd be ashore again in a couple of days, so we arranged to meet up at the same time and place. My messmates were as good as gold, because when I met Wills again he handed over £5 to me.

I immediately hit the road again, tracking up the A3 towards the smoke. I passed through Waterlooville and Petersfield before I was dropped off in Godalming, a place that brought back troubled memories regarding my father. After he retired from the RAF he lived nearby in Witley, and I'd stayed with him a couple of years back during a summer holiday when I was at college in Manchester. It was a total disaster. He got drunk every night and one time we had a fight. I say fight, but really it was *deja vu*. It was a re-enactment of the time he chinned me when we lived together in that Northamptonshire village, when Dad was stationed at the missile base. I'd reacted in the same way as when he came at me previously. I was powerless to strike him and he decked me again. I was older this time, and afterwards swore to myself that this would never happen again. I remember how I packed my bag that night and left in a hurry. I trudged through the darkest woods to Witley railway station, only to find it was locked up for the night. I had no option but to return through the same dark nightmare woods, trying to hurry along with screech owls screaming and scaring the living daylights out of me. When I returned to the cottage I half expected an apology, or some sign of regret from my father; but no chance. Instead he just stood there, swaying in his alcoholic stupor, laughing at me. I was the butt of his amusement for making a fruitless three-mile journey in the middle of the night. I went straight to bed and left early the next morning without a word. I was sixteen then and decided I'd have nothing more to do with him. And now tonight, although geographically close to him as I passed through

Godalming, I was a million miles from him as far as I was concerned. I remained resolute that I was never going to have anything to do with him again; he was no longer part of my life.

It was late at night when I reached the other side of Godalming and, unbelievably, managed to hitch one of my best lifts ever. In hitch-hiking terms I'd reached the despondent stage that night; I'd walked for miles through the town and stood at the side of the road for hours. Sometimes, when this happens, you become convinced no one is going to stop and offer you a ride. I always imagined that the main reasons why no one stopped for you was because you were either soaking wet or they didn't like the look of you; or it was either too late or too dark. I was on the verge of giving up that night and began thinking about where I could kip, when a big artic pulled over.

We drove right through the night, through the bright neon of London, as well as a red light over Tower Bridge. It happened because we were (or I was) talking too much, mostly about my broken home, and the last day I saw my mum. How I sensed something was wrong the morning she left, how I asked if I could go with her. She said, *'We'll see.'* I remembered it as if it was yesterday. And when I returned from infant school that day she'd gone and taken my baby sister Rosemary with her. I never saw her again. I told the truck driver about this and other sad times, and how I'd missed my mum all my life. He said he was going to tell his wife my story when he got home. He said it would make her cry, and I thought about how I used to cry when I thought about my mum.

I think her leaving made me cold and indifferent, especially when I heard sob stories from others. I couldn't bear to listen to their heartaches; I'd often walk away, turn my back on them, and distance myself from their pain. I felt I'd developed a couldn't-care-less attitude towards the misery of others; it was something I wasn't proud of. It was my defence mechanism. When others accused me of having a chip on my shoulder, I'd reply, *No I haven't, I've got a King Edward potato!*

We trucked on up the A12 until he dropped me off on the outskirts of Chelmsford; early-morning light was just breaking across the eastern skyline. It was close to a newly constructed bridge, which straddled a stream and a field full of cows. I thought how the angles underneath each end of the bridge would be too acute for the cows to access; there should be some sheltered space there, somewhere safe and clean where I can rest my head. I chose the end under the bridge that was partially hidden from view. My suspicions were confirmed when I crawled underneath, as it was free from the presence of cows and their pancakes. The brown dirt underfoot was hard, dry and clean, and low enough to prevent cows from getting in too close. I crawled under and pushed my gear into the angle, before I settled down inside my sleeping bag and caught up with some much-needed sleep.

When I awoke it was afternoon. I looked around for any sign of a farmer in the field, but no one was about. I covered my sleeping bag and rucksack with some branches and leaves, and walked into town. I planned to get something to eat but had less money than I thought. I sought out the local SS for a handout.

'*How can I help?*' asked a guy in a shirt and tie.

'*I'm wondering if you can fund me to get to Lowestoft. I'm applying for a job there on the fishing trawlers.*'

'*What's your name?*' He had a pad in front of him.

'*Joe Davis.*'

'*Have you got ID any on you?*' Silence. I gave him an impromptu look of genuine amazement.

'*Oh, God,*' I said, slapping my forehead. '*I never thought of that. You know, I never gave it a thought.*'

'*For all I know, you could be Fred Bloggs,*' he said.

'*Right. You're right. Honestly. I didn't give it a thought. And I've left all my stuff on the outskirts of town, about two miles away. I spent last night sleeping under a bridge. And I've left everything there – hidden away.*'

He was scrutinising me. I could tell he wasn't sure. I reasserted, '*Look, if you could just give me enough to get to Lowestoft, I'll be alright. Honest. Just my fare and a bite to eat. That's all I'm asking.*'

'*Wait here.*' And he disappeared through a door behind the counter.

When he emerged twenty minutes later he said they would give me something, but not the train fare to where I wanted to go. He said they'd give me enough to get back to London, buy something to eat and pay for a night's hostel accommodation. The fact that it was now late in the day helped my cause. There was no way I could have gone back to collect some (non-existent) identification from my belongings and returned to their office before it closed.

The proof of ID became irrelevant; I was happy to leave there with some cash. I compromised on food and bought some liquorice papers and a small pouch of baccy. I rolled a few cigs, enjoyed a smoke and hit the road again. I made sure I had enough cash left to get something to eat when I arrived in Lowestoft.

It was around ten the next morning when I reached the harbour area in Lowestoft. I approached some guys fixing nets and baskets on the quayside and asked them if they knew where I should go if I was looking for work on the trawlers. They directed me to a large three-storey Victorian building opposite the harbour, next to the junction between Waveney Road and Denmark Street. I stepped inside through an open front door, then another door that led into a dimly lit hallway, where a row of empty chairs were lined up along the wall on the left-hand side. A door opposite opened and a man stepped out and asked if I was so-and-so. I replied I wasn't, but asked if I could have an interview although I didn't have an appointment. He said they'd be happy to see me, but not until the end of the day after the last interview was over.

'*It'll be around five-thirtyish,*' he added.

'*That's okay,*' I said. '*I'll be here.*'

I passed the hours by going for walks, visiting a fish and chip shop for lunch, and having cups of tea in a nearby cafe. I made sure I was back for my interview by five-o'clock. I'd also spent some time inventing a story about my circumstances during the couple of years since I'd left school. I needed to be clear as to why I couldn't produce an NI number (under my assumed name), something that had weighed heavily on my mind. I knew I had to convince them that there was a genuine reason for not having an NI record. When I returned to Denmark Street for my interview, I knew I needed a well-rehearsed a story. I'd have to take my chance.

The man I'd spoken to earlier invited me into the office where another guy was already sitting behind a desk. They were both mid-thirties and casually dressed with short-sleeved shirts and sleeveless pullovers. They were lookalikes; I thought they might be brothers, or twins.

'What's your name?' asked the one who ushered me in.

'Joe Davis.' I used the same surname I'd adopted for the SS; it was easy to remember as Davis was the surname of my adopted family in Manchester. The interviewers employed the tennis-match technique, questioning me alternately. I concentrated; I had to make sure I didn't slip up with my answers. For a while I sat there mesmerised. My head switched continuously from one to the other, left to right and back again; I felt like a spectator watching a long, drawn-out point at Wimbledon.

'Tell us about yourself, John.'

'Yes. What have you been doing, John?' asked the other.

'I don't really have a family,' I began. 'My mum left when I was about four years old and my dad put me in a home. He drank too much – and still does – so I stayed there. I managed to get a part-time job on a farm when I was about thirteen. The woman who owned it called it a smallholding. There were lots of different animals there. She was a widow and when I was old enough to leave the home she took me *in. Anything was better than living in the home. And so when I left school I lived there, and I've been there for the last three years; well, until now that is.'*

As I told my story they each took turns to rapidly nod their heads at me as I finished a sentence; someone could have had strings and been working them from above. I found it hard to keep a straight face because I knew what I was telling them was mostly bullshit, but they appeared to be listening so intently. When I'd finished they turned and faced one another but didn't say anything. The gist of the tale I fed them was another gem spawned from the conversation I'd had with that squaddie I'd met on a train. He'd mentioned how he'd been involved in a relationship with an older woman who'd fed and kept him.

'*So what made you leave, Joe?*' said one.

'*Yes, what made you take off, Joe?*' said the other.

'*I decided to make a break. It was getting too much – she was a lot older than me. I started thinking I've got to make my own way in the world – see what's out there. I felt trapped, hemmed in.*'

I didn't want to admit there was more to our relationship. I thought, *Leave them wondering, suspecting. Let them work it out.* I wanted to come across as reticent, coy.

'*I'm grateful to her, for her looking after me and everything. But I think she was expecting too much. I had to get out, see what's going on, find my own way in the world. Before it was too late.*'

They were both nodding again vigorously.

'*We understand,*' said one.

'Yes, we both do,' said the other. '*You're saying she was making unfair demands on you.*' I remained silent for a moment before I answered.

'Yes, sir. *And they were demands I didn't feel I could meet.*' Another pause. '*And that's why I needed to get out of there and meet other people, people of my own age. And that's why I don't have any NI records. I've never needed them. She fed and clothed me and I had a roof over my head. In return I helped her out. But it was getting too much. But I'm not sure about the National Insurance thing. Will it be a problem?*'

'*No. I'm sure we can sort that out,*' said one.

'*Yes, I agree, it shouldn't be a problem,*' said the other.

They sat there looking at me. Silence prevailed. I just looked from one to the other until first one spoke and then the other.

'*Look, Joe. I think if you can wait outside in the hall...*'

'*Yes, we need a few minutes...*'

'*We won't keep you long.*'

'*No. We'll be as quick as we can. If you can just hang on?*'

'*We'll be with you shortly – thanks.*'

I waited in the hall and they were as good as their word. After about fifteen minutes they summoned me back into the office.

'*We've thought about your situation, Joe, and we think you deserve a break.*'

'*Yes. It's time you had a chance.*'

'*We can send you to college, to the local Tech...*'

'*To learn basic seamanship...*'

'You can start as a deckie learner...'

'A trainee deckhand – what do you say?'

The deal was done. They gave me an address for some digs further along Denmark Street, which they'd pay for, and said they expected me to be down at the harbour entrance at 6am on Monday morning. I was to join the *Elsa Rosa*. *Wow!* I thought. *I'm sorted.*

The *Elsa Rosa* was a sidewinder trawler, about 110 feet from stern to bow, with a beam of approximately 20 feet, a small ship by any stretch of the imagination. Sidewinders cast their nets over the side, which was the common way to trawl in those days, dragging their nets just above or along the sea bed. The *Elsa* trawled the North Sea and I didn't realise how shallow it was until that trip; in the southern waters of the continental shelf it could only be 30–35 metres to the seabed.

On that first trip the crew numbered ten, excluding yours truly. There were four young but experienced trawler men from Fleetwood, an engineer and his mate, a cook, two local hands, and the skipper. All the deckies assembled below in the crew's quarters as we chugged out from the inner harbour, and through the outer harbour, into the expansive dark blue-green North Sea. The Fleetwood four had been drinking the night before and were the worse for wear. They sat around a table in the centre of our sleeping quarters, which had raised edges on top to stop anything from sliding off; there were two benches, one on either side, and everything was bolted to the deck. The quarters were cramped with five veneered wooden double bunks spaced either side of lockers. A short curtained rail ran along the side of your bunk which, apart from offering limited privacy, also protected your eyes from the direct glare of the mess light that remained switched on for the entire trip.

I rested on my bunk, a top one of two, with my curtain open and ate the sandwiches my landlady had prepared. One of the local lads suggested I could get a brew from the galley if I wanted. *'But don't bend over in front of the cook.'* He smiled. *'He likes young boys.'* This raised a few chuckles and effeminate responses from the Fleetwood four. *'Ooo, get you,'* said one. *'I say!'* said another. *'Mmm – I'll see you later.'* And so on.

I learned these guys had travelled across the country to see what it was like to work on a trawler that fished from Lowestoft. *Pretty much the same as Fleetwood,* I thought. They had been eating crisps, chocolate, packets of biscuits and drinking cans of fizzy pop since they arrived on board. Sobriety was slowly returning to them just as nausea was gradually kicking into me. I knew this was more to do with the weight inside my stomach rather than the quality of my sandwiches. The contents of my gut became heavier, bouncing, swaying and heaving around, totally at odds with the turbulent motion of the *Elsa*. The further we went out to sea the worse I felt. Eventually things came to a head when I knew I was going to be physically sick. Prevention was out of the question. One of the local guys recognised my symptoms and offered some salutary advice in the nick of time:

'*Get up on deck. And get your head over the side.*' I didn't need persuading. I was up there in a jiffy and grabbed a rope that was keeping the nets in place. I wedged myself between the side of the trawler and some hoisting tackle, then leaned over the side as far as I could. I feared for my safety as my head was spinning and feet were slipping; waves splashed up and soaked my face. I desperately needed to be sick, and so held on to the rope for dear life and stuck my fingers down my throat to hasten the process. Images of what was happening and what might happen flashed through my mind: *Don't lean over too far… For God's sake, keep hanging on… Am I dangling over too far…Don't let go or you'll be over the side…What if an angry wave crashes into me and swallows me up…?* Thankfully I managed to hold on, haul myself back up on deck and steady myself.

I had no idea when we slipped anchor that we'd be heading out into the North Sea for at least six hours before we reached the fishing grounds where we trawled. I guess that's not that far when you think our cruising speed was approximately10 knots an hour, but the *Elsa* was now really rocking, rolling and reeling, up and down and from side to side, like taking a ride on a giant roller coaster. When I returned back down below advice and encouragement flowed from my shipmates: '*Carry on eating; you might not feel like it – but keep on eating. It'll pass.*'

Yes it will, I thought, *one way or the other.*

'*You'll see,*' they insisted, '*carry on as normal – don't stop eating – you'll soon get over it.*' When I eventually ventured down to the galley for a brew the cook reinforced the same message: *'Keep eating as if you don't feel sick at all; and if you do feel sick, you should still keep on eating.'*

I retired to my bunk and tried to get some shut-eye, but it was impossible. The queasiness inside my stomach was relentless; I continually felt I was going to vomit again at any moment. But I was only physically sick once, in spite of all the hours we took to get to the familiar North Sea fishing grounds where we finally cast our nets. I thought the best policy was to still try and get some sleep, the great healer, no matter how long it would take me. I rationalised the current state of my health as I lay there: *I'm ill. I feel ill, so I must be ill. I'm certainly too ill to work. I need to rest and get some sleep; rest will cure it. They'll have to manage on deck without me, until I feel better; they'll have to wait until I'm fully recovered.*

I later learned it was about two in the morning when the big ginger *"gett"* (wild hair, scruffy beard, wild eyes), from Fleetwood, ripped aside my privacy curtain:

'Wake up, you twat! You f…ing bastard. If you don't get out of your f….g bunk for the next catch, you're f….g dead! D'yer hear me! I'll tell yer what, you twat, you'll be over side! I mean it! I'll throw yer over side! I f…ing mean it! No one'll know…'

Funny, I was thinking exactly the same thing as his expletives exploded through my eardrums. I thought, *Who would know if I disappeared?* There'd be no way of proving a crime had been committed; no one knew I was on board. *Well, not the real me.* And then if I was reported as *missing,* who could say what had happened? The skipper might conclude: *'He must have fallen overboard.'* So what? And in the greater scheme of things I'm not sure anyone would miss me anyway. Such crazy thoughts raced through my brain. Needless to say I was out of my bunk dressed in oilskins, and up on deck ready for the next catch before you could say *wet fillet of cod*. Ginger bollocks had scared the shit out of me.

I was still feeling rough and half-expecting to throw up again, but the threat to my life had forced me out of my bunk. Self-preservation was my priority; I had no option but to get on with it. Ginger's solution didn't bear thinking about. I now needed an alternative plan, as clearly I wasn't cut out for a life on the ocean waves. And certainly not for a life on the trawlers. I smiled to myself. *If only they knew I was in the Royal Navy.* I was a sailor who hadn't been to sea, a sailor who was as sick as a dog, but obviously not a *sea-dog*. It was then I decided to confess my deception to the skipper. I'd tell him I was a deserter from the RN and shouldn't be on board. I made my way up to the bridge and confessed my true identity to him, adding that I was still feeling very ill. He said all he could do was contact the harbour master in Lowestoft. He thought, as we weren't too far out to sea, they might send another vessel out and take me back to shore. I was in total agreement with his plan as I could see no end to the sickness and misery that consumed me. I also thought, if he was to let the authorities know they had a deserter on board, it might extend my life expectancy. As things transpired no one came out to take me back to Lowestoft, but at least people now knew where I was should anything happen to me.

Thankfully the sea sickness passed within the next 24 hours, which surprised me as I continued to eat regularly in spite of constantly feeling sick. I was now up on deck during each watch, hauling the catch in along with everybody else. We wound the nets up and over the side every four hours; it was a non-stop day-and-night routine for the entire trip. During that time I learned to winch in the nets and gut the fish with the best of them. Cod and flat fish, mainly sole and plaice, were the main bulk of the catch, but the beauty of the silver-bellied mackerel with their marbled iridescent blue-green colours and black barred scales blew me away.

The Fleetwood four had their fun mainly at my expense, sending me down to the engine room to ask the engineer for a bucket of steam and a long stand. He told me to 'hang around' whilst he went and fetched the stand? Yes, I was caught out with that one, but not with the bucket of steam. The Fleetwood four also held a competition amongst themselves to see if they could lasso a seagull. This sport usually occurred when we'd gutted the fish and threw the entrails back overboard, a time when gulls targeted the waters around us. With so many gulls surrounding us you'd think they would be easy prey; but I only saw them manage to lasso one and it untangled itself as soon as it was caught.

On the day we headed back into port I learned there was a shower on board. This was something no one had mentioned, probably because no one felt they needed one as there was nowhere to go. I suppose the consensus was that if you were to be up on deck every four hours, and dressed in oilskins and smelling of fish – what's the point in taking a shower?

I observed our approach on deck as we chugged into Lowestoft harbour early one Sunday morning. The rhythmic throbbing of the engine was an affront to the peace and tranquillity that surrounded us as we sliced through the glass-like waters. I'd almost forgotten the slumbering world of Sunday mornings, even though we'd only been away for a fortnight. We drifted on towards our mooring, passing boats, tugs and trawlers, each resplendent under the sunshine in their colours of white, red, black and blue. There was no movement in the harbour except us, as the sun captured and framed the scene, lighting up the town behind the vessels with its golden glow, a real picture-postcard scene.

I felt pleased with myself, as if I'd achieved something. I was glad I'd stuck it out and come through it, as I looked back to that first day on the *Elsa,* when I was so sick I was ready to give up after only a few hours out at sea. I was now a picture of health, both physically and mentally; my seasickness was now a distant memory. As I stepped ashore I was as buoyant as the *Elsa* had been riding those high North Sea rollers. I was looking forward to picking up some pay and enjoying a night out with my Fleetwood companions as I strode out along the jetty. Trawler tradition had it that the whole crew would now breakfast together before parting and going their separate ways. I was thinking how everything had worked out well in the end, until that is, I reached the end of the quay. It was there that two boys in blue jumped out of a police panda car. They'd received the message from the harbour master two weeks before but had waited until we docked before taking me into custody. They escorted me to the police station where they informed the Andrew that I was now in their care. I spent the rest of the day and that night in a Lowestoft police cell, where I didn't sleep too badly.

But when I awoke the next morning it was as if I was still on the *Elsa Rosa*, rocking and riding on the North Sea. I got up to collect my breakfast tray and was all over the place, crashing into one wall and then staggering across the cell and hitting the opposite wall. There was no doubt that I'd acquired my sea legs, and for some time afterwards I couldn't escape the reeling, rolling and sideways motion that had hijacked my mobility over the past two weeks.

I was escorted back to HMS *Victory* barracks in Pompey and held in the cells at recess; this meant I was held in custody until my trial. It was May 1968 because my beloved United were in the European Cup Final. And fair play to the regs on duty that night for unlocking our cell doors, leaving them open and letting us listen to the radio commentary of the match.

When I arrived in recess I was greeted by another guy in one of the cells, a cheeky cockney sparrow. He saw my sleeping bag and haversack as I went through the admission procedure and found it amusing.

'*Wo! It's the 'appy travler!*' he shouted as he spied me hand over my baggage. He was a happy-go-lucky character himself, someone else who didn't fancy a life in the RN. He found a funny side to most things in life; a common denominator amongst most cockneys I came across. We introduced ourselves, exchanged pleasantries, and described to each other how we came to be in recess. I said I just wanted *"out."* and was working my ticket. The cockney then told me his story. He said he was arrested back home in London for being as pissed as a fart. He said he'd gone AWOL and had found work as an usher at the Houses of Parliament, something that mainly involved opening doors for MPs. When he was eventually apprehended for being drunk and disorderly and went to court, he said the copper that arrested him was called to the witness box. He said the bobby opened his notebook and read out the circumstances surrounding his arrest, something he, personally, had no recollection of.

'On being apprehended the defendant said, "Don't worry, cocker, I'm backing Britain."' I thought this was brilliant. The *I'm Backing Britain* slogan was introduced by the government to boost the economy. It was emblazoned on carrier bags with a Union Jack backdrop, and in the mid-sixties you saw them everywhere you went. London was swinging then, with Twiggy, Mary Quant and Carnaby Street. The Beatles were in full flow as were the Stones and The Who. Mods and rockers were followed by hippies and free love (thanks largely to the pill, which made contraception easy). Young people in the UK and USA instigated a social revolution that proclaimed freedom and peace, partly against the war in Vietnam. I wanted to be part of this scene. I was desperate to get back into civvy street, to grow my hair and lose my virginity. I wanted to be free to *live* through what I thought were the best years of my life.

When I went in front of the commodore at Victory barracks I was asked if I had anything to say. *'I made a mistake signing on, sir. A big mistake. I need to get out, sir. I'm not cut out for Navy life, a life in the Armed Forces. I formally request a discharge, Sir. Please let me go, Sir. I made a big mistake. I'm asking – begging you, Sir, to give me the discharge I desire. That's all I ask, Sir – a discharge from Her Majesty's Forces.'*

'I'm sorry you feel that way, Alcock. It's something I'm not at liberty to do. I can't do it, do you understand? It is not within my powers.' He looked straight at me. *Oh yes it is,* I thought, and returned his stare. I stood there unblinking, motionless. I didn't care about protocol anymore. I just wanted out.

'You should have thought about all this before you signed on, Alcock. My advice to you is to stick your chest out, stand up straight and be a man, someone the Royal Navy can be proud of. You need to buckle down, carry on and serve the time you signed on for. I sentence you to 28 days' detention suspended for a year.'

This meant I'd have to keep my nose clean for 12 months. If I was charged again with something else within a year, I'd have to serve the 28-day suspended sentence plus any additional days I'd receive for any new offence.

After I was released from recess I was instructed to report to the regulators at the main gates; there I had to collect a railway warrant and a couple of quid in cash, which would be deducted from my pay. I'd assumed the *Happy H* had sailed out of Pompey dockyard some time ago, and so it came as a surprise when I was instructed to join her. I thought my plan for another draft, possibly on a smaller ship, had worked. The truth was the *H* had sailed, but she hadn't left UK waters; she was currently off the coast of Scotland carrying out sea trials.

Whilst waiting for my railway warrant the regs quizzed me about my family and why I had absconded. When I explained my circumstances, they remarked how they were continually surprised by the number of personnel from broken homes who ended up in trouble. I guess it merely reflected the number of young guys from fragmented families who adopted the Armed Forces as their home. I'd seen a few of these guys already, guys who often stayed on board when they were due to go on leave, because they had nowhere else to go. I remember times when I packed my bags to go home on leave and consciously kept my head down because I felt guilty. I didn't want to look a messmate in the eye when I knew I was leaving them to spend their leave in an empty mess. I thought how lucky I was to have somewhere to go to even though it wasn't with my own family.

The train journey to Scotland was an arduous one. Portsmouth to Waterloo, across London to Kings Cross, KC to Aberdeen, change at Aberdeen for Inverness. Upon arrival at Inverness I was escorted to the port at Lossiemouth and onto a trawler, similar in size to the one I'd been on in Lowestoft. This time I experienced no qualms or queasiness as we slipped out of Moray Firth and into the North Sea.

We found the *Happy H* anchored and motionless, as we bobbed and tossed our way towards her. She was a huge grey monster of a ship, a floating naval airbase with a hangar, and a runway approximately 220m long by 44m wide. The *H* carried thirty operational aircraft and completely dwarfed the tug I was now on.

As we approached I spotted two of my messmates, Wills and Doog, leaning over the starboard boat deck having a smoke. They saw me and waved, but I ignored them; I wasn't too happy about being caught and brought back to the *H*. I wondered how I was going to get back on board as we drew alongside. *Perhaps they'll drop one of those winches,* I thought. No chance. A rope ladder appeared from nowhere and landed on the deck of the trawler. I made hard work of clambering halfway up this giant carrier to the safety of the lower boat deck. Later I had a laugh with Wills and Doog when I learned Wills had remonstrated with Doog for waving at me. Apparently he'd said, *'Don't wave; he's working on the trawlers.'* He remembered our meeting in Pompey when he organised a whip-round for me to help me on my way to Lowestoft. He thought Doog might blow my cover; they both hadn't realised my time on the run was over.

FIRST STOP
CAPE TOWN

When we finally set sail for the Far East you wouldn't have known we were at sea. The *Happy H*, with its 23,000 tonne displacement (28,000 when fully loaded), meant that, for all the motion, you could have been taking a walk in the park. Apart from the slight engine vibration, which soon became oblivious to the senses, there was no apparent movement between decks. Our floating village sailed along merrily without incident, until we hit the Bay of Biscay. It was then that there was noticeable momentum on board, a gradual rocking and rolling between bow and stern, port and starboard. Someone had been up on the flight deck and reported we were crashing into 20-foot-high waves. This was not uncommon in the Bay of Biscay, where winds blow in from America to Europe and cause waves to climb as they gather speed from west to east. These swells can be even greater when accelerated by the high winds. I had to smile at Doog who, along with some others, was throwing up in the mess. I was grateful for my experience on the trawlers as it had stood me in good stead and enabled me to wander around the ship like a true salt; sea sickness, for me, was a thing of the past.

We sailed into Cape Town on the last day of July and dropped anchor for a five-day (four-night) sojourn. I was up on the boat deck nearest to our mess when I witnessed our approach from the Atlantic. The spectacular vista of the Cape in all its splendour was something to behold. I still regard it as one of greatest sights I've ever seen. On that particular day the view was ably supported by a bright cornflower-blue sky. It was a perfect backdrop to the immense mesa of Table Mountain, with Lion's Head to the east and Devil's Peak to the west. The mountainous panorama reflected in bright sunshine contrasted sharply with the brilliant white residential properties, which were all sandwiched below between the mountains and the surrounding blue sea coastline. It was a sublime sight that took my breath away. I stood and paused, momentarily, captured by my capacity for wonder. I felt privileged to view one of the world's outstanding sights from the vantage point of the ocean.

The duty watch system on board alternated between port and starboard, and each crew member was either in one or the other. When at sea your duty watch was every other day, but when in port this was relaxed to a one-in-four duty watch system. During our stay in Cape Town this meant that there was plenty of time to see the sights the city had to offer.

In those days the apartheid system ruled in South Africa. It was divided into four racial groups: white, Indian, black and coloured. The latter included people of mixed race or other non-whites that didn't fit into the non-white categories. It was a crazy, unjust system, where non-whites were not allowed to vote; all had to use separate schools, hospitals and public services. It was a crime for a white person to have sexual relations with someone from another race; but if they were found out then it would be the person from the other race, and not the white person, who would be prosecuted.

One of the guys had a letter from his old man saying he had a friend who lived in Cape Town, someone he'd known during the last World War, and asked if he could look him up. He'd forwarded an address and so three of us set out on what we saw as an adventure. Shore leave in Cape Town was declared a *"rigger's run,"* which meant uniform had to be worn if you went ashore. It was quite a trek to the address we'd been given and meant catching a train, but we viewed it as an opportunity to see something of everyday life in Cape Town.

The train journey brought us face to face with apartheid. Since we had to travel in uniform it was obvious to any South African that we were visitors and not residents. The carriages were segregated, but when we boarded we hadn't noticed we were sitting in a *Blacks Only* carriage. We didn't mind who we sat next to and thought, probably through some misguided belief, that if we sat amongst blacks in SA we were supporting their fight for equality.

After we'd joined the RN a few of us had become good mates. Our short regulation haircuts meant we could could still identify with a young generation in civvy street; the modernist (mods) movement. Earning regularly meant we could buy fashionable clothes (through a naval tailor), and we followed the black music of reggae, soul and tamla motown. We idolised performers like, Otis Redding, Joe Tex, The Temptations and Smokey Robinson. They were soul music heroes to us; it didn't matter about the colour of their skin.

Back on the train a solitary black man got on and sat across the aisle from us; he was the only other occupant in the carriage. He sat staring at us. I began to feel uncomfortable and decided I needed to explain how we felt about things: *'Look, man, we don't mind sitting here.'*

'No,' added Doog. *'We're all one, the same.'*

'Yeah, we're all equal, same as you,' said Wills, whose father's friend we were travelling to meet. *'You don't mind, do you?'* he added.

The black man just sat, stared and said nothing. It was at this point a white guard entered to check tickets. Upon seeing us he came over and stated we weren't allowed in this carriage and we needed to move along to another one. As an afterthought he then asked if the black guy was disturbing us. He told us not to worry as he could easily report him if he'd been a nuisance. He then repeated this as though we hadn't heard him. He asked us again if we wanted to make a complaint. It sounded as though he was expecting us to complain against the black man. I was sure he wanted us to, even though this guy had done nothing wrong and it was our fault that we were sitting in the wrong carriage. We said we were quite happy where we were and that the black man had done nothing wrong. We reiterated again there was no problem, and said we didn't see any point in moving. We said we had nothing against black people. The guard's demeanour changed. He became louder and more aggressive when he realised we weren't going to move or complain. He now insisted we move to a *Whites Only* carriage. He said if we didn't comply he'd pull the emergency cord and stop the train; he threatened to have us physically removed. As soon as he said this the train began to slow down and Wills, who had a map, declared it was our stop. We all stood up and got off the train. *Funny how fate sometimes plays a hand.*

We found our way to a dark door on the fourth floor of a tower block. After knocking a few times (there was no bell) and getting no answer, we gave up. We had purposely planned to travel during early evening, thinking there was a better chance of catching someone at home outside of working hours. It was dusk, rapidly descending into darkness, and half the corridor lights didn't work because of blown or missing bulbs. The lift didn't work and the littered stairwell was also blacked out.

We groped our way down to the street in semi-darkness, and then decided to high-tail it back to the bright lights and relative safety of Cape Town city centre, only this time in a *Whites Only* carriage.

The splendid architecture of old Cape Town with its colonial buildings and boulevards was impressive, but underneath this civilised facade lay a perceptible tension. A persistent undercurrent of threatened violence existed that wouldn't go away; something that was more pronounced after sunset. I thought maybe I was overreacting, and it was merely a reflection of Jolly Jack's predisposition to visit the seedier parts of city nightlife. But no, there was definitely an air of foreboding, something that made you constantly check to see who was around or look nervously over your shoulder to see if you were being followed. We stayed mindful as we wanted to remain safe, and were well aware that intoxicated sailors out on the town were easy prey. It was these runs ashore (with 2,000 sailors on the loose) that I'd always dreaded; they weren't my idea of a good time. When we got off the train we headed to the nearest bar and bought a cheap bottle of Cape Brandy. We downed this between us and then decided to take another along to a nightclub. It was common practice then (and cheaper) to take your own booze into clubs.

The club we entered was aptly named The Crypt, as it was full of zombie-like characters who were completely out of it. Stupefied, through alcohol or drugs or both, they flowed constantly between tables, toilets and the bar, lurching and stumbling across a floor that stuck to your shoes as if it had been recently varnished. The air, heavy with spiralling cigarette smoke, permeated around the dim lighting and made it impossible to see across to the far side of the room. We passed a pretty girl at the bar leaning between an old man's legs. She had one arm around his neck, whilst the other hand cupped his chin as she kissed him full on the mouth. He looked about seventy, twice her age, and had his hand up her skirt. I was sober, and a not quite innocent eighteen-year-old, but my stomach churned. It was a complete turn off.

We plotted our way across the room and found space on some bench seats that backed onto a wall. In front was a Formica-topped table with a couple of empty chairs. I noticed that most of the tables were covered with spilt drinks, fallen bottles or cans, and overflowing ashtrays. Everywhere guys were either half-asleep or resting their heads across tables if there was space. Women, too, were out of it; some had spread-eagled themselves across chairs, with their legs stretched out at weird angles; others had skirts hoisted that high you could see their knickers. Couples groped one another in dark corners amongst all the littered debris. Everyone who remained conscious had a cigarette on the go, even the gropers. The whole place was a mess.

It was then we spotted him. Taff, from our mess, eighteen like me, in one of the dingy corners with an old woman on his knee. She was old enough to have been his grandmother, or even great-grandmother; it was an age and gender reversal of the couple we'd passed earlier by the bar. Again my stomach turned over; I couldn't believe what I was seeing. I quizzed Taff the next day about his *party* at the nightclub. He said he had no regrets and had had a good night. I didn't delve into how the evening ended with her. But I did ask him if that was the kind of run ashore he expected when he'd signed on? *A run ashore and a bag-*

off with a pensioner? Taff didn't comment further on his previous night's entertainment, but he admitted he had little option but to enlist in the Navy. He said he'd appeared in court for breaking into a cheese factory and then having a dump amongst the cheeses. The judge gave him a choice: sign up for the RN or spend time in borstal. His defence claimed Taff was in the process of joining the RN at the time and that he was drunk when he broke into the factory and committed the offence. Taff confessed he was absolutely legless, but had never been in trouble before. I wasn't sure whether Taff was from Caerphilly, but I've always steered clear of any Welsh cheeses since his revelation.

Unfortunately our next run ashore coincided with a visit to our mess by the eminent heart surgeon Dr Christiaan Barnard. He was world famous at the time for performing the first human-to-human heart transplant in 1967. Phillips, a three-badge Killick in charge of the mess, had invited him on board to share a tot of rum. Dr B duly obliged. Although I didn't see him personally, it lifted the spirits of everyone who was present in the mess. It showed that someone of his stature actually had a heart. He showed humility, respect and saw us flunkies as equals. In spite of the inequality that existed in the South African regime, Dr Barnard chose not to discriminate and managed to transcend his country's prejudices. His conduct was in stark contrast to a lot of *pigs* I'd encountered in the senior service, who were quite happy to patronise ratings from the lower decks. They made sure the barrier of *them and us* was firmly in place, a legacy of the UK class system still prevalent at the time.

When we next went ashore we were accosted by a coloured woman old enough to be our mother. She shouted and waved at us from the opposite side of a main road, so we crossed over to see what she wanted. She wasn't black but mixed race, and said there was a party that night with girls, music, dancing and drinking. And did we want to go? It cost two rand each and we all happily chipped in. She gave us an address in District Six and said the action would start around 7.00pm. We were aware that the whole of the ship's company had been briefed about this area of Cape Town: *District 6 is strictly "off limits"*. It was a black area that was regarded as dangerous for whites to enter. To us the colour of the woman, like the black man on the train, made no difference. She could have been white, brown, black, green or purple; we were young bucks on our first voyage, in our first port of call, and looking for good times and adventure. We had no hesitation in accepting her offer of wine, women and song.

The taxi driver drove slowly up a narrow, litter-strewn street, passing rows of white single-storey adobe buildings, where many black people sat outside on low walls next to the pavement. They smoked and stared at us as the taxi crawled by. The flat-roofed houses with square fronts had a few concrete steps that led up to the front doors. They were constructed in blocks of two or three, and each block was divided by narrow, uneven alleyways, where giant rusty oil drums had been discarded on the corners to collect refuse. It was close to twilight and groups of black, brown and mixed-race ragamuffins played outside, running around with sticks and rolling tyres; the obligatory pack of roaming mongrel dogs sniffed, urinated and skirmished indiscriminately with each other. When some kids saw our taxi crawling down their street they abandoned their games and ran right up to the taxi windows and stared inside; some pulled faces and stuck out their tongues. The driver continued along the street at a snail's pace, checking out house numbers.

Eventually we pulled up where a black guy was standing on top of some steps outside one of the front doors, as if he was keeping guard. He ignored our arrival but continued, as before, looking intently up and down the street. He was dressed all in black leather from head to toe, with a black leather trilby over what I imagined was a shiny bald head. His hat complemented a full-length black leather coat and black leather trousers. He could have stepped straight out of an old World War II film as a member of the Gestapo. When the taxi driver pulled in and wound down his window, leather man danced down the steps to the curbside; he asked what we wanted. We had the right place because he said, *'You're early.'* But we all got out and followed him up the steps, through the front door and down a long corridor with doors leading off on both sides. Halfway down on the right, our host threw open a door. *'Wait in here until we're ready.'*

I was about to step inside when a mangy dog leapt off a bed that was partially hidden behind the door. It bolted straight towards us and wriggled through the tangle of legs that filled the doorway. I turned back and saw a skinny old hag sit up on the bed; she struggled to kick off a filthy sheet that had become wrapped up in her legs. Dressed in a manky nightshirt that matched the sheet on the bed, she eventually set herself free and made a beeline towards us all standing by the door. She elbowed herself through and quickly disappeared down the corridor. The whole scene unnerved me. Skags, immediately behind me, and Jimmy behind him, were still hovering in the doorway, neither in nor out, as the dog and the woman rushed between them. The room stank. I worded Jim before he managed to enter the room: *'Stick your foot in the door, Jim.'* I didn't want Gestapo man shutting us in. *'I don't fancy it. What do you think?'*

'Na, f--- it,' said Skags behind me.

'Let's f--- off,' said Jim.

We told leather man to keep the two rand we'd each paid and said we couldn't be bothered to wait. It was still just about light outside and so we set off down the road the way we had come.

After we arrived back on board we heard of other horror stories about matelots who'd ventured off limits into District 6. One was when a taxi accidentally strayed into that area, only for the taxi driver to pull over and do a runner. Fortunately the guys inside had the presence of mind to lock the doors before black faces appeared at the windows. Unable to gain access they rocked the cab back and forth, as if to roll it over. Luckily the cab driver returned and took them back into town; needless to say he didn't get his fare. Another episode was when a couple of guys visited a bar nearby, only to be targeted and followed by three big burly black guys. Apparently these guys were definitely gaining on our shipmates when the sailors turned a corner and luckily bumped into three other sailors they knew. The additional strength in numbers was enough to make the would-be muggers disappear.

There happened to be an unfortunate end to our stay in Cape Town. A rumour spread around our mess that two ratings had disappeared and it was thought they'd gone on the run. Allegedly some clothes were found on a beach, and there was speculation that this was part of their disappearing act, to make it look as though they'd drowned. Unfortunately it wasn't true that they'd gone AWOL, but it was true that they had drowned. A host family had invited them to stay with them for the weekend, and they'd gone for a day out to Camps Bay beach. The *Cape Times* reported that the host had warned them of the strong currents there, but the sailors were determined to go for a swim. His account stated that he was playing with his children when he realised the sailors had got into difficulties. He said he tried to reach them, but the current was too strong and he, too, had to be rescued. He said there was nothing he could do. By the time a SAR helicopter from Hermes was deployed, it was too late to save them.

ON TO SINGERS

We slipped anchor and headed for Singapore approximately 5,000 miles away. The *H* hugged the coast around the Cape of Good Hope to avoid the strong Aghulas current, which was against us. Although a steward lives below decks there's always the opportunity, when off watch, to take a breather and view coastal sights and high seas from the boat decks above. I managed to see the town of Port Elizabeth and miles of golden beach as we headed up the eastern coast of South Africa. We then made a north-east beeline and headed towards Madagascar and Mauritius, and straight into a Force 8–9 gale, with 20–30 foot high waves and 85mph gusts. We hadn't experienced such rough seas since the Bay of Biscay.

As we entered the Indian Ocean the ship slowed down, but not before she'd crashed through dense streaks of white foam that rose, fell and floated on giant rollers. Up on the boat deck I was splattered with spray. I tasted the salt of the ocean on my face, and thought, *This is what it's all about.* I was alive. And then, paradoxically, I began to fathom more about the sea. I saw a different side to the calm, romantic vista of blue that had first enticed me to sail away when I stood on the dock in Southampton. I now witnessed the might of the Atlantic and Indian oceans colliding, the uncontrollable surges that could roll a 25,000-tonne ship like a rocking chair. I stood in awe of a turbulent, tempestuous sea. I was captivated, hypnotised.

The wildness of gigantic waves drew me in like a magnet and begged me to take the plunge. A voice in my head said, *Come on, it's easy; there's nothing to it; don't wait, come on in; jump over the side.* Trance-like, as in a dream, I pictured myself floating momentarily, my arms flailing, trying to stay afloat amongst the giant rollers. And then another thirty-foot wave would swamp me. I'd scramble, waving my arms frantically up and down, trying to stay up, keep my head up above water, until finally I'd succumb and be sucked under, disappearing into the depths below. And the voice persisted again: *Come on; you can do it. End it all; it'll only take a minute and you'll be gone. You'll be free; no more worries; no more cares. And who'd care anyway? Who's going to miss you?* The roaring angry sea wouldn't let go. It had me in its grasp. I stood there, swaying, getting wet, pondering: *Shall I? Shall I... end it all?* And then a giant wave rolled the ship. I lunged forward and banged my chest into the safety rail; I instinctively grabbed hold of it and held on for dear life. More spray slapped my face and the spell was broken. I stood there soaked, closed my eyes and inhaled deeply. I knew then I didn't want to die. From that moment on I didn't want to give in; I wasn't going to let them win. I knew I'd had a close call. I pushed myself free and scrambled back down the ladder and into the sanctuary of *4 Papa 1* mess. There were many nights afterwards when I lay awake in my bunk and reflected on how easy it would have been to end it all. I could so easily have banished the misery that consumed my life. But now I was relieved to be alive; I found solace in the fact that I'd confronted and overcame one of nature's most ferocious, yet beguiling, forces. I made a conscious decision that such destructive thoughts weren't going to possess me again. My near miss strengthened my resolve and made me more determined than ever to get out of the RN. I had hardly begun my life, but now I wanted to make sure I lived way beyond the time when I made my mistake at seventeen.

Two weeks later we sailed on up past Sumatra and into the Malacca Straits towards an island off Malaysia, Pulau Penang, where we dropped anchor. We were involved in "exercises" with other RN ships and submarines, as well as warships from both the Australian and New Zealand navies. One exercise, Operation Awkward Stations, involved divers trying to attach mines to the hull of the ship. Naturally we had to be anchored since divers wouldn't be able to keep up with a ship sailing at 20–30 knots; however the exercise was abandoned because a diver got into difficulty. And then we heard all the other divers were withdrawn, too, due to *"a heavy swell?"*. *How farcical is that,* I wondered. A war being called off through bad weather?

We were involved in other sea-going exercises before we finally dropped anchor off Langkawi. Liberty boats took us ashore for a *banyan*. As stewards we had access to victuals and so took ashore pork chops, salads and bread. It wasn't long before the pork was sizzling over a fire, some beer was downed and a lazy afternoon was spent *bronzying* on a deserted tropical beach. We were led to believe it was an uninhabited island, but when we ventured further inland to look around we came across discarded Coke cans and bottles. Some native guys then appeared out of nowhere and tried to sell us beer. The day passed all too quickly for me, but it was a welcome break from the claustrophobic, overcrowded atmosphere of *4 Papa 1* mess.

We finally docked in Singapore at the end of August and berthed on the north side of the island in Sembawang Naval Dockyard. This covered over 20 square miles and had the largest dry dock in the world. Apart from *Jolly Jack (JJ)*, hundreds, if not thousands, of local workers used to stream in and out of the dockyard every day.

Opposite the main gates and over the road from the dockyard lay a strip of bars: The Oasis, New Paris, Melbourne, which all had their resident coquettes. These girls, mainly of Chinese, Malay, Indian or Eurasian heritage, were specifically employed to prey on *JJ* as he ventured ashore for a night out. Their western dress sense and young unblemished skin positively glowed under the subdued lighting of the bar. They enhanced their appearance with long eyelashes that fluttered over deep, intoxicating, inkwell eyes, and pouting cherry-red lips. Invariably, you'd find these girls sitting at the bar with skirts high on the thigh. To the uninitiated, the tantalising allure they projected provoked the possibility of an exotic liaison with one of them; this often enticed the unsuspecting customer to dally a little longer than they initially intended. This was a fruitless exercise as these girls hardly ever drank alcohol, and the most you could hope for was to buy them tea or a soft drink and share their company. Many a rookie matelot must have rued his decision to stop off in one of these bars for a quick drink, only to linger longer than they intended and spend more cash than they planned. Me and my mates had been wisened up to the bar-girl ruse from our old and trusted messman, *killick* Phillips. The thing about those girls then, which still holds with me today, is the fascination I had with their hair. I've always marvelled at the rich black colour and texture of Asian hair; how its iridescent blue-blackness can shimmer like silk. I don't know why, but that glossy sheen always conjures up an image in my mind of a raven's plumage, reflected at night as it flies across the bright white light of a silvery full moon.

But the must-see night-time venue for any visitor to Singapore then was Bugis (pronounced Boogie) Street. You could go there anytime after nightfall and soak up a constantly buzzing atmosphere, which was replicated each and every night. Bugis Street was a crowded narrow street, full of hustle and bustle, where hawkers had ramshackle stalls that sold their wares of meat and vegetables, trinkets and jewellery, on both sides of the road. These stalls were interspersed with *al fresco* food vendors, who laid out bamboo chairs and tables indiscriminately, and so further restricted what was already a limited amount of space.

Coloured lights, hanging from the street stall lanterns, cast shadows at odd angles and made the whole scene appear surreal. Bugis Street was a *pasar malam* and I'm sure, at the time, it must have been one of the busiest streets on the planet. You'd be jostled to and fro, have to wait for others to pass by, get bumped, and, if you were to make any progress yourself, be the instigator of some bumping; always apologetically, of course. For all the diverse humanity that passed through that street and bumped into one another, I cannot recall any serious hostilities that got out of hand.

Everyone there appeared relaxed, and the mixed cacophony of the ensemble was not dissimilar to the trill of wildlife under the canopy of a rainforest. The mood was convivial; a certain *bonhomie* existed as you drifted along, soaking up the jingle-jangle world of the east on warm balmy nights. There were many exotic aromas that tantalised your nostrils from the food stalls; Indian, Malay and Chinese vendors vied for trade, titillating your senses with *dim sum,* noodles and roast meat. Other aromatic perfumes, spices and incense filled the air. I remember standing still at the end of the street one night and closing my eyes, trying to soak up and savour this unique oriental experience.

Amidst all the chaos young street urchins threaded there way in and out of the crowded melee, zig-zagging from table to table with small plastic boards and pens. Up and down the street they'd go until the early hours, when it would have been long past their bedtime back in the UK. They'd challenge anyone to a game of noughts and crosses for a Singapore dollar. On a nearby table one night the female companion of a four-ringer played and lost; nothing remarkable in that as the kids usually won. But then I heard her say, in a haughty, high-pitched voice that rose way above the incessant babble of the street, *'My God, he's got a brain in his little head.'*

It reminded me of my time back at Osprey, when I was waiting-on at a *pig's* function. It was FA Cup Final week when I heard one of the females say, *'Oh, I do hope Spurs win, because I really don't like Tottenham.'*

She, too, sounded so superior; yet it was obvious she didn't know what she was talking about. I found this supercilious manner particularly irksome; it was all too prevalent amongst *pigs* and their peers. I've always thought we are all victims of circumstance. So why do some people think they have the God-given right to look down on those less fortunate than themselves? I found this condescending attitude endemic amongst officers in the RN; it was another annoying thing that gnawed away at me, a constant reminder that I had to get out of *the Andrew.*

One of the main attractions in Bugis Street was the parade of the *Kai Thais,* which took place late at night and pulled in visitors from all over the globe. Many of the sisters, as they called themselves, dressed vividly in dazzling silks and satins.

Some wore long cocktail dresses in every colour of the rainbow, with splits from the ankle to the top of the thigh, whilst others squeezed into very short tight skirts and dresses. Their perfect make-up, bouffant hair and glimpse of cleavage only added to the shimmering exotic spectacle that was Bugis Street at night.

When midnight approached as many as thirty of the sisters would sashay up and down the street using it as a catwalk, whilst simultaneously touting for business. Apart from homing in on half-drunk sailors, particularly if they were Americans taking some *R&R* from the Vietnam War, they would immerse themselves in the spirit of the street. They'd stop at tables to cajole and tease, sit on laps, and agree to be photographed, all for a price. You could sense their proximity as the crescendo of audible conversation became more raucous; patrons became more animated, until the excitement reached fever pitch. You could smell the unmistakeable floral fragrance of perfume as they passed close by; it was intoxicating, yet at times overbearing. Often when the sisters, also known locally as Beany Boys, stopped at tables, they'd be provoked with lewd suggestions and coarse behaviour, but few ever complained. It was their innate instinct to survive and to continue to play their part in the street drama that was Bugis Street.

Many of the *Kai Thais* in Bugis Street had seen far worse times. They were young men who discovered they were *"different"* whilst still at school. They became socially ostracised and over time were disowned by their families; they sought solace with others who felt the same and didn't *"fit in"*. Often cast out on the street with no money, no home and no job, many of these transexuals were drawn into prostitution. The Bugis Street area was an obvious choice for them since it had been a red-light district for generations. Many of the Beany Boys used hormone injections to enhance their breast size and were saving up for transgender surgery. The extravagantly over-dressed and glamorous sisters were easily distinguishable from the local females, who wore plain and simple clothing. And yet mistakes were made.

O'Connell, a mouthy Irishman from our mess, made just such a mistake. He'd taken a sister back to her room for some sexual gratification, genuinely thinking he was accompanying a beautiful woman. He said when they arrived he paid up front and things were definitely *"looking up"*, as she was pleasuring him orally. Things progressed nicely up to the stage of undress, which was when O'Connell discovered *"she"* was still packed with meat and two veg. He blew up, as was his want, and demanded his money back. Things got out of hand and he was, literally, caught with his pants down. He/she came at him with a knife and scarred him in his nether regions. He escaped with his life, he said. No lasting physical damage was done, although he received treatment from the MO on board. All he was left with was injured pride, but at least it shut him up for a while.

The other highlight to an evening's entertainment in Bugis Street, centred around a filthy public toilet situated at one end of the street. Thank God I never had to sit down in there. The place was rank, with an overpowering stench of ammonia that emanated from a floor constantly flooded with urine. I'm sure I would have suffocated or passed out if I'd had to stay in there too long. The *Kai Thais* occasionally clambered up on to the flat roof and performed an impromptu striptease, although usually it was the Aussie and Kiwi sailors who shimmied up there. Once on the roof, two or three of them would strip off and perform what became a hallowed tradition: the *Dance of the Flaming Arseholes.* This became a ritualistic performance where crowds gathered below and chanted, '*Haul 'em down, you Zulu Warriors; haul 'em down, you Zulu Warriors!*'

The sailors would prance about on the roof and then stick rolled newspaper between the cheeks of their arse and set fire to it. Although they tried to ensure the paper stuck out far enough before they lit it, many miscalculated. I called it *Dance of the Burning Bums,* since you often heard the participants roaring and bellowing as they cavorted around wildly until the flames were extinguished, usually by beer hurled up from the captivated audience below. Such entertainment occurred around midnight, but Bugis Street could be an all-night venue if you wanted it to be.

Me and some of my mates – Wills, Jimmy, Doog and Skags – had ten days' leave due, and decided to take it in Singapore where we'd be docked for over a fortnight. We booked into the Union Jack Club (UJC) which was located near the centre of Singapore, and although it was dormitory accommodation it made a welcome break from the overcrowded confinement of *4 Papa 1* mess on board.

4 Papa 1 was an underground chamber with no natural light. It was home to over 60 men who slept in bunks that were stacked in threes, one on top of the other. The majority of bunks were housed in a number of grots (cul-de-sacs) with six bunks on each side (two stacks of three). The grot was wide enough for one man to stand on the deck in-between the bunks, but impossible for two to stand side by side. And if the twelve inhabitants of a grott queued up in single file between the bunks, then there would be an overspill where half of them would have to occupy space outside the grot. Most of the ratings in our mess were housed in these grots, the exception being a larger communal area, where a table and chairs were battened down in the centre. Eighteen bunks (again in triple tiers) surrounded the communal area, and due to my earlier AWOL excursion (hence my delayed arrival on board) I had no option but to accept the only bunk available, which was in this area.

If finding privacy in a grott was nigh on impossible, then finding it in the mess communal area *was* impossible. Everyone used the added facilities of table and chairs at one time or another. It was the focal point for those who played *uckers* – the Royal Navy's variation on the game of Ludo. And there were plenty of these obsessives who rolled the dice night and day. I'd often go to sleep with dice rattling in my head and wake up in the morning to the same rhythm, as if they'd been playing all night. Another downside to my bunk location was that it was right next to the mess tannoy speaker. I turned my bedding around, head to tail, to distance myself from it, but it was the lesser of two evils. I moved my head away from the blare of music, the blast of Captain's Orders, the piping on board of various dignitaries, only to find myself closer to the head of another sailor in the bunk directly below mine. The problem with this guy was that he was a prolific smoker; don't get me wrong, we all smoked, and at eight bob for three hundred Blue Liners who could blame us? The real problem with him was that he was a chain-smoker who slept with his ciggies and lighter under his pillow. The first thing he'd do in the morning, whether it was five, six or seven am, was to light up. And to compound the problem, he refused to lie the opposite way round in his bunk, which would have allowed his smoke to filter up over my feet instead of my face. I was in a perpetual smog when he lit up; there was no escape; I'd have to vacate my bunk as soon as he woke up. Thankfully, we were on opposite watches, which meant I could lie smoke-free for a few hours each day when he was on watch.

Life on board had become too claustrophobic for me, and so when me and my mates discussed taking some leave in Singapore, I was the first to get on board, although *I wouldn't be on board*, if you know what I mean. I made a promise to myself that I'd spend every minute of my ten days' leave ashore and so escape life underground in *4 Papa 1* mess.

When we checked into the Union Jack Club (UJC) we soon developed a routine where we'd rise early, shower and head downtown for some breakfast, taking our towels and swimming trunks with us. We'd pass a school on the way where all the kids performed exercises on a playground before disappearing into classes. We'd stop and watch this, fascinated, as we'd seen nothing like it in the UK. Afterwards we'd seek out a street hawker who sold us iced coconut milk; then find another one further on who sold us nuts wrapped up in newspaper cones. I usually went for a mix of peanuts, cashews and walnuts, and always saved some of my milk to wash the last of my nuts down. The cost of living – as well as life itself – was cheap back then.

After breakfast we'd drop in at the Brit Club, situated directly opposite Raffles Hotel, where there was a huge swimming pool at the rear of the building. It was a magnet for sunbathers, and since we wanted to get a glorious suntan, we spent each day bronzying there. We mingled alongside bikini-clad wives and daughters, family members of those serving in the Armed Forces, who were mainly stationed out there long term. The females were a welcome attraction, as well as a pleasant distraction, to us. Although no serious relationships developed between us and the wives and daughters, it was refreshing to socialise with females from back home in the UK.

We'd always grab a bite to eat at the Brit Club before returning to the UJC. On our journey back to the UJC we passed the Capitol cinema, where a guy would sit playing his guitar inside the arched main entrance. Each time we stopped by he'd give us his rendition of *Blood Red River,* a blues number by Bill Jackson. Next to him was a notice board written in Chinese and English saying he needed money to continue his journey to Australia. He seemed to do OK as his upturned hippie hat always had a few notes and coins inside; later on we'd catch him dining *al fresco* in Bugis Street.

Evening entertainment usually kicked off back at The Brit with a few *Tiger beers* before we moved on. For almost a week we'd end up on Bugis Street; that is until our money ran out. One by one the guys drifted back to live on board; this was something you could do, stay on leave but sleep and eat on board. I was determined to stay loose and hang out at the UJC for as long as possible; although I was forced to return to the *Happy H* to borrow some money in order to stay ashore. For me, the whole point of taking leave was to get away from the oppressive living conditions that existed on board. I couldn't stomach the thought of living back in our mess when I was supposed to be on leave. The idea of living on board made me sick; but then, unlike my mates, I didn't want to be in the Navy full stop. I knew I'd be getting myself into debt, but I also knew we'd soon be rolling on the high seas again with no immediate plans for a run ashore once we left Singers. I would have plenty of time to pay off any debts before our next port of call.

Although my messmates on board ship were still on leave, it made little difference to our routine. We still met up in the Brit, sunbathed and took things from there. One afternoon, when Jim and I were the only ones out of the four of us bronzing behind the Brit, a monsoon downpour on a grand scale crashed out of the heavens. It provoked a human tsunami when everyone deserted the pool area and made a mad scramble for the safety and shelter inside the Brit. This thunder storm and downpour lasted much longer than normal, which led to Jim and I taking some refreshment inside. Eventually we decided to abandon our bronzing for rest of the day and changed back into our civvies. We spent the rest of the afternoon in the Brit becoming too familiar with that intoxicating elixir Tiger beer. Too much went down too quickly; consequently we were ready for some action much earlier than usual.

By the time we tumbled down the steps outside the Brit it was late afternoon and we were the worse for wear. Taxi drivers and other street hawkers descended upon what they must have thought was easy prey. We were engulfed as soon as we stepped outside:

'*You wan watch, Joe… you wan watch… Seiko?*'

'*Taxi, Joe, you wan taxi… I take you anywhere… Where you wan go? I take you…*'

One grabbed my arm as they swarmed around us; the fresh air hit me and left my head spinning. I didn't know what I wanted or where I wanted to go. I felt lost and disorientated.

'*Joe, young girl… you wan young girl… virgin Joe, Joe…*'

'*My name's Peter,*' I shouted. '*My name's Peter!*'

'*Peter, you wan young girl? Clean girl? Peter…?*'

In my stupor I was trying to deflect attention; but in reality I wasn't sure what I was doing. Their incessant haranguing didn't stop. I realised you couldn't win. Jim grabbed my arm and led me round the corner. He said we'd get a cab and then decide what we'd do. He found a driver he recognised and trusted, and so we both fell into the back seat of the yellow and black Mercedes. We drove off and all I could hear was Jim shouting:

'*Down flip-flop, Chuck; down flip-flop, Chuck!*'

'*Where go? Where go…?*' came the response.

'*Anywhere, Chuck. Anywhere!*'

Chuck drove around for a while until Jim suggested a bag off. We still had plenty of time to kill before our rendezvous with the others in Bugis Street. As time passed, and my head semi-cleared, I became more inclined towards Jim's way of thinking. *Let's go for it,* I thought. My main concern had always been catching a dose – VD. I needed to be sure that if I was to partake in the delights of the flesh, I wasn't going to catch anything. *How could I be sure?* It would be a momentous occasion for me if it happened, and I didn't want the memory to be tainted any more than it had to be. I hadn't given any serious thought to my virginity recently, but I'd often wondered about how and when I might lose it. I never imagined it would be with a prostitute and that I'd be paying for the privilege. If that wasn't sordid enough, I certainly didn't want to compound the circumstances surrounding *the event* by contracting an STD. I shuddered at the thought. *Now that really would be a momentous occasion.*

A couple of *nearly* episodes, with regards to losing my virginity, flashed through my mind. One was when I was sleeping rough in the Chines at Bournemouth. I shared my sleeping bag one night with a raven-haired vamp who was older than me, something adolescent guys dream about. Her dark eyes promised to take me where I'd never been before. I kissed her luscious lips. She pressed my buttocks into her groin. I knew she wanted more. I was seventeen and slightly built; she was voluptuous and larger than I; yet we both managed to squeeze inside my single sleeping bag. The only problem was when we were both inside; there was little room for manoeuvre. We couldn't move freely without our knees, elbows, arms and legs getting in the way. I managed to half escape and take my shirt off; she did likewise and took off her top from a sitting position. I wriggled out, stood up, undid my kecks and took them off. I was starkers when I got back inside. Meanwhile my dream had undone her jeans and shuffled them down past her knees. I felt the warmth of her breasts as I lay on top of her; it was heaven, where I wanted to be: flesh on flesh. My member, tucked somewhere between her thighs or underneath her, felt like a missile on its launching pad, and it was getting closer to countdown. I knew blast-off was fast approaching, but a lack of mobility persisted. Her legs were tied around her ankles by her jeans, and I couldn't lock-in; time was running out. There was a lot of rubbing and grinding as we French kissed passionately. Finally, I was left with no other option but to explode into orbit without her. She was okay about it and no harm was done. I thought her casual acceptance of my premature *rush* came as no surprise to her.

The only other time I nearly lost my virginity, and I can recall it because it *was the only other time* I nearly lost it, was when Rib and I were on the roads in Scotland.

I'd met Annie in Princes Street gardens; she was a sweet Scots girl who lived in some high-rise flats on the outskirts of Edinburgh. I walked her home from work one day, and we got into some heavy petting under the stairwell of the block of flats where she lived. Again I got too excited and left things too late; this time, as I approached the critical moment, I fumbled and panicked. I was still in the throes of a passionate kiss, when I found I couldn't unfasten the zip of my jeans; it was snagged.

And by the time I managed to free myself it was all over. I'd failed miserably again. Thankfully Annie didn't make a fuss about it. We never consummated our relationship because soon afterwards we broke up. And so my ambition to relinquish my virginity, during the freedom I enjoyed on the roads, never materialised. I was seventeen when I joined the Royal Navy and, yes, I was still a virgin.

Back in the taxi the decision to kill some time by getting laid was agreed. I had never mentioned my virginity to anyone before, either to friends at home or messmates on board. I had always referred to my two close *nearly* sexual encounters as if I'd gone all the way. And when I referred to them in conversation with my peers, it sounded as though I was more experienced than I was. I always let it flow and thought let them believe what they want; it was up to them. I was happy to live the lie without admitting I was still a virgin. Now, it seemed, in a semi-alcoholic haze in Singapore, I was about to put the absence of my first full-blown sexual encounter *to bed,* so to speak. After losing my virginity I'd be able to hold my head up high in any company; I'd be able look *men of the world* in the eye and reveal the truth behind my sexual experiences. To be honest, I think in those days the kudos attached to losing your virginity was grossly overrated.

'Are you sure it'll be a clean girl?' I asked the taxi driver.

'Yes, *very clean young girl,'* Chuck responded. *'Look. See for yourself.'*

Chuck passed a little notebook back over his shoulder to us sitting in the back. Jim took it and opened it. He read aloud: 'This man is is one of the most honest men in Singapore.' Jim skipped a couple of pages.

'Chuck knows the youngest, best-looking girls in the area... I'd trust this man with my life. Please believe what he says – he won't con you! The girls he takes you to are clean, young and beautiful. You won't find a better guide in the whole of Malaysia!'

We settled the deal with Chuck, and it wasn't long before we arrived at a large white detached residence. There was a half-moon pebble-dash drive and a pillared entrance to the front door. It was certainly upmarket compared to anything we'd previously seen. I was bursting for a pee when we pulled up and so went around the side of the building to relieve myself. Jim was waiting by the front door with Chuck; they'd rung the bell. A Chinese woman who looked about thirty answered. She and Chuck exchanged pleasantries before Chuck appeared to ingratiate himself to her; it sounded like he wanted to make sure she knew it was him who'd brought business to the establishment. Eventually she ushered us in.

We followed her down a wooden-floored hallway with waist-high panelled walls that led into an open-spaced area. The lady who answered the door pointed us towards a soft cushioned three-seater settee, situated against a wall on the right-hand side. She waved an open hand as she swept passed it, intimating we should sit and wait there, whilst she carried on and disappeared through a door on the far side of the room.

I looked around the place whilst we sat and waited, and thought how it was a throwback to a more grandiose era.

An antique, crimson, velvet-cushioned chair was placed directly opposite the settee; behind this you could just make out a wide, carpeted staircase that led up to a balustraded balcony. The suffused half-light of the space we sat in was illuminated by lanterns and candles that left dark shadows in the corners. The gentle sound of traditional Chinese music, plucked from a lute or *pipa,* started up. The lady returned and lit some joss sticks of cinnamon and lavender which now mingled with the music. I closed my eyes and let the oriental ambience tantalise my senses. I wondered what eastern promises were in store for us.

My daydream was broken when I heard a door open and the sound of approaching footsteps. An African American guy, immaculately suited and booted, appeared out of the gloom. His shiny grey suit, with razor-creased trousers, dazzling white shirt and contrasting tie, all screamed *sharp.* He looked *the business.* The disconcerting thing for me was his huge sunglasses; you couldn't look him in the eye.

Well, you could, but it was impossible to see what lay behind those glasses. He sat down in the velvet chair opposite, motionless, staring. I'm not sure if he was actually staring; it was hard to tell. Was he weighing us up? Suddenly he raised his right hand high above his head and snapped his fingers twice in rapid succession. Out of nowhere eight girls appeared and assembled alongside him, four on either side. From where I sat they all looked tall, and I mean *TALL.* I'd have put them at seven foot; they were older than us, too. I was surprised, shocked and disappointed. I looked at Jim, who stared at the women and didn't say anything. I felt threatened. I remained silent, too. I didn't fancy any of these girls. The silence became uncomfortable but continued. It seemed like an impasse. Eventually I felt I had to say something. I leaned forward and said, '*Have you got any younger girls?*' The black guy stopped chewing his gum; I hadn't noticed he had been chewing. He then straightened himself up in his chair with a shrug of the shoulders and leaned forward towards me.

I got the distinct impression he *was* now staring directly at me; his shades had me hypnotised. He looked as though he had monstrous, black, giant bumble-bee eyes. I'm not sure if my head was *buzzing*, when he said, '*Are you calling my girls old?*'

'*No. No. I… I'm just thinking, well… well, I've only just turned eighteen myself. I was only wondering if…*' I left it hanging there. We were all paralysed for a few seconds until he eased back in his chair. *Phew*, I thought. Moments passed before he raised his arm and snapped his fingers twice more. Half a dozen more girls appeared, again divided on both sides of his chair as the others melted away. I knew I'd now have to make a decision; they were younger, but they all still looked so tall.

Funny how thoughts flash through your mind in micro-seconds. I recalled girls at school, when I had this thing about not being seen with a girl who was taller than me. Mind you, I was small for my age then, and I'd grown a bit since, and it didn't really matter now. I studied the faces of each these girls and knew I had to choose one. I was nervous as I searched for a pretty face. I wanted a girl I could kiss and hold. I wanted a girl I was attracted to, someone I'd be happy to be with. I suppose I'd always imagined losing my virginity with someone who meant something to me. Reflecting back I realised this didn't have to be the case; I knew it would mean absolutely nothing to her.

I struggled to my feet and was amazed to find that *all the girls* were shorter than me. I could see over the hair on their heads. I couldn't believe it. I turned around and looked at the settee, and for the first time I noticed how low it was; we'd been sitting on cushions barely a foot above the floor. I hastily picked out a sweet-faced Eurasian girl. Her skin was the colour of cappuccino coffee and her long, flowing black hair was pinned to one side with a floral clasp. She wore a short pink and white rose-patterned dress that matched her earrings. Her look reminded me of some Hawaiian girls I'd seen in an Elvis Presley film. As I approached her I thought I'd take her hand, lean forward and kiss her gently on the cheek. I didn't want to appear overzealous, and I thought a more modest, gentlemanly approach would convey how significant this experience was for me. Then I spotted old *bumble-bee head* watching us and I immediately abandoned my idea. Instead, I took her hand and let her lead me towards the winding staircase.

'*What's your name?*' I asked.

'*Lucy – what's yours?*' Joe, I told her. She giggled.

'*What's the matter?*' I asked.

'*Did you say John?*'

'No – Joe.'

'*Oh, sorry,*' she said, and giggled again behind her hand.

I should have said Peter, I thought, as we climbed the stairs. She let go of my hand and began stroking my inner thigh. I put my arm around her waist and pulled her closer. She moved her hand further up and rubbed me over my fly. At the top of the stairway we turned right and headed along the balcony past a few doors, until we came to one that was almost above where we'd been sitting. She opened the door and stepped back.

'*Wait here. You get ready. I won't be long.*'

She left and closed the door behind me. The room was sparsely furnished with a dressing table and mirror opposite the door, and some drawn curtains to the side. Cosmetics were strewn across the top of the table. The double bed to the right had an empty dining chair on either side. I decided to undress and so stripped down to my *chinky nicks*. I hung my clothes over one of the chairs.

I'd forgotten I was wearing pink nicks with roses on, which coincided with Lucy's dress. I then wondered if this was meant to be. I checked my reflection in the mirror on the dressing table and flexed my muscles with a couple of Charles Atlas poses. Although there wasn't much of me, I thought there wasn't much of her either. At least my sunbathing at the Brit had given me a healthy sheen. I sat on the bed and waited for Lucy to return. When she did she said, '*Twenty dollar. You pay now.*'

I retrieved my wallet from my trousers and paid her; this was expensive. Some of the guys on board had said that in Singers you could get all night in for ten dollars. I consoled myself by thinking that at least with Lucy I was paying for class; the place was clean and hopefully she was. Surely I wouldn't catch anything.

'*You have rubber?*' she asked. I shook my head. Condoms were free issue from the sick bay on board and you were encouraged to use them. I hadn't bothered to collect any as I hadn't planned such an excursion.

'*I have one.*' She held out her hand and unfurled her fingers. There, in the palm of her hand was one in its foil. '*Put it on.*' I was happy to oblige, as the last thing I wanted was an infection; but then I discovered I had trouble in the arousal department. I struggled with the condom. Lucy, meanwhile, slipped out of the satin robe she had returned to the room in. *This isn't how it's supposed to be,* I thought. *It's not meant to be like this.* I needed stimulation; I wanted to be turned on. I wanted some passion, some affection. I started to feel the whole thing was unnatural – unreal. I'd always dreamed my first time would be something to be savoured. I thought it would be with someone I cared for and they cared for me, that we shared true feelings with one another. I leant forward to kiss Lucy but she turned her head away and my lips brushed her neck instead. '*No kissey,*' she said, and then helped me with the condom. I stroked her back and was about to touch her breasts, when she lay back on the bed and pulled me on top of her. Although we engaged physically, I still wasn't fully aroused. I put this down to my earlier drinking bout and subsequent pee after we arrived. Schoolboy gossip had suggested to me years before that if you relieve yourself, just before intercourse, then it affects your ability to become aroused and prolongs performance. At the time I believed this to be true. I recalled Rib back in our Bournemouth days when he took Yvonne, a pretty young blonde girl, up to the Chines. He confessed afterwards he *couldn't get a hard on.* At the time I thought, *Wow!* But then Rib admitted he'd taken a leak just prior to getting down to business; we both believed this was the reason for him being unable to perform. We happily accepted it then. I now automatically assumed this was why I had erection problems with Lucy. It took me an age to get going, and I thought of loads of reasons as to why this might be. Was it the sterile atmosphere? The lack of emotion? Passion? The absence of touch? Taking a pee? Maybe it was a combination of all of these factors. When I finally completed the task and made my way downstairs, I found Jim waiting outside.

'Where have you been, man? What have you been doing? You've been so long.'

'I was just doing it, man. Having the ride.'

'Well, you took your time. Some kind of stud, eh?'

I didn't answer. I thought if Jim wants to think that, let him. I was happy for him to spread the word.

One morning, when the lads were back on board and I was buying breakfast with the street vendors, a little Malay girl of about six or seven years old appeared by my side. I'd just had a mouthful of nut mix when she thrust her hand out in front of me. I shuffled some nuts into it before she cupped both her palms together; I tilted the cone of nuts so that more spilled into her palms. She was ravenous and scoffed them all down before I could finish another mouthful; her voracious appetite forced me to buy another cone for us to share. After that first meeting by the street vendors I found her there waiting every morning.

I nicknamed her little *"Bunga,"* which I heard meant *flower* in Malay. She was a street urchin with tangled, dishevelled black hair, and large ebony eyes that appeared too big for her face. Each day she wore the same stained T-shirt, with scruffy shorts over liquorice-stick legs, and grubby feet that slid around in well worn flip-flops. There was a sadness in her eyes when she stared up at me, as if kindness had been a stranger to her and wasn't to be trusted. We'd sit in the sunshine by the roadside and eat in silence, watching Singapore wake up and wind its way to work. The incessant cacophony of car horns blasted their warnings to hundreds of rickshaw drivers, who risked their lives daily as they weaved in and out of the traffic boom.

I'd ask little Bunga if she was, *'Okay?'* But she never answered and never smiled. After we'd finished eating she'd just get up and walk away. Ironically, on my last day of leave, when I knew I wouldn't see her again, she got up, turned, waved and smiled, before she skipped away. I smiled and waved back at her, even though I knew it was goodbye. It reminded me that life is full of *goodbyes*. Not long afterwards we put to sea for more trials and exercises, before sailing south and down to Oz.

DEBAUCHERY AND DENIAL

It was mid-October when we berthed at Garden Island, Sydney Harbour, with the harbour bridge, affectionately known as the Coat Hanger, on our port side. Further along we could see the completed exterior of the famous opera house, with its grand shell-like roof; although there was still much work to be done inside before it was completed. From our jetty it was a sight to behold each time we stepped ashore and gazed across the bay.

We were docked in Sydney for a fortnight, but during that time I saw little of real interest, either in the city or the surrounding area. The nocturnal neon of Kings Cross, Sydney's red-light district, drew me and my messmates in like bees to nectar. I regard my time spent there as "*a nightclub blurrrrrr"*, since almost all of my runs ashore were lost in an alcoholic haze. I seemed to drown myself in drink every time I went ashore for a night out, something I vowed I'd never do after living with my alcoholic father. I made a promise to myself that I wasn't going to follow his drunken behaviour. I was proud that I managed an alcohol-free day on my eighteenth birthday, but it didn't take long afterwards for life on board to suck me in. Personal promises, much like NYE resolutions, became meaningless.

There was a heavyweight boxer in our mess who fought in the Far East championships, and when he was in training he'd sell his *grog* for a shilling. I started to pre-book this with him whenever I was going ashore. I'd combine his tot with our free daily entitlement of two cans of beer, which were standard issue then for naval personnel serving in the Far East. By the time I went down the gangway I was already light-headed and had that mellow feeling inside. I was on the road to oblivion – but didn't realise it at the time. It hadn't taken me long to fall into the drinking habits of my shipmates. From Pompey to Singers, and now in Sydney, each time we had a run ashore me and my oppos drank until we were either legless or incapable. We went out with the sole aim of getting drunk; but for me it was a quest that couldn't satiate an unquenchable thirst. As much as I wanted to extricate myself from the ways of my father, and distance myself from the drinking culture synonymous with *Jolly Jack Tar,* I couldn't. I was too weak.

At the time I didn't think about what was happening to me. I didn't care. I believed I was drinking to blot out the life I'd consigned myself to, the nine years of misery I still had to serve. I was trapped, wasting the best years of my life. I believed my youth would be lost and gone forever, and this was something that constantly preyed on my mind.

Sometimes I'd wake up on board in the early hours of the morning after a run ashore, with my tongue stuck to the roof of my mouth. I was so parched I'd struggle to prise it free. Once, when I was that dry, I had to check my pillow to see if I'd bitten into it as my mouth felt as though it was full of feathers. After another night ashore, when I'd end up getting wrecked, I'd always have to get up bleary-eyed in the small hours, and stumble through hatches searching for water. Whenever I found a tap I'd fill up until satisfied, only to feel intoxicated again. I'd then have to claw my way back to my bunk, reeling and colliding into hatches and bulkheads along the way. When I eventually woke up to turn to for duty watch, I rarely remembered how I'd managed to get back on board the night before. So many of my runs ashore were lost due to excess drinking; but then it's easy to blame the situation I found myself in as the reason behind this. I think it was more than that.

We must have hit Kings Cross nearly every night. I thought of it as a mirror image of Soho in London: a compact inner-city area that offered entertainment and vice. It was full of night clubs, strip joints, bars and restaurants, and was a Mecca for tourists and servicemen. The yanks, in particular, headed there in their droves to escape the horrors of Vietnam and indulge in some serious R&R. One night at around half-past two in the morning I was sitting on the pavement outside the *Whisky a Go Go,* a nightclub on William Street. I'd gone outside as I'd had way too much to drink and couldn't breathe; I felt claustrophobic. One of the working girls followed me out and tried to get me to stand up and go home with her, but I wasn't interested. I knew I was incapable.

At some point Wills appeared and sat down next to me. We both fell asleep, right there on the pavement. When we awoke and clambered to our feet it was getting light; everywhere was quieter and virtually deserted. We got up and started running downhill until we were flying, helter-skelter, so fast and unstoppable. Once our legs adapted to the regular rhythmic cycle of one leg rapidly passing in front of the other, we just kept going. We managed to stay upright and balanced, and by accident knocked over a rubbish bin that was standing on the curbside. Its contents shot over the road. All of the waste bins were lined up like this, but once that first one went over, we made sure all the others suffered a similar fate. One by one we shoved them out over the road as we ran madly by, shouting and cheering as we went. A constabulary meat van appeared on the scene, lying in wait at the bottom of the hill, something we failed to notice. They soon caught us and we were unceremoniously bundled into the back, and taken into custody until we were sober. When they released us they said we were lucky to be in HM forces, otherwise we'd be facing the local magistrate later that morning.

I met a few girls in the night clubs we frequented, good-looking girls looking for a good time. We'd often dance, smooch and arrange to meet up again, with the promise of closer intimacy high on the agenda. But, just like the night at the *Whisky a Go Go,* I'd end up legless; and when I sobered up I couldn't be bothered to go through with any pre-arranged date. A temporary respite from drinking almost always followed a night on the lash. I'd promise myself, *Never again;* but it wasn't long before the whole cycle repeated itself. I couldn't help myself.

We visited a few nightclubs in Sydney. One, the Pink Panther, was our first and only visit to a strip club; I believe once you've seen striptease, then you've seen it. The exception was Les Girls nightclub, where the strip show doubled as a cabaret; the strippers there were all drag artistes, guys dressed as girls. We also visited a Playboy Club as a one-off because admission was free. We ordered Cokes there which was all we could afford, but achieved our ambition to be served by a Bunny Girl. She bent right over as she placed our drinks on the table and then wiggled her white pom-pom tail in Skags' face.

But our main venue of choice, which we frequented quite often, was Martin's Place, which was named after the business area in the city called Martin Place. It had a unique feature at the time with telephones installed on the tables inside; these allowed you to call another table and ask if you could join the occupants or buy them a drink. The lights were dimmed on the dance floor, where brick pillars were strategically placed from floor to ceiling. These offered seclusion from the prying eyes of others. Each time I went there I hooked up with the same girl, Marie. She was a couple of years older than me and was married, but her husband was away serving in the Army.

Every time I asked her to dance she agreed, but even after that first dance I knew I could dance with her for the rest of the night if I wanted to. She was dark-skinned, as if she was part Aborigine, but she was fun, could dance, and her full-on figure knocked me out. They played some great records at Martin's Place: one, *Second That Emotion* by Smokey Robinson & the Miracles; and another, *Unchained Melody* by The Righteous Brothers.

It was to this last record that we danced so close, and pressed into each other so hard, that I felt an impression of our bodies must be moulded into one another. We were kissing, with Marie giving as good as she got. We continued to smooch and kiss until Marie began to stroke me over the area of my flies. I was getting excited and, almost in a quickstep, we danced across the floor, and took refuge behind one of the pillars that offered seclusion. Once out of sight she put her hand down my trousers and grasped my growing member. I was bursting and struggled with the clasp and zip at the top of my pants; finally they burst open. Her eyes lit up with delight as she pushed and pulled at me. A maniacal grin froze across her face as her eyes stared wildly into mine. I was at her mercy. As soon as she heard me gasp and groan, she swiftly ducked down and took me in her mouth. I was ecstatic, yet simultaneously grateful; she'd avoided what otherwise would have been a considerable mess. We both knew we wanted each other, and so arranged a follow-up date in Manly Park. *'Marie in Manly Park,'* I whispered in her ear. She replied in similar fashion, *'Joe Alcock – the coxswain.'* Unfortunately it turned out to be another no-show on my part, something

I regretted and reflected upon afterwards. I wondered what was wrong with me, and came to the conclusion that I needed to be twisted before I could face up to the outside world. I put it down to shyness and a lack of confidence with members of the opposite sex. But it made me reflect once more on what was going on with my life. I had nothing – no money, no skills, no prospects – and as far as I could see no future. I had nothing to offer anybody, least of all myself. At eighteen I hadn't a clue where I was heading and what the future might hold for me. The same recurring thought still haunted me: I had to get out of *the Andrew*. My mantra became, *I've gotta get out; I've gotta get out…*

During one of my sober runs ashore, probably because it was early afternoon, me and my messmates visited Bondi Beach. It was a famous landmark even back then in the sixties, and it happened to be the only place of interest (outside of Kings Cross) that I took the trouble to see. We were walking across the fine golden sands to the water's edge, when suddenly *Hey Jude,* by The Beatles, blasted out from a transistor radio planted amongst a bevy of bikini-clad girls. They were part of the bronzed sun-bathing surf brigade, and as we passed them we paused to join in the *Nana na na* refrain. This provoked some giggles from them, but I think they were laughing at us, rather than with us, as we were fully dressed in trousers and jackets and ready for a night on the town. I'm not sure what I was expecting to see at Bondi Beach, but I'd always imagined it was going to be a quiet, secluded, idyllic beach, a place of beauty, somewhere special. Instead I found it was an overcrowded crush of humanity, much like modern-day Benidorm in high season, a place where you had to plot your way carefully to the water's edge, making sure you didn't step on anyone or anything. Bondi was suburban; a main road ran behind the beach, with shops, cafes and accommodation blocks on the far side of the road. It was a big disappointment. All I could say afterwards was, '*Well, I've been there.*' But all of us agreed it wasn't worth the taxi fare for the experience.

I thought I'd send Jenny, a girl I'd met back home, a picture postcard of Bondi; but after visiting I changed my mind. Instead I sent her a night shot of Sydney harbour, lit up with a picture of the *Coat hanger* bridge and the opera house; it was more romantic and looked impressive. On the reverse I wrote how I missed her and kept thinking of her. I added that OC Smith, who was in the charts with his hit *Son of Hickory Holler's Tramp*, was performing here in Sydney. She later told me her school friends were more excited about OC Smith appearing in Sydney than the pic of the harbour lit up at night.

I'd met Jenny, my *dream girl*, one bank holiday weekend when I went to Blackpool with my old college friend, Huw. I literally bumped into her in the Tower Ballroom and immediately apologised for not looking where I was going. She was fine about it, but her infectious smile rendered me helpless. I couldn't take my eyes off this heavenly face in front of me. Her pert nose, kissable lips and large, wide-awake eyes left you in no doubt that you were the focus of her attention when you spoke with her. Her unblemished skin showed little sign of make-up, yet her face glowed under the artificial lights inside the ballroom. She had her hair pinned back in a pony-tail, revealing large daisy earrings that complemented her natural beauty. I thought someone had flicked a switch in my head when I met her, and turned Blackpool Illuminations on. I was smitten, and knew I couldn't just let this girl wander off and out of my life. I nervously fired questions at her: *What are you doing? Where are you going? Who are you with?* I surprised myself, because I'd always found it difficult to chat up girls and hold a conversation with them.

I was the guy who'd go to dances and stand on the periphery of the dance floor, watching and waiting for the right moment to make a move and ask a girl to dance. I'd scan the floor, searching for the perfect girl: someone I fancied, someone who looked genuine and wasn't going to ridicule my dancing. And then, when I finally had the courage to venture out onto the dance floor to ask a girl to dance, either the record would end or I'd find some other guy had stepped in before me. I tried to remain cool as I jabbered away to Jenny. I could feel my heart banging like a drum; I wondered if she sensed my nervousness. After we'd exchanged pleasantries (and that's how I found out her name), I suggested we take a walk along the Golden Mile. I nearly fell over when she agreed. Luckily she was with her sister, who kept Huw occupied whilst we chatted away. When we wandered off it was agreed that we'd meet up again at the railway station, as Huw and I had a train to catch back to Manchester.

Jenny and I walked and talked and learned more about one another; we promised to keep in touch. Inside a quiet sea-front shelter we kissed until time caught us out, and we had to rush to the train station. We said our hurried goodbyes, and in the process forgot to exchange addresses. I couldn't stop thinking about her on the journey home, and it was only when I replayed the time we'd spent together that I realised I hadn't got her details. I was seventeen then and felt I was in love. I knew I had to find Jenny again; I couldn't get her out of my head. Although Huw didn't click with Jenny's sister, I persuaded him to return to Blackpool with me the next day. I had to try and find Jenny, although I realised this would be an impossible task.

When we returned to Blackpool we searched everywhere: up and down the prom, around the funfair, until finally we ended up inside Tower Ballroom again. I couldn't believe it when I saw her there. We replayed the Golden Mile stroll and entered a small photography booth along the front, where we had some small black and white passport-sized photos taken. I kept two and folded them over, one framed on top of the other, and put them in my wallet for safekeeping. It was these two little photographs of Jenny, with her smiling face and piercing eyes that radiated back through the lens at me, that I took with me as I voyaged halfway around the world.

When I sent Jenny that picture postcard of Sydney at night I took those two photos out of my wallet as I wrote; she seemed so far away. It was something I did every now and again, especially when I felt sad. I wanted to see her smiling face. She gave me hope, comforted me; especially when I found it hard to carry on. I'd look at her and remind myself that there was another life, a life beyond the RN.

Through her letters I learned Jenny was staying on in sixth form at school to take A levels, and had ambitions to be a teacher. I also knew she had other admirers. As time went on I wondered what I could offer her; she seemed to have her future mapped out. I hoped she'd still be interested in me when I eventually got back home. She was a long way from me physically, but I didn't realise how far apart we were emotionally. I was too busy living in the moment, too busy surviving to make sense of the future. My present circumstances determined I wasn't in a position to make plans. I couldn't think about tomorrow when I felt trapped in the RN. I knew that when, and if, I ever got out of the Navy I'd have to start living my life all over again. I knew I had nothing but couldn't bear to think that realistically it would probably be too late for me and Jenny to have any sort of a future together.

During our stay in Sydney we lost one of our guys in Kings Cross. He was a mod stores assistant called Carey. The story I heard was that he'd overdone it on amphetamines and booze when he frequented one of the nightclubs along the strip. A bouncer tried to evict him, but Carey had lashed out with a glass in his hand and caught him square across the face. Some other bouncers jumped in and took Carey outside to the back of the club, where they gave him a good pasting before handing him over to the police. He was held in custody and placed on remand for 1,000 Australian dollars. Apparently his folks at home were contacted for the cash, but his plea fell on deaf ears and he was left to suffer the consequences of his actions. The ship sailed without him and it was only much later, when I bumped into an ex-matelot, that I learned about Carey's demise. He said Carey eventually received six months' hard labour, as well as being discharged from HM Forces. He added that after Carey finished his sentence he moved back to Singapore where he married a Sembawang prostitute. *There but for the grace of God*, I thought; it could have been any one of us in the nightclub that night.

During that stay in Sydney I learned more about my shipmates than at any other time I spent on board. Jimmy, whom I'd known since Part II training at Pembroke, and spent six months with at *Osprey*, revisited Les Girls. He stayed on after the show had finished one night, when the girls mingled and had a drink with customers. He was attracted to one of the cast and bought her a few drinks. Her name was Diana, and I remember how she was a dead-ringer for Diana Ross when he showed me a photograph of her. She had the same build, skin colour and texture, but it was her hairstyle, with that long, curved cut and shape down one side of her face, that clinched it for me.

Jim said, '*I couldn't help it – I had to take her home...*'
'*Yeah, so what happened?*' I asked.
'*She was beautiful.*'
'*Yes, but what happened?*'
'*I had to,*' he responded. '*I had no choice.*'
'*What do you mean?*'
'*I couldn't help myself.*'
'*Yes, but what do you mean?*'

'*I did it with her face to face,*' he said.

'*So – how does that work?*'

'*Face to face – like you would with a woman. It's like when they're on stage – you can see nothing because they have this amazing tape. They pull everything back and up – underneath – tight – and the tape hides everything.*'

'*Well, where did you put it?*'

'*Under, somehow – underneath – between her legs, but underneath. It was OK. I felt... I treated her as if she was a woman. I kissed her, kissed her breasts. I just thought I was in bed with a woman.*' Jim paused briefly. '*There was something, though, that put me off...*'

'*Oh yeah, what was that?*' I asked.

'*Her stubble in the morning,*' he said. '*I didn't want to kiss her then. I couldn't kiss her goodbye; the stubble put me off.*'

I couldn't quite get my head around Jim's confession, his last comment about facial hair. Going to bed with a beautiful woman (who was a man) was something I'd never done or considered before – but *hey, whatever turns you on*. And then there was Rib, the guy I'd lived on the roads with for over three months, when we hitch-hiked around the UK. His story unfolded after Jordy, a guy in our mess, couldn't make it ashore. Jordy asked me to pick up his watch from a jewellers in a shopping mall. I was with Wills and when we came out of the shop with the watch, we were immediately approached by an old guy in his fifties. He came straight up to us as we left the shop.

'*Is that Eddie's watch?*' he asked in an effeminate voice.

'*No. Who are you?*' I said.

'*I'm a friend.*'

'*No, it's Jordy's watch.*' And then I remembered Jordy's first name was Eddie.

'*Shall I take it?*' he persisted, and held out his hand. He then smiled sweetly and said, '*I'll be seeing him soon.*' How he knew we'd just picked up Jordy's watch I'll never know. But since neither of us were interested or his way inclined, we told him to forget it and left him standing there.

When we returned back on board with the wristwatch, I quizzed Jordy about our encounter. He said he'd met this acquaintance through Rib and we should ask him how they'd met. I took this up with Rib. He said the guy who had approached us was a captain in the Australian Army and they'd met in a bar. Rib had gone back to the captain's place and later again, when he was ashore with Jordy. The captain had paid for them to share a prostitute. He said the captain got a kick out of watching others perform. He also said the guy liked to masturbate whilst Rib pissed in his mouth and all over his face. Rib said in exchange for such services the captain had provided him with treats, such as taking him out for meals at expensive restaurants. He said the captain had also taken him out for the day, when they drove up into the Blue Mountains.

Rib's revelations about his exploits with the captain were something I found hard to believe. Such perverse sexual activity didn't interest me, but it made me think long and hard about the time I spent with Rib on the roads. I guessed that when we met at seventeen he must have been unsure of his sexuality. I recalled that time he'd taken Yvonne up to the Chines in Bournemouth, only to find he couldn't get an erection and give her what she so desperately wanted. *Pity,* I thought, as she was a pretty girl, but she only had eyes for Rib. We had reasoned at the time that Rib's lack of enthusiasm was probably due to him taking a leak prior to intercourse. Now I knew that was a load of crap, and so was it Yvonne (as a female) who didn't turn him on? And then there was the hitch-hiking episode when this guy picked us up. The driver insisted one of us sit in the front with him. *'Or you can forget it,'* he had said. I was adamant I wasn't going to sit there and quickly jumped in the back. Rib duly obliged. After we were dropped off Rib said he didn't mind sitting in the front. I thought he was doing us both a favour, but later the same guy came back, did a u-turn, and offered to drop us off further up the road, where he said it was easier for motorists to pull over and offer us a lift. This time Rib didn't hesitate and jumped straight in the front. When I later quizzed him about this he admitted that the first time around the guy had stroked his thigh and he hadn't minded. I now tried to rationalise these incidents that had occurred on our journey that summer. I thought Rib must have been confused back then, that he had an internal struggle over his sexual identity. All I can say is that I never had any doubts about my own heterosexual desires. And during the whole time Rib and I spent hitch-hiking and sleeping rough together on the roads, I can't recall that he ever made a sexual advance towards me.

When we sailed on and through the Far East there was a growing coterie of characters from the steward's branch who were personally sidelined to work in the wardroom bar. These included Rib, Jordy and his younger cousin Keith, as well as some others, including the petty officer in charge. Whenever I passed that PO he always smelt sweeter than any *Madam* in her boudoir. Working in the wardroom bar was always regarded a cushy number, with occasional perks; it was a coveted position and much sought after among ordinary rate stewards. On the *Happy H* it became obvious that those selected to work behind the bar had to be of a certain sexual persuasion, poles apart from those who took pleasure in the act of procreating. I'm not sure if any of those chosen to work there were required to perform additional duties, but they were all well qualified to do so. And I'm sure they would have been happy to oblige if and when such services were requested.

We left Sydney at the end of October and within a couple of days I was pulled up on a charge by one of our CPOs. I had a button missing off the cuff of my Number 8 working shirt, which ordinarily would have gone unnoticed as I often kept my shirt sleeves rolled up. I was well aware of other ratings wandering around the decks with buttons missing in far more conspicuous places than mine, usually on the front of their shirts. It made me wonder why this CPO had suddenly collared me, as he'd never troubled me before; but then our paths had rarely crossed during the time we'd been at sea. He reminded me of an adult Billy Bunter wih his circular-framed NHS spectacles, chubby face and round girth; every time I spotted him I pictured him stuffing his face with a cream cake. Although this CPO hadn't bothered me previously, I now seriously considered if he was singling me out for some reason. He'd recently removed me from waiting-on duties in the wardroom, and placed me in the washing up area behind the servery; somewhere where I was out of sight and sound. Personally, I didn't mind this move as I could dress down and wear working rig – a Number 8 shirt and trousers each day. I didn't have to worry about wearing a clean and ironed white front, or pressed bell bottom trousers (with seven horizontal creases in each leg) every time I went on duty. But the CPO's decision could be interpreted as an oblique demotion, something which made me wonder why he had done it. I wasn't aware of any particular reason for his decision, and he never offered me one. Perhaps *a pig* in the wardroom was sick of my miserable face, or my forlorn, churlish manner – who knows? Perhaps he'd been asked to remove me. I wondered if it was the CPO's intention to offend or embarrass me by relegating me to the wash-up; but then I wasn't bothered about performing menial tasks and he'd inadvertently made my life easier. If it was the chief's intention to demean me (by reducing my duties and responsibilities) then I felt it had backfired on him. But it didn't stop me wondering why he appeared to be singling me out; why was he suddenly trying to make life on board more difficult for me?

I didn't find out what was behind his thinking, but he was determined to see the offending shirt cuff with a button on it by the next day. I didn't bother sewing the button on and forgot about it until the chief came to see me. When he saw the button still missing he ordered me to present my kit via a kit muster. He gave me a two-hour deadline to present all my kit and lay it out on top of my bunk. This would be a real bind because we lived towards aft on four deck and most of my kit was stored *for'ard*, and below on six deck. The storage compartment down there was where hundreds of kit bags and cases were stashed, virtually for the whole of the ship's company. I immediately thought, *If the chief thinks I'm going to rummage through all that luggage in the hold to find my bag and case, and then drag my kit up ladders and through hatches, for nearly the whole length of the ship, then he needs to think again.* Slowly memories of HMS Pembroke returned, and how unjust the severity of the punishment had been for a trivial misdemeanour. I thought justice in the RN was flawed. I'd seen so many ratings with buttons missing off their shirts, walking around with shirts undone and hanging out of their trousers; others with longer than regulation hair, long sideburns and unshaven. And yet none had been punished. It only convinced me more that the chief was picking on me. If someone in the RN wanted to get you, or to make life as difficult and miserable as possible for you, then no one would stop them; there was nothing you could do about it.

When the appointed time arrived for my kit muster I was summoned to the entrance of the mess where the chief was waiting. He asked me to lead him to where my kit was laid out for him. I took him to the main grott area and pointed towards my bunk. He stared and then looked around at all the bunks:

'*Well, where is it?*' he asked.

'*There,*' I said, pointing to my bunk.

'*But there's nothing there!*'

'*Yes, I know. I'm not doing it.*'

'*I'll give you one hour, Alcock.*'

'*I don't want an hour – that's it.*'

'*One hour, Alcock.*' And with that he abruptly did an about turn and left the mess. I knew I wasn't going to do it and didn't need the hour's grace offered. When the chief reappeared we replayed the earlier scene all over again; I led him to the communal grott area where my empty bunk confronted him once more. This time he put me on a charge for Wilful Disobedience. I appeared before the Officer of the Day (OOD) the following morning and admitted my guilt. I was then passed up to the duty commander followed by the captain; they both listened to my defence which was always the same:

'*I made a mistake, sir – when I enlisted. A terrible mistake. I need to get out, sir. The Navy is not for me. I shouldn't have joined. I made a mistake. Please let me go, sir – I'm not suitable.*' I'd recently learned that new recruits, who weren't suited to service life could now buy themselves out within three months of signing on. I asked the captain if they would review my case in light of this, as I'd only missed the deadline by a few months. Again my pleas were ignored.

There was another alternative: you could buy yourself out after six years' service, but this wasn't an option for me. I'd been in nearly two years, but only one year had counted towards the nine I'd signed on for. I wasn't prepared to wait another five years to gain my freedom. I realised I was now at a point of no return; I wasn't going to serve any longer than I had to.

I was found guilty for the charge of Wilful Disobedience and sentenced to 32 days' detention in a Military Corrective Training Centre (MCTC). As I still had the 28-day suspended sentence hanging over my head, from my stint on the run when I worked on the trawlers, my full sentence in detention amounted to 60 days. There was a MCTC situated in Tanglin, Singapore, and so me and my RN escort were to be airlifted from the *Happy H* courtesy of an 849 Squadron COD Fairey Gannet. The COD usually had an additional passenger seat reserved for VIPs, and although I wasn't a VIP I felt like one. Fairey Gannets had double-folding wings and two propeller blades that rotated in opposite directions in front of the pilot's cockpit. The opportunity for stewards to fly off an aircraft carrier was almost unheard of.

Any feelings of trepidation I had about being incarcerated in a military boot camp for a couple of months paled into insignificance in comparison to the excitement I felt about flying off an aircraft carrier at sea. I knew most of my oppos in *4 Papa 1* mess would never get this opportunity. I viewed this as a once-in-a-lifetime experience, something I couldn't help but look forward to. I planned to relish every moment and soak up the whole experience.

We clambered on board via a quick-release ladder which had fasteners attached to the side of the plane. Once strapped in, the propellers were fired up and we were hooked up, ready to be catapulted off the ship's flight deck. I swear to God, if we hadn't reached the end of the flight deck when we did, I would have gone through the back of my seat, such was the g-force encountered. I was pressed further and further back into my seat as I clung on to the sides for dear life. Take-off only lasted a few seconds, but the end of the flight deck couldn't come soon enough. As we left the bow of the *H* we dipped slightly towards the surface of the ocean, before we wheeled up, straightened out and flew on to our destination in New Guinea.

We flew to Madang airport (if you could call it an airport), a small single strip of runway that hadn't the capacity for large commercial aircraft to use. It could only accommodate light aircraft, whether they were landing or taking off, and after we landed and came to a halt I had to jump down from the plane. I was about to make my way off towards some small single-storey huts and buildings, that I'd spotted on my near side, when the navigator shouted down: *'We need your flying suit – take it off and throw it up.'* I unzipped and stripped it off, and then hurled it up to him as he crouched by the hatch door. Unfortunately he missed catching it, as it got caught in the backdraught of the propellers. The Gannet was programmed to take off and return to Hermes as soon as we disembarked, and so the propellers were still whirring at almost full throttle. My one-piece olive-green flying suit, designed like a pair of overalls, instantly ballooned up in the warm air. The arms and legs became bloated, stretched out and it took off over the aircraft and down the runway, performing somersaults and cartwheels like some obsessed acrobatic gymnast.

For a moment I was caught off guard. I stared after the suit before I realised it was me who had to chase after it. The flying suit was well on its way, and I had some ground to make up if I was to catch it. I sprinted back down the runway in hot pursuit, but was forced to look over to my far left when I heard what sounded like shouting, cheering and laughing. I couldn't believe what I saw 200 yards away; lined up along the full length of the perimeter fence, which ran parallel to the runway, was a continuous line of black bodies crammed in, faces pressed up against the fence. I know I was running and didn't stop to look for too long, but I couldn't see a single gap or empty viewing space along the whole length of the fence. All I could make out was black skin, white teeth and gleaming eyes. Everyone appeared to be jumping up and down; waving and banging long sticks; laughing, joking and cheering. My race with blow-up man was undoubtedly the source of all the noise and gaiety. I put a final burst in until I managed to catch and grab hold of the errant flying suit.

I guessed that watching light aircraft land and take off every day was a favourite pastime for locals living in Madang. I smiled to myself afterwards, as I imagined how I must have looked to the indigenous population. No wonder they got excited; I would have cheered a white boy making a fool of himself if I'd been a casual observer. I doubted whether my audience had seen anything like it before and doubted they'd see anything like it again. I still rank it as one of my most embarrassing moments and am just grateful there was no one else there who could retell the tale and cause me further embarrassment.

We took an internal flight from Madang across NG to Port Moresby, where we had to catch a flight back to Sydney, and from there another flight to Singapore; there my escort would deliver me to the military at MCTC, Tanglin. Most of my time in NG was spent waiting in and around both airports at Madang and Port Moresby, and so my experience of life there was pretty limited. All I saw, when we flew across this wild tropical island, was steaming primeval rainforests and swampy lowlands that bordered rivers and lakes. Although you could make out the contours of the land, as it rose and fell beneath the packed dark-green jungle canopy, the hillside and mountain scars remained hidden from view. I stared down at this mass of greenery and couldn't help wondering at how primitive life must be down there.

At the time NG was governed by Australia and in Port Moresby I engaged in conversation with an Australian teacher. I made a comment to my Royal Naval escort when I noticed a woman sitting opposite us smoking a cigarette. She was inhaling deeply, but I wasn't sure how much of her inhalation reached her lungs. My fascination, and I admit I was staring at her, although she was oblivious to this, centred on the fact that she had no nose. The hole in her face was the exact size of where her nose should have been; but she continuously stared at her feet and never once looked up. I wondered if she felt intimidated because she was sitting directly opposite white men; or was it just because we were male? She didn't seem self-conscious about her facial cavity when she regularly drew on her cigarette, and appeared oblivious to the permanent cloud of smoke that shrouded her face.

'*I think she's got leprosy,*' I commented to the RNP sitting next to me. The Aussie teacher had just sat down on my other side.

'*It's cancer,*' he said. '*It's quite common out here.*'

The three of us then, coincidentally, decided to go outside for a smoke and stretch our legs, even though the humidity was over 30 degrees. We exchanged a few pleasantries about where we were travelling to, and who we were, before I asked the Aussie what life was like out here. I asked about the native NG people; what were they like? He told me how it was still pretty primitive, that many of the inhabitants still lived in clans or tribes in their villages. Each community had their chiefs, leaders and senior members, who took on the responsibility of looking after the less fortunate members of their village. They cared for those with disabilities, illness or disease, as well as those who didn't possess the means to feed and clothe themselves. The teacher explained that many villages were self-sufficient; they rarely found the need to venture beyond their own boundary. The difficult terrain was also a disincentive to travel far; this meant many tribes had remained cut off from each other for generations, and so often spoke in only their own language. There was a common language called *wantak* – which literally means one talk – but there were still many who spoke only in their own tribal language. He said there were over 800 native languages in NG, which equated to over a third of the languages in the entire world. *Wow!* I found that truly amazing.

I mentioned to the Aussie teacher that I'd seen men at Madang airport openly strolling around holding hands and putting their arms around one another. I thought, *Homosexuality must be rife in NG,* yet it was still illegal in the UK when I signed on. He said I was mistaken and that such affectionate behaviour openly displayed by male adults was part of NG culture. He explained that when young males were old enough to leave the family home, they'd move out to go and live with other males in a shared house; similarly, the custom for women was to share a house together until they got married. Polygamy was part of NG culture too, and so to find a shortage of women and a surfeit of males was not uncommon.

We left for our flights and it wasn't long before we were passing through the main gates at MCTC Tanglin Barracks, Singapore. This was where I first caught sight of a Gurkha who happened to be on guard duty. I was immediately struck by how smart he looked in his military fatigues. My eyes were drawn to the dazzling sunlight that bounced off the toe caps of his boots, and then his razor-sharp creases in his shorts, which complemented an immaculately pressed shirt. His whole demeanour displayed crisp military smartness; he exuded an aura of pride and discipline. He wandered over and stared at us through the tilly van window whilst our papers were being checked. Once we were cleared we moved on to the detention block.

The Army buildings at Tanglin were a mixture of local and colonial architecture with plenty of open windows and doorways; these allowed fresh air to enter and circulate freely. The huge tiled roofs overhung wide open verandahs that were supported by large pillars. Although the covered verandahs provided shelter from the frequent monsoon downpours, they did little to counteract the hot, humid and sticky Asian climate. I caught a whiff of frangipani or jasmine as I unloaded my kit and made my way inside the detention block. I couldn't help but inhale the sweet scent and thought how *some things can never be taken from you,* even when you are denied freedom and life gets you down. I knew that fond personal memories can stay with you and would help me get through some of the tough times inside detention.

My cell was small, perhaps eight or nine feet long by six feet wide, with a hard wooden bed (bunk) bolted to the floor. A mesh-covered open window was high up in the wall opposite the cell door, and below it was where I'd lay my head. A small wooden table was placed next to the bed within arm's reach, and there were two semi-circular shelves, one above the other, in the corner of the opposite wall. I stored my toiletries and brass cleaning paraphernalia there. A pocket-sized bible was on top of the table next to my bunk and a plastic piss-pot underneath the bed. This, apart from my kit, amounted to the total contents of my cell.

When we checked in I had to relinquish my personal effects, but I managed to keep the two passport-size photographs of Jenny from our time in Blackpool. Other personal possessions such as my lighter, cigarettes, watch, crucifix and chain, were sealed in an A4 envelope which I could reclaim when I was released. After I'd sorted things inside my cell I took out the photos of Jenny and kissed her beautiful face. I looked for a safe place, other than my pockets, where I could keep and preserve her pictures. I spotted the pocket-sized bible again and placed them inside the front cover; I couldn't believe how they fitted inside perfectly. It was as if these photos of Jenny had always been destined to be housed in such a safe and sacred place. I knew they'd be a source of comfort to me during the long, lonely days and nights that lay ahead.

I next saw Garung the Gurkha (which is what the pongo staff called him) when he was on sentry duty again and I was sitting in the back of an Army truck. We'd stopped, momentarily, by the main gates whilst the duty staff who were accompanying us were completing signing-out procedures at the gatehouse. We were on our way to an unknown destination about five miles away, where we would be dropped off on some back road and left to double all the way back to the MCTC; the Army called it an endurance march.

At first I couldn't quite see what Garung was up to as he was half-turned with his back to me; he crouched slightly forward with a stick in one hand. He manoeuvred sideways, and then I caught a glimpse of a king cobra snake that was the focus of his attention. I was fascinated. It must have been ten feet long, as its head with splayed-out hood, appeared to be at least three feet above the ground. Garung was facing it about six feet away; he moved the stick slowly from left to right, whilst the king cobra's head mimicked the side-to-side movement of the stick Garung was holding. It seemed to be trying to second guess the stick's movement. I was surprised by how sleek and lithe the cobra looked, when suddenly Garung recoiled; but then he immediately lunged forward, much as a fencer might do when performing a riposte. I think he must have caught the snake with his stick because the king cobra ducked to one side, lowered itself and then slid away towards a monsoon ditch by the roadside. I later learned from another member of staff that the king cobra had hissed and fired venom at Garung during his face-off. Cobras usually aim for the eyes, and so Garung was lucky to escape unscathed as the venom fell short and missed him. It was the only living snake I saw in the wild during my time in the Far East, although on our marches beyond the perimeter fence we passed a couple of dead ones lying by the roadside.

Life inside MCTC, Tanglin, meant detainees had to march everywhere in double-quick time; it was integral to their punishment. I couldn't get my head around this ultra-quick style of marching and fell foul of this crazy Army practice almost immediately. It was the day after I arrived, when I was in a small detail marching off to stores to get my issue of webbing, that I had to break ranks. I was mesmerised by the others in front of me and tried copying them in an effort to keep up. I flung my arms up and down, forwards and backwards as fast as I could; but try as I may, I couldn't get my legs marching at twice their normal speed and keep them in time with such frenzied arm-swinging. The pictures inside my head triggered memories of a popular TV series called *Mad Movies,* which featured clips from old silent films starring Charlie Chaplin and the Keystone Cops, who whizzed around film sets at breakneck speed, either being chased or chasing others. These images filled my head, and I couldn't help but fall out and collapse by the side of the road. I was in hysterics and had a prolonged fit of the giggles. I was a hopeless mess. The staff in charge kept bellowing at me to fall in, but it took me a while to recover. When I was almost there, but still had tears in my eyes, I was marched straight back to my cell.

On the way there I still tried, but failed miserably, to master this rapid marching routine. I was dumped back in my cell to cool off, but for days afterwards that episode was a constant source of amusement to me. I couldn't help laughing to myself whenever I replayed that scenario inside my head. I was put on a charge for insubordination and immediately lost some remission; this now meant I'd be spending Christmas Day inside the MCTC, but the initial memory, of me trying to replicate that crazy marching technique, undoubtedly lightened the load for me during those first few days of detention.

Much of the time spent in army detention involved stripping down and cleaning SLRs (self loading rifles) and SMGs (sub machine guns), before reassembling them. Route marches were a regular feature of our sentence as were endurance marches. The former involved a truck journey to some back of the beyond location in Malaysia, where we'd be dumped and have to march back to camp. Endurance marches were similar, as we were still dropped off somewhere beyond the main gates, but this time we had to double all the way back to the MCTC. Although physically demanding these exercises were a welcome diversion to the monotony of life inside. It meant we weren't completely cut off from the outside world; we were privy to life beyond the perimeter fence and had a limited view of others going about their business. This *freedom* was an alternative to being caged up and helped me cope mentally; it offered some respite and I think it also helped time pass more quickly inside.

Other daily activities performed inside detention involved completing the *in situ* assault course. And time spent locked in your cells was for cleaning your pattern webbing: pouches, belt buckles and straps, and a water bottle carrier. All of this kit had brass fittings and fastenings, which, when polished, had to shine and sparkle without leaving any visible traces of metal polish.

There were a couple of other unplanned diversions which occurred during my time inside MCTC. Both provided some welcome relief to the mundanity of life inside and took place in and around the vicinity of the assault course. The first involved a vile, pungent smell, which became stronger over the course of a few days. It eventually became unbearable, and even the staff found they could no longer stand it. This putrid stench became so overpowering that a couple of inmates were reduced to breaking ranks and retching amongst the undergrowth. Thankfully, the staff in charge saw sense when this happened and immediately abandoned assault course activities for the day. Instead, we were instructed to fan out in pairs and search the grounds along the perimeter fence. Everyone thought it must be something dead, a rotting carcass lying somewhere. And true enough we discovered the source of the fetid stink within the hour. A dead python nearly 20 feet long had managed to slip its head, as well as half its body, through the diamond-patterned chain-linked fence. It must then have become stuck, with the thick bulge of its midriff split open, revealing the remains of what must have been its last meal. The back end of a large part-digested rat was clearly visible; its whip-like tail dangled out between torn flesh. We were all relieved that regular Army personnel, stationed at the main camp further up the road from us, were assigned to python disposal duties.

The other incident happened when we were actually tackling the assault course, which consisted of some pretty basic obstacles. There were some hurdles to jump, posts to zig-zag in and out of, netting to crawl underneath and tunnels to crawl through. There was also a ten-foot wall to scale (with the help of others), and a twenty-foot-high rope obstacle that you had to climb up, scramble over and descend down the other side. This obstacle had twelve-inch square holes in the rope pattern, which was where you'd place your hands and feet as you climbed up and over it.

It was about a week after the python episode when we approached this rope-climbing obstacle only to hear a loud rattling noise high up above. It appeared to be coming from inside the rope bindings at the very top. These ropes were wrapped around the top of the wooden structure, and once everyone became aware of the alien crackle up there no one was willing to take the first step onto the rope apparatus. Everyone arrived and stopped at the base of the obstacle and then stared up at the summit. No one was brave enough to take that first step. We were apprehensive and decided we weren't going to climb it. Instead we milled around the base, pacing around in slow motion. All you could hear was the rattle and crackle overhead, as if someone was tightening a bolt with a ratchet spanner. We speculated as to what could be making a noise like that. My thoughts turned to the python incident, and I wondered if it could be a rattlesnake. Eventually Himmler, the duty staff member, caught us up. He was called Himmler because he wore small, round, metal-framed spectacles and sported a ridiculous little moustache.

'*You!*' He pointed at the only Malay inmate. '*Get your arse up there! And the rest of you follow!*' The diminutive Malay soldier just looked around at the rest of us; we all stared at him. I was standing right next to him; I shrugged my shoulders and thought, *Hard luck, mate, he's picked you not me.* I think everyone was glad they hadn't been singled out.

'*No. No. Not me,*' the Malay cried. '*I not goin' up.*'

'*Alcock! Get up there!*' shouted Himmler at me.

'*I'm not going up there,*' I retorted. '*It could be a rattlesnake!*'

'*They don't have rattlesnakes in Malaya,*' shouted Himmler. '*Now get up there!*' Panic set in as I looked around. I spotted the royal marine who was standing on the other side of me, a member of 42nd Command.

'*You go,*' I shouted, looking at him. '*You're trained to kill.*' Momentary silence.

'*Ah, yes.*' Himmler had weighed up the situation and turned on him. '*You ARE. You're trained to kill! Now get up there and see what it is!*'

I'm not sure whether the marine didn't want to lose face, or whether he didn't want Himmler to put him on a charge, but, fair play, the marine started to climb the ropework. We all stood in silence watching him from below. The incessant buzzing was ringing in our ears as he got closer and closer to the top. As he got there Himmler shouted:

'*What is it?*'

'*Dunno, Staff!*'

'*Well, what can you see?*'

'*Nothing, Staff.*' And with that he wrapped one arm around the horizontal wooden beam at the top of the structure for support, and then started to poke through the end of the rope on one of the bindings; bit by bit he pushed it through. As soon as he'd pushed the end through he'd grab it again, and repeat the process; all the time that crazy crackling noise was getting louder. The Green Beret was now hanging off the frame at arm's length, since the binding was almost free of the frame; then, suddenly, a giant black hornet escaped from underneath the ropework and took off. Himmler claimed afterwards that these hornets had been known to kill a human being. *Wow!* We all cheered and clapped, and agreed the bootneck really was trained to kill. Once the binding was threaded back to its original state again, normal assault course service was resumed. And, although I couldn't swear to it, I thought I caught a flicker of a smile on Himmler's face, something I hadn't seen before and something I never saw again.

A major rule in MCTC was that we weren't allowed to talk to each other and could only speak to staff if they gave their permission. This wasn't strictly adhered to all of the time, and it often depended upon which member of staff you were addressing. There was only one staff member from the RN stationed in the MCTC, a regulating petty officer called Steve (short for Stephens). All the other staff were pongos, but Steve was someone I'd met previously when he was on duty and I was locked up in the cells at HMS Osprey. He'd allowed me to smoke during the time I'd spent in there, something which was strictly prohibited. He'd even given me a cigarette when I had none. I remembered him from those days because often such simple acts of kindness stay with you, especially when you feel you're taking on the whole world. Steve was a good hand and one of the few regulators I met who showed any semblance of humanity. I could talk to him, and I remember we shared a joke once; although he made sure no one was around at the time.

I was well into serving my time in Tanglin, and believed I was coping as well as anybody despite all the mind-numbing routines. The weather was its usual tropical self with thrashing downpours of rain that stopped abruptly; clouds that quickly evaporated into blistering sunshine; hot, sticky, humid temperatures, where the sweat inside your shirt made it stick to your back. In short, I wasn't aware of anything that unduly bothered me and didn't feel emotionally disturbed. I thought I was in control. And then it happened.

I was sleeping in my cell one night when I was jolted awake. It was as if something had disturbed me. As soon as I awoke I lay perfectly still and listened intently. I was waiting for a noise inside my cell, or for a sound, any sound, whether inside, or outside through the mesh window above my head. I was sure if I lay awake listening I'd hear something; silence prevailed. I was hot and clammy but lay there quite still, holding my breath. The dampness on my vest became cold and uncomfortable. I stirred and raised myself up on one elbow; automatically I reached for the pocket bible on the bedside table and felt inside the cover for my pictures of Jenny. They weren't there. I sat up and flicked through all the pages. Nothing. Instinctively (and I don't know why I did this) I rolled out of bed and groped underneath for my piss-pot and pulled it out. And there she was. Floating below, drowning in my piss. I couldn't believe it. I sunk my hand in and grabbed her from the urine. I dried the pictures, rubbing them carefully on my blanket. I was dumbstruck. How could my only source of comfort, the focus of my resolve to see things through, end up floating in my urine? I didn't understand it. I sat back on my bunk totally perplexed.

My mind turned to unexplained phenomena: spirits, ghosts, poltergeists. I wondered if there was some unearthly presence in my cell, something evil trying to break me. And then I thought of God. I closed my eyes and, as I'd always done since my mother left when I was four years old, I prayed silently for help. I wasn't that religious, and not a regular church-goer, but a silent cry for support had stood me in good stead over the years. Whenever I was scared as a child, or in the depths of despair and wondered what was going to happen, I'd resort to an intimate conversation with God, Jesus or the Lord. It was always when I needed someone. Sometimes I felt guilty because I'd only call on whoever as a last resort, when I was worried, desperate, felt I couldn't cope and needed inner strength. After my mum left it became a habit; talking to Jesus had stopped me crying, kept the nightmares away and helped me get to sleep.

I now needed help to try and solve this mystery. I needed to speak to someone and the padre sprang to mind. I knew every ship had one; so the Army should have a chaplain. I decided to put in a request to see whoever was responsible for Godly affairs. I planned to ask them for their interpretation on what they thought had happened. I wanted to confer with someone I could trust, someone in authority who had an unbiased perspective. It was whilst I was contemplating my next move that the observation hole in my cell door slid sideways and exposed a beady eye. This was quickly followed by a jangle of keys, and the rhythmic clunk, clack, click of the cell door unlocking before it was thrown open. Steve stood there in the doorway, neither entering nor receding. *Thank God, it's him*, I thought. He spoke before I could:

'*Are you alright?*'

'*I'm not sure. Why? What's the matter?*'

'*Well, you were shouting out in your sleep last night.*'

'*Eh? You're joking – what did I say?*'

'*Well, you went on a bit. All I could hear was, "Why don't you leave me alone?" Or, "Why won't you leave me alone? Leave me alone."*' He paused, as I did. I was stuck for words. I couldn't believe what he'd just said. All my earlier reasoning and thoughts, that centred on how well I was coping with life inside, immediately evaporated. And with them any plans I had to meet up with the Army chaplain.

'Well, as long as you're alright then,' said Steve, and with that he swung the door back to and locked it. So I was talking in my sleep, and not only that, *they (the system)* **were getting through to me, frying my brain.** I couldn't believe how messed up I sounded, especially when I thought I was coping and everything was A-OK. The realisation that I must have been the villain of the piece slowly filtered through to me. I was responsible for throwing my pictures of Jenny into a pot full of piss. Who else could it be? I found the whole thing hard to accept, and from what Steve had said about me talking and shouting out in my sleep, however implausible it sounded, it appeared to be the only logical explanation. I was responsible for trying to destroy the thing I loved most. I was shaken, but it was something I would have to live with.

Another member of military staff in charge of us was called Midge. I initially thought it was because he was annoying, irritating and a pest like a mosquito. I learned later it was an abbreviation of midget, and merely reflected his short stature. Midge happened to be a stickler for all things Army. I concluded quite early on that he was totally brainwashed. I remember his instruction on how to mark time:

'*When you hear the order to "mark time", you raise your right leg until the thigh is parallel to the ground, with the foot hanging at a natural angle. As you slam this foot down to the ground, raise your left foot immediately, to a similar angle, again with the thigh parallel to the*

*ground and the foot again hanging at a natural angle –
like this...'*

At this point Midge demonstrated the technique,
but by now his eyes had glazed over and sputum was
secreting from the corners of his mouth. He had a look in
his eyes that travelled beyond you, over the horizon and
into a distant past. He was lost in another world, as more
white saliva bubbled and transmuted itself into a frothy
substance where his lips met his cheeks.

'Left-right. Left-right. Left-right. Left-right.' He barked
on monotonously, continuing with this exercise as if we
were stupid. Whilst this was going on a couple of naval
sayings flashed through my mind: *It's mind over matter;
I don't mind and you don't matter.* And the other one,
which was often said with contempt when leading hands
sneered at able rates: *You're not paid to think – just do it!*
Although leading hands were only one up from us on the
promotion ladder they took great pleasure in pulling rank
and asserting their seniority. They always reminded me of
Tennyson's immortal lines:

'Theirs is not to reason why, theirs is but to do and die...'

Midge's next frothing-of-the-mouth incident, again
accompanied by his glazed expression, only convinced me
of his mental instability. He waxed lyrical one day when he
described the beauty of the hand grenade:

*'It's one of the most wonderful weapons ever invented.
And it's particularly effective when thrown into a small
confined space. When a grenade is used in an enclosed area
it can do most damage. I remember once when we were in
Aden...'*

And so, trance-like, he mutated into this other being, extolling the virtues of causing havoc and carnage with hand grenades. I'm sure, at times, he was completely oblivious as to where he was and whose company he was in.

On one endurance march Midge really *got through to me*. Words were spoken between us yet, surprisingly, I managed to have my say without getting into trouble.

The new boots I'd been issued with had ripped the skin off the tops of my toes. The strenuous daily exercise had caused blisters which had now broken. The exposed red-raw flesh was soldered to the inside of my thick, navy, woollen socks. I'd long passed the agony stage. I could hardly feel the stubby digits at the end of my feet because of the numbness. I'd heard that if you became ill on one of these marches outside camp, or were too injured to carry on, then you could get transported back to Tanglin in an Army truck. I was in agony when we stopped and sat down by the side of the Bukit Timah Road for a rest and drink of water. I complained about the state of my feet; I felt I was in too much pain to carry on. I thought I'd give this ploy of getting a lift back to the camp a try. I complained to Midge:

'I've got to get these boots off. They're killing me. You should see the blisters I've got.'

'What do you think you're doing?' Midge responded, when he saw I was untying my laces.

'I've got blisters, Staff – they're killing me. I've got to get these boots off.'

'What? Blisters? You've got blisters? I've got blisters. I can show you what blisters look like.' And with that he started to undo his boot laces.

'I don't want to see your blisters,' I said.

'I'll show you blisters,' he said, tugging at his boots.

'I don't want to see your blisters! I'm not interested!'

'I'll show you blisters. You don't know what blisters are. I've got real blisters!'

'I don't want to see your blisters. I've got my own.'

Midge struggled with his socks, pulling them off. 'There,' he said. 'That's what I call blisters – take a look.'

'No,' I said. 'I'm not looking. You look at mine.'

Midge continued, 'There! Look at that one – a beauty.'

'I'm not looking. I'm not interested in your stupid blisters.' It was an impasse. He wasn't listening. He wasn't interested in my blisters and I certainly wasn't interested in his. I poured some water from my canteen over my toes, dabbed them carefully, then replaced my socks. I poured some more water over the sock toe-ends before I put my boots back on again. The cooling effect of the water provided some relief, but it was obvious that Midge wasn't interested in my sore feet. I just thought he was looking for an excuse to get his own boots off; he certainly wasn't interested in anyone else's pain or discomfort. I realised I was living in dreamland if I thought I could get a free ride back to Tanglin.

When Christmas Day arrived we experienced staff role-reversal. It was a tradition for custodial staff on duty that day to wait on their charges during the course of the festive meal. Our portions on that particular day exceeded the norm, but this was purely down to a quirk of fate, rather than any benevolent Christian gesture on the part of the Army. The caterers always pre-ordered supplies a few days in advance, based on the number of inmates at that time, and it just so happened that four or five detainees were released on Christmas Eve. This allowed the rest of us (now 12 in number) to share sixteen or seventeen men's victuals. However, the opposite had applied on many previous occasions, when the number of admissions exceeded the releases, which meant smaller portions for those already serving their time.

Apart from sitting down and being waited on by staff, we were all spoiled with glasses of lemonade. We each had a cracker to pull and everyone had to wear the paper hat inside, which they did. We were also allowed to smoke our daily ration of two cigarettes as part of the event, one before and one after the meal. Before the meal Himmler said grace, and afterwards we all held up our glasses for a communal toast of *God Bless the Queen*. It was as if she had smiled down on us, rather than the Almighty, and rewarded us with the gift of extra scran. Himmler and Steve were on duty that day and discipline, as far as talking amongst ourselves was concerned, was relaxed. They both pulled crackers and wore their paper crowns too. Himmler looked ridiculous in his, as it was far too big for his head and ended up resting on his ears; it kept slipping down over his spectacles and covering his face, which provided us with a few giggles at his expense.

Everything was relaxed and amiable until the end of the meal, when someone made a light-hearted comment directed at Himmler:

'You'd make someone a good wife, Staff.' Himmler must have misheard him because it set him off:

'I don't need a good wife, son. I've got one! I married a Filipino. And let me tell you, they make damn good wives. Yes. She'll do anything for me. I don't have to step into the kitchen; she can cook anything. I just have to ask. I can ask her for anything. And she'll do anything for me. Look at this...' And with that he stretched out his arms, held the palms of his hands open and stared down at his tunic, trousers and boots. His novelty hat, as if on cue, came down over his eyes again. We laughed as he quickly re-adjusted it: *'I don't have to do any dhobying or ironing; everything is washed and pressed for me. My boots are polished without me having to ask. Look at them shining. Gleaming! Damn good wives they make – and make no mistake about it. You won't find a better wife anywhere in the world.'* I wondered if he had married a wife or a slave. And then if love had ever been part of the equation.

'Well, I won't be coming in here again,' I said, deliberately being contentious. *'If I end up in here again, say the same time next year, I'll escape. That's what I'll do; I'll go over the wall.'* Himmler immediately bit.

'No, you won't Alcock. I'll see to that. You won't escape when I'm on watch.' I grinned at him as he stared back, unsmiling. I couldn't believe that he'd taken my outburst seriously. Still, I'd stopped him pontificating about how clever he'd been in choosing a slave instead of a wife.

The day before I was due to be discharged from Tanglin a seaman from the *H* was admitted. He was a mod named Wilson, but everyone called him Pickett, after the soul singer. I first met him ashore when we discussed music and clothes and found we had quite a lot in common. I was in the dinner queue when he arrived and heard someone humming and singing *The Happy Song* by Otis Redding, so I immediately started up with a refrain from *The Sad Song*. We then recognised one another, had a laugh about it and shook hands. He'd just arrived singing *The Happy Song* and I'd been in way too long and sang *The Sad Song;* but maybe it should have been the other way around. It was just another of life's little coincidences that stays with you.

SO LONG
SINGERS

I completed my detention in Tanglin between Christmas and New Year in 1968, and returned to the *Happy H* which was now docked back in Sembawang. As I entered the main grot area where my bunk was housed I saw Sam, a good mate of mine, who was fast asleep; he was facing the bulkhead and had his back to me. Not only had we played football together at HMS Terror during our last visit to Singers, but we'd shared some great runs ashore. I didn't want to wake him and thought, *I'll wake him later on; it'll be a surprise.* I knew we'd both be pleased to see one another and I was looking forward to chewing the fat with him again.

When he eventually woke up I discovered it wasn't him. Wills later informed me that Sam had flown home on compassionate leave as his wife was pregnant. The problem for Sam was that we'd left the UK nearly nine months ago, and she'd only just discovered she was expecting a baby. It was a sorry state of affairs and I felt for Sam. All the divorce stories about unfaithful husbands and wives connected to family life in the armed forces returned. Apart from my own personal experiences when my mum left me and my dad fifteen years before, I recalled the comments *the regs* made at Victory barracks when I was released from recess; they seemed to reinforce the belief that fragmented families came with the job whenever you served in the Armed Forces.

It was YG who had now requisitioned Sam's bunk. I remembered him from HMS Osprey: the braggart who said he could jump over five feet but had then failed miserably. He'd arrived on board during my absence as a replacement for Sam. I noticed a considerable difference in his demeanour since those cocky days at Osprey. Then he'd seemed harmless enough, but now YG was more morose, agitated. He was more introverted, had mood swings and constantly muttered to himself. And then one night I heard him sobbing and moaning to himself in his bunk. The next morning I asked him if he was OK? He confessed he found it hard to sleep, that he had started to lose things, personal things. A lot of this was kit, which he hadn't stowed away but had left lying around his bunk space. He told me he was having to repeatedly buy replacement white fronts, number eight trousers, caps and ribbons; the list seemed endless. He said his pay wasn't covering what it was costing him to live on board. He couldn't afford to go ashore. He became scruffy through wearing the same clothes too often. He couldn't cope. Killicks (senior hands) picked on him. He became increasingly disturbed as the days passed into weeks. It was sad to see. I'd never encountered the demise of a human being before, witnessed someone who became dysfunctional. I was ashore when YG was eventually escorted to the sick bay. Our messman told me that he cracked up; started talking gibberish and developed breathing problems; hyperventilation was mentioned. YG returned to the UK and I never saw him again.

I still had a habit of switching off when I heard sob stories from others. I'd dismiss them out of hand and walk away. I used to think, *So you think you've got it bad, how do you think I feel?* My defence mechanism had been reinforced with, *Don't think about bad things.* This was how I managed the life I was now consigned to. I'd developed a cold side to my nature. I knew I could be soulless and unloving whenever I wanted to be. There were times when I still didn't care about others, but then there were times when I didn't care about myself. I felt I'd become sullen, like YG, with similar mood swings. I still used the snap retort, that a giant King Edward was on my shoulder, weighing me down. And, although I only used this ploy to deflect attention away from me, I also knew, deep down, that there was a ring of truth about it when others pointed the finger.

During the time I spent serving my sentence in MCTC I'd missed a couple of HMS Hermes stopovers. One was in Okinawa, a Japanese island, and the other in Hong Kong. From what I heard when I returned back on board I don't think I missed much. In Okinawa there was another surfeit of Yanks (not surprising since there were a number of US bases there) but also, unsurprisingly, there was a conspicuous absence of available females to spend time with. I again recalled my thoughts as to why I had wanted a small ship when we sailed into foreign ports. *Never mind the number of Yanks – what chance have I got to meet pretty local girls when 2,000 Jolly Jack Tars are on the loose!*

I also learned of more tragic news when I returned back on board. Four more of our crew had died whilst I'd been away. The first crew member passed away in Okinawa, where my messmates agreed there was little to do there but drink. A cheap and extremely potent brand of booze (sounded like something akin to meths or boot polish) was produced locally and readily available in many of the nearby bars. A stoker had had too many wets during a run ashore, before he went on to sample this lethal concoction. Allegedly his oppos managed to carry him back on board without being challenged by the duty watch and put him to bed. However some hours later, when someone tried to wake him, they found paralysis had set in and he couldn't be saved. From what I heard about drinking in Okinawa and the lack of female companionship, I felt lucky to have missed the whole trip. And a couple of enforced months on the wagon for me at MCTC, coupled with strenuous exercise, hadn't done me any harm.

The other three who lost their lives were aircrew. And once again, I couldn't help thinking how fortunate I'd been when I flew off the *H* in a Fairey Gannet. A couple of weeks after my flight there were two flight accidents, which immediately followed one another, and both involved Fairey Gannets. The first happened late one Friday, when the plane was attempting to land on the flight-deck but failed to grab the arrester cable. Usually the pilot receives a signal on deck to notify him that the cable hasn't grabbed, so he opens up the throttle and takes off again. This occurred and another landing was attempted, which again failed. The pilot tried to land a third time, but the arrester wire still failed to hook up. The general consensus as to what happened was that when the pilot attempted to take off for a third time, the engine choked out; which meant it decelerated and couldn't take off again and so ended up in the drink. Miraculously the Gannet sat on top of a rolling sea, allowing the pilot and crew enough time to get out before they were rescued by the ship's SAR helicopter. Available statistics suggested it was very rare for the whole crew of a Gannet to be rescued when it ends up in the sea.

The second incident occurred the following Monday morning, when one of the Gannet's wings folded as it attempted to take off; it plunged straight off the flight deck and into the oggin. One of the crew managed to be winched from the sea, but he was dead by the time they got him back on board. I heard they searched all day for the other two crew members and any signs of wreckage but found nothing. This suggested the Gannet was probably under three hundred feet of water. The other two crew members were reported as *missing, presumed dead.*

Memories of how I felt when I blasted off for New Guinea a few weeks earlier came back to haunt me. How we took off at over 120mph in a matter of seconds; I shivered as I thought of those guys in their final moments. They must have been buzzing, in a state of heightened nervous anticipation (as I was) before take-off. The adrenalin would have initially pumped them up; it would have then transmuted into accelerated panic as they nosedived into the sea and realised they had to fight for their lives. It's hard to believe that life can be snatched away in an instant and I wondered if some things were preordained. I thought it could have easily been me on that flight but for a couple of weeks. *Thank God it wasn't.*

When I arrived back on board from MCTC Tanglin, I'd hoped a few of us – Wills, Doog, Skags, Sam and myself, – would have a run ashore. Things didn't pan out that way as Sam had flown home; Skags was on duty when the rest of us were off watch; Doog, who'd been to the sick bay because he was having problems with his waterworks, was unbelievably grounded. He was experiencing a burning sensation when taking a leak, a pus-like discharge and had soreness around the end of his penis. The medics confirmed he had a dose of the clap!

I asked Doog if he knew how he'd been infected, and he said he could only validate it through one recent experience. He'd attended a party in Singers just before Christmas when I was still banged up in Tanglin. He said he'd met a girl in a bar who was a Christian, and she invited him to her church hall where there was a carol service. Afterwards there was music, dancing and socialising, with some nibbles and wine. Later on they had ventured outside for some fresh air and began kissing in a secluded spot at the back of the building. Deli, the girl he was with, was worried that the party might finish and they would be locked in, but she was happy to carry on as long as they could still hear music playing from inside the hall. Amorous feelings quickly escalated, until a lot of fondling resulted in their passion becoming *overheated;* Doog's word not mine. They soon reached a point of no return and, so he said, he heard the refrain, *ding-dong merrily on high,* just as he reached his climax with her. *Some coincidence,* I thought.

Although the RN encouraged us to use condoms and provided them free, Doog said he hadn't bothered to collect any for protection. He said this decision had crossed his mind prior to penetration, but he'd reassured himself he'd be alright. His passion continued unabated, certain he would be safe with this wholesome, willing, beautiful Christian Eurasian girl. I couldn't help thinking, as Doog relayed the details of his sexual encounter, how I'd visited various houses of ill repute in the Far East and remained STD-free. Yes, it was true, I'd paid for my pleasure, but a sense of self-satisfaction surrounded the fact that I'd managed to remain disease-free. And when Doog had finally reached the end of his monologue, and concluded that it *must* have been that girl, I couldn't resist reminding him of how *God works in mysterious ways.*

Wills and I were the only two available for our planned run ashore. He'd heard about a discotheque called The Fireplace from some other mods on board, somewhere he had yet to visit. We decided to give it a try. It was situated on the Bukit Timah road, heading out of Singapore towards the Causeway and Johor Baru. We caught a cab and discovered it was a stand-alone shophouse on a quiet stretch of road. On the ground floor was a hairdressers, with the nightclub occupying the two floors above. This building was unusual as shophouses were often built in blocks or rows, consisting of three or four together. Many similar structures lined the streets in Singapore, where families would live above the shop they owned below.

When we arrived at The Fireplace it was still early and quiet, with only a handful of people there. As we stepped out of the yellow and black Mercedes taxi the distinctive sound of Tamla Motown and soul music escaped from the top floor. We entered through a side door and climbed up a bare hardwood staircase to a lounge and cocktail bar on the first floor. The low lighting complemented crimson velvet wallpaper, adding an intimate and warm ambience to the room. Two couples were sitting inside, cradling drinks on soft leather armchairs, whilst two Malay girls sat at the bar waiting for customers. We politely declined their advances to join them and moved along and ordered some Tiger beers. We then ventured upstairs and sought out the source of the soul music we could hear. It was a room with a dance floor, and the only occupants were two black US sailors practising some synchronised dancing; they reminded me of the Temptations or Four Tops. The relaxed privacy of the surroundings gave me the confidence to go over and ask if they could show me some of their steps. They were happy to oblige and introduced me to the *boogaloo*, a popular dance at the time. We prasticed a few moves to the sweet soul sound of Otis (Redding) singing *My Girl*.

The place got busier as the evening progressed and I recognised a girl I'd seen at the Brit Club during our sunbathing days. There weren't many English girls around, but she was young and pretty, and so I ventured over and asked for a dance. Although she didn't recognise me from the Brit, she admitted she'd been there sunbathing and this initiated some conversation. Meeting her that night didn't lead to any romantic entanglement, but I was made up when we danced to a few records and she complimented me on some of my dance moves.

There was an added bonus when we bumped into those two Yanks that night; they literally *lit up* the evening for us. After my dance lesson, but well before the The Fireplace got too busy, they rolled a couple of joints and passed them around between us. I inhaled deeply, held the essence of the weed inside my lungs for a few seconds (as they did) and felt totally elated as I exhaled. It was the first time I'd smoked real grass, or that *old Molly J,* as we later called it. The aroma of those spliffs was intoxicating and unmistakable, a sweet, floral bonfire smell never to be forgotten. We learned from the US sailors that their supplier was none other than the barman downstairs; and so before the night was over Wills and I struck up a deal with him. $10 would get us enough for a couple of decent joints, and so we went for $20 worth. He said we could pick it up the following night, although he wouldn't bring it into the club, as he was worried about the police who periodically raided the place. He promised to leave it in a bag further on down, on the opposite side of the road behind a large boulder that straddled the monsoon ditch.

We thought he might gyp us, but he was as good as his word. And so we collected our first *stash of hash, man,* the following night.

The true beauty of that score was fully appreciated back on board, when I turned on one night just prior to going on duty in the wash-up. The *pigs* were enjoying a gala evening with onshore guests, and posh-nosh was central to proceedings. I rolled and smoked a four-skinner with Wills before making my way to the wash-up. I floated through the flats as if I had giant marshmallows glued to the soles of my boots. I grooved and bounced along in slo-mo with a beautiful spring in my step. Whilst on duty that evening I had a fit of the giggles, but it was the sweetest time I ever spent in the company of a dishwasher. And then for me the *pièce de résistance* was when I tasted my first-ever plate of succulent fresh crab meat, apparently the best bit pulled from the back legs. I couldn't believe how the *pigs* had failed to finish off something so delicious.

I had only been out of detention in Tanglin for a few days when I was put on a charge. It was a crazy situation. I'd gone to collect my beer allowance, which was an entitlement of two cans a day for those serving in the hot and humid climate of the Far East. When you went to claim this allowance a leading hand regulator clipped your card to indicate you'd received your cans for that day. On this particular occasion the aptly named regulator, Pricky Price, (because he was *a prick*) was on duty. He duly clipped my card, but as he went to hand it back he hesitated and quickly withdrew it.

'Aha!' he said. 'I think we need a haircut.'

'You what?'

'Haircut! And your sideburns need shortening.'

'You've got to be joking. I've only just come out of DQs. I had a regulation haircut when I was in there.'

'Listen, mate – you get a haircut and take those sideburns up – or no more beer for you.'

'You're joking! I don't need a haircut.'

'What are you in? The men's navy – or the boys'?'

'With all this talk about haircuts, it sounds as if I'm in the boys.'

'Well, I'll tell you what; we'll get you a haircut right now!'

And with that Pricky Price rushed round and through the hatch door that separated us and started to manhandle me. I was having none of it and grabbed the side of the hatch and the locks that secured them. He couldn't shift me on his own and so shouted for help and assistance from other regulators in the office. Two more were soon in attendance; one grappled with my arms, whilst I grabbed at the pipes that ran along the bulkheads. Pricky then held me in a head-lock, and one of the others grabbed my legs. Between them they managed to lift me up horizontally and charge for'ard. When I realised we'd passed the hairdressers I stopped struggling and relaxed. We passed through the dining area at a rate of knots. Wills, who was having some scran at the time, saw the whole drama played out in front of his eyes. He later recalled the scene to me: 'Joe, you came through there like a battering ram. The three of them had hold of you, charging, just like a battering ram!'

It was a pity Wills didn't see the end of my journey after we'd passed him in the dining area. We went beyond the galley and through another hatch, until we arrived at a ladder that led down beyond the lower deck to another ladder, and to the deck below. The regs took great pleasure in releasing me when we reached the top of the first ladder and letting me fall. I went crashing, tumbling and bouncing off steel steps, down to the deck below; there was no other exit and so I had to descend down the next ladder. I scrambled to my feet before they caught up with me, and flew down this second ladder as fast as I could. I was lucky to escape serious injury. At the bottom of the second ladder I was confronted by a cell door, something I didn't know existed. There was nowhere else to go; I was now in the bowels of the ship.

When I was locked up inside the cell I realised there was nothing on board further for'ard than this. The bulkhead directly opposite the cell door was the only thing that separated me from the Pacific Ocean, the largest and deepest ocean on earth. I must have been close to or just below sea level, as I could hear huge waves roaring and crashing into the prow of the ship. The *H* rose and fell in time to the sound of those thundering waves and left me feeling both scared and uncomfortable. After a while the incessant sound of the sea battering into the bow allowed my fears to subside. I eventually accepted the fact that the sea was not going to burst through the steel bulkhead and wash me away, although it sounded as though it might.

Fair play to my messmates. They visited me whilst I was held in there and passed me drinks and chocolate through the small-barred eye-level opening in the cell door. The next day I was hauled in front of the OOD and charged by Pricky Price for disobeying an order. He saw Pricky first and then asked me for my version of events. I explained how I was asked the question: *Was I in the boys' navy or the men's?* And I told Pricky what I thought was an honest answer. The OOD reached his verdict and the case was dismissed. I believe Pricky got a bollocking for wasting the OOD's time.

Although Jim and I were both skint we borrowed some money and decided to have one last run ashore before we left Singers. A bag off was high on the agenda as we knew we'd be sailing away but didn't know how many weeks we'd be at sea before we reached our next port of call. After we'd had a few wets downtown we grabbed a taxi and explained our predicament to the driver on the way back to the ship; we were short of funds but wanted female company. I think he took us to the only place in Asia where something was on offer for almost nothing; *all night in* for less than ten Singapore dollars. The taxi pulled up outside a single-storey prefabricated dwelling in Nee Soon village. Inside were small, partitioned square-shaped rooms with a 12-inch gap between the top of the partition and the ceiling. The last thing I thought of, as I sat down on the sparsely covered bed to get undressed, was: *Do I really want to do this?* Again I wondered about catching a dose. The girl I was with was young and had a bit of a belly; I wondered if she was pregnant. I *really* didn't want to be here and so shouted over the partition to Jim in the next room, '*What are you doing, man?*' Jim's lady, of about thirty, was old to us, and if I said she was large that would be a *gross* understatement. She was twice our size, and I couldn't see how the two of them were going to share a single bed together. The realisation that I felt I was making a mistake made me shout out to Jim over the partition and ask him what he was doing.

'*I'm doing her, man. I'm doing her!*' Jim shouted. And then gasps, sighs, grunting, heavy breathing and bed-banging, drowned out any thoughts I had of abandoning the situation. I'd had too much to drink and realised I couldn't back down. I was past caring and so, as far as I knew, went through with the dirty deed. I guess I must have crashed out immediately afterwards because I woke up alone in bed. I had no recollection of my performance the night before, and if she'd been lying next to me in the morning I'd have wondered who she was and where I was. I tried to familiarise myself with my surroundings and struggled to piece together the events of the previous evening. It was at this point that Jim clawed his way into my box room in a state of undress.

'*Where are your clothes, man?*' he asked. I sat up, rubbed my eyes and looked around before pointing to my gear straggled across a chair at the foot of the bed.

'*My clothes are gone, man. They've been nicked. Someone's nicked all my gear,*' Jim said.

'*No,*' I replied. '*They can't have. You've got your socks on.*'

'*I never took them off, man. I wore them in bed. I'm telling you, all my clothes have gone; they've been stolen.*' I jumped out of bed, quickly got dressed and went to look for the main man who ran the establishment. I bumped into a couple of girls and asked them if they could find whoever was in charge. I couldn't tell if either of them had been the girl I thought I'd been intimate with the night before; eventually a middle-aged guy appeared. He wanted to know what the problem was, so I explained. He didn't appear to be the slightest bit concerned, as if stealing someone's clothes and leaving them stark-bollock naked was part of the deal. He said not to worry; he'd sort something out for Jim to wear. He soon returned with a bundle of clothes for Jim to put on.

I left Jim and pursued the guy outside to explain our current situation. We now had no money and I told him that what we did have had disappeared with Jim's clothes. I told him we needed a taxi to get back on board ship at Sembawang dockyard. I explained that because we had no money one of us would wait in the taxi when we arrived at the ship's gangway, whilst the other went on board to borrow some money for the taxi fare. I stressed he needed to translate this message to the taxi driver, something he agreed to do.

I was outside having a cigarette when Jim appeared. He looked gorgeous. He had on a see-through white chiffon blouse and long, tight, bright pink, velvet flared trousers. His shoes were replaced with red flip-flops, which were mainly hidden by his trousers, but when they weren't they went well with his outfit. Jim was embarrassed and didn't want to go back in women's clothes. We spoke to the main man again but he was adamant that he could do no more; those clothes were all he could lay his hands on. '*Sorry; nothing else,*' he said.

When our taxi arrived the main man explained our predicament and we headed back to the dockyard. As we pulled up next to the ship on the jetty I volunteered to go to the mess and borrow ten bucks for the fare. I explained the situation to the guys in the mess and had no problem borrowing the money. I then implored everyone present to go up to the boat deck and give Jim the welcome he so richly deserved. I paid the driver and Jim stepped out from the taxi to hear rapturous applause; he was greeted with a variety of wolf-whistles, cheers and cat-calls. A raucous shrill followed him all the way up the gangway from the jetty; and again when he finally stepped inside the mess. He wasn't allowed to forget his drag act entrance for the next few thousand nautical miles.

WELCOME WA

We arrived in Fremantle, Western Australia (WA), early one bright and sunny February morning, having sailed over two and a half thousand miles from Singapore in approximately a week. Fremantle (known colloquially as *Freo* and pronounced Freeo) was bathed in blue sky but a lot cooler than Perth (the capital of WA), which is only fifteen miles away but inland. Freo, being on the coast, is at the mercy of a local wind known as the Freo Doctor, which blows in off the ocean at up to 20 kilometres an hour.

The next day the local newspaper heralded our arrival:

This is the only major warship in the Royal Navy that does not carry guns. She is equipped entirely with missiles. The aircraft carrier is HMS Hermes... she entered Fremantle yesterday.

A couple of days later Wills and I went on our first run ashore in WA. We thought we'd try Freo first to see what it was like, but knew if we wanted more entertainment we could always catch a cab into Perth. We were anchored in WA for two weeks and right outside the docks was a scruffy old pub called The Ship. I thought we'd give it a miss, but Wills wanted to buy some cigs as he'd forgotten to bring his Blue Liners ashore.

When he darted through a side door I followed. Initially we were both blinded by the glare from a low-hanging light over a pool table and had to shield our eyes. But when the door slammed shut behind us, the hubbub of conversation inside the room petered out and left a palpable silence. My eyes adjusted to the light within seconds and revealed a snapshot of suspended animation inside the room; everyone was static and staring at us. The pool table dominated most of the space in the centre of the room, and there were small tables and chairs pushed up against the walls on either side. Abbo or mixed-race women occupied most of these, whilst four bronzed white guys, each armed with a cue, played pool. They all stood guarding their side of the table and looked similar, with their long, tousled, sun-bleached hair, cut-off denim shorts, singlets and work boots. It was about eight o'clock and I guessed they'd arrived at the pub straight from work.

I looked around and there was hardly any space between the feet of the sitting women and the pool table. At the far end of the room was an archway that led to a bar, and this was where we needed to get to for Wills to buy his cigarettes. The guy standing on our side of the pool table stood between us and the archway, blocking the entrance to the bar. He had rippling biceps, as thick as my thighs, and was chalking his cue as Wills carefully plotted his way along between the tables, chairs and pool table, ensuring he didn't tread on the toes of the Abbo women. As he reached the blond giant, who towered over us both, the guy stopped Wills in his tracks. He pushed the freshly chalked tip of his pool cue into Wills' chest.

'*Where'r' ya from, mite?*' demanded the blonde Neanderthal. Wills looked down at the cue pressing into the lapel of his jacket. He then knocked it sideways with his left hand and dusted the chalk mark away with his right hand.

'*Watch the suit, mate.*' The Aussie took half a step back, surprised at Wills' response. His hesitation allowed Wills to glide passed him and make his way through the archway and into the bar area. Now it was my turn. The big Aussie quickly refocused and pointed his cue directly at me as I approached. Uproar ensued:

'*Leave them alone! Leave them alone!*' came a chorus from the Abbo women. '*Let them be – they're doing no harm.*' But the big ox ignored them.

'*Are you off that big ship?*' he asked.

'*Yeah.*'

'*You're off that big ship – in the harbour?*'

'*Yeah – that's right,*' I confirmed.

'*Well, you're a c – – t!*'

'*Yeah – that's right,*' I agreed, and smiled. Again this guy looked bewildered. He took a step back and let the pool cue drop to his side. It was all I needed to slip past him and join Wills at the bar. I was about to say, *'Don't bother buying a drink,'* when a pool cue came flying through the air and crashed into the bar beside us. As soon as Wills paid for his cigarettes we were out of there, through another exit close to the bar.

It's funny, but we'd been warned about the sort of reception we could expect in Australia by a killick in our mess, although we hadn't taken him seriously at the time. He said Aussies had an innate hatred of anything associated with Britain or the British, and we were often referred to as *POME bastards* (POME, meaning Prisoner of Mother England and pronounced Pommy). On a previous visit to Oz the killick referred to an incident when he'd been having a quiet drink at a bar when an Aussie guy kept asking him, *'How are the bogs?'* The killick replied that he didn't know as he hadn't been. The Ozzie kept on and on asking, until the killick eventually challenged him with, *'What the hell are you talking about? I haven't been to the bogs,'* meaning the toilet. However it transpired that the Ozzie was referring to the UK as *the bogs.*

I had a few runs ashore with my messmates during that fortnight in Fremantle, but needless to say we headed straight into Perth and gave Freo a miss after our earlier encounter. We visited a few nightclubs in the city, The Blue Meanies, The Firecracker, and The Waldorf. There were always plenty of girls in the clubs since it was half price or free admission for females. Whilst we were docked in Fremantle and clubbing it in Perth, I didn't make it with any girls, or take any home, but I enjoyed their company by having a few drinks and dances with them during our stay. The tuition at The Fireplace disco in Singapore had certainly given me the confidence to approach girls both on and off the dance floor. I felt I didn't need as much Dutch courage as I had in the past when approaching members of the opposite sex.

We were near the end of our stay in Freo when I heard about a couple of guys who planned to jump ship and go on the run in Australia. It had been something I'd been thinking about for a while; but it was only when I heard of their plans that I decided I'd let the *Happy H* sail home without me too. One guy was a stoker and the other an Airey Fairey, and we met up just a few days before the ship sailed. We decided to go ashore separately on the day before she sailed, and to meet up in the lounge of the Swan Hotel, which was directly opposite Perth railway station. We agreed that whoever arrived first would book a room for the night, and then wait in the lounge bar for the others to arrive. We'd split the cost of the room between us, as we were all going to spend the night in the one room.

Before we jumped ship I realised I needed some additional funds. It was lucky that another payday coincided with our last week on board, but I still needed to boost my cash reserves. I flogged my rabbits (presents to take home) and also my treasured LP record collection of soul and Motown. I'd built up quite a collection and was sad to let Otis Redding, Joe Tex, The Temptations and Smokey Robinson go.

But I knew I needed as much cash as I could muster to support me on the run. I'd had little time to prepare as it had been a last-minute decision for me.

The three of us made a pact to stick together in Perth; we knew we were out on our own and that it was a big step to take: to suddenly arrive in an unfamiliar country with nowhere to live, no job and no income. We applied the safety in numbers rule, three heads being better than one. The only plan we had, besides sticking together, was to find somewhere to live as soon as possible.

I was last to arrive at the Swan as I'd been on duty. Wills helped me with my case when it was time to disembark, as I thought it would look pretty odd carrying a suitcase off the ship when it was due to sail within 24 hours. I'm not sure that, *'just popping to the launderette,'* would have cut the mustard with the duty watch liberty boatmen; particularly when we had a Chinese laundry on board. Wills took my suitcase down a covered gangway amidships that wasn't being used, whilst I disembarked in the normal manner. It was dusk when I went ashore in my civvies, whilst Wills snuck down the redundant gangway and waited with my case. I walked along the jetty checking that no one was about who would see me. It would obviously arouse suspicion if I was seen tampering with the rigging at the bottom of a gangway alongside a Royal Navy warship. It was a relief to collect my case without incident; I said goodbye to Wills, a good mate, and to the *Happy H.*

I met up with the others in the lounge of the Swan Hotel as agreed. They both appeared relaxed, sitting at a table and sharing a jug of Swan lager. They'd been chatting to the waitress who worked there, Yvette, a girl from Bolton who'd recently emigrated. The jukebox was playing

Marvin Gaye's *I Heard It Through the Grapevine.* I thought, *I hope she hasn't heard about us on the grapevine,* but Yvette didn't seem concerned that three Brits had suddenly rolled up and were spending the night at the hotel. We ordered another jug of lager but were well aware that we needed to take it steady. That evening we discovered more about one another. Billy, the stoker, was short, stocky and had jet-black hair. He was from Billingsgate, in London, and was a real chirpy, cheeky cockney, who always had a smile across his *north and south,* as he would say. He was full of all the cockney rhyming slang and would try to bamboozle you with it. Rod, the Airey Fairey, was taller, slimmer, with blond hair and hailed from Birmingham. He was quieter and seemed more insular. Sometimes, the combination of his Brummy accent and quiet nature made you ask him to repeat what he'd just said. When I arrived they both had plans to grow moustaches. They said they wanted to disguise their appearance in case any photos of them had been passed on to the local authorities by the RN. Rod claimed it was common practice for *the regs* to report details of missing crew members whenever a ship left harbour. He said he'd heard they usually notified the police, who themselves probably weren't that bothered, but he thought they might pass on details of deserters to boys' brigades, such as the sea cadets, and ask them to keep a look out for us.

As it got near to closing time Yvette came and joined us and had a couple of middies from our jug. She asked where we'd come from and what we were doing. We told her we'd moved from quaint old Freo to the big city, and that we were looking for *"digs"*. Yvette went and fetched us the hotel copy of *The West Australian* so that we could scan the advertisement columns. We'd only booked the Swan for one night and didn't want to book another night unless we had to; preserving our funds was a priority for all of us. I mentioned our suitcases needed stowing somewhere, since we didn't want to be carrying them around with us when viewing accommodation. Thankfully, Yvette came to our rescue and suggested we could leave our luggage in her room. She lived in at the hotel and said she'd catch us over breakfast to arrange this. The next morning Yvette was as good as her word and we smuggled our cases into her room.

She shared her room with an older girl, who was still in bed when we entered the room and transferred our luggage. Her roommate was attractive with blonde hair and an angelic face – probably in her mid-twenties. I thought she was someone I'd seen before. It wasn't until she scrambled out of bed and limped her way to the bathroom that I remembered where I'd seen her. I was returning back on board in a taxi from Perth a few nights ago, at around two in the morning. A fight had spilled into the street outside a nightclub, forcing the taxi driver to slow right down, almost to a standstill. We crawled past, where a couple of Yankee sailors were shouting and trying to get at each another. A small crowd had gathered, intrigued by the spectacle, and a woman was screaming at them to stop. She was running forwards and backwards, in-between them, trying to keep them apart. It was bedlam with the onlookers cheering and goading them on. She became framed in my mind because she looked beautiful, real class; she seemed totally out of place in the middle of such chaos. She wore a satin evening gown that shimmered in the semi-darkness; I thought she wouldn't have been out of place at a gala ball, never mind refereeing a street fight in the early hours. Her hair, pinned up in a pre-Raphaelite style, exposed long earrings that sparkled under the lamplight. I noticed her limp when she ran between the sailors pleading with them to stop, and I wondered what had caused her affliction. It was her limp now that ignited my memory; there was no doubt in my mind that this was the same woman I'd seen in the street fight. I realised things weren't what they seemed and, intuitively, that we weren't in the presence of angels.

That first day we dropped lucky with our house-hunting, finding two rooms in the same house to share between the three of us. And as strangers in the city it was an easy address to find from the centre of Perth. If you went down William Street, which was to the left of the railway station as you faced it, and crossed over the railway lines via a horseshoe-shaped bridge, and kept on going, you'd walk into and through Northbridge, heading out of the city towards Mount Lawley. Eventually you'd come to Hyde Park on the left, and our new address was directly opposite the park on the other side of the road.

It was a large house with other occupants already living there. Liz, in her early twenties, was a few years older than us. And then there were two orphaned brothers, Arnold and Toby, about our age. Rod, Billy and myself met up with our fellow residents in a shared lounge area. We were looking around, familiarising ourselves with the communal areas in our new home, when they sought us out; they appeared keen to meet us. It was a fortuitous meeting as far as I was concerned, since my shortage of funds meant I needed to find a job (any job) ASAP. Arnold was confident that there was an opportunity with his employer doing some window cleaning. And so it proved. I got up early with him the next morning and met the employer who gave me a start straight away. Arnold primed me beforehand; he said, *'You'll be asked about call-up.'* This was National Service enlistment, as Australia was involved in the Vietnam War. He told me to say, *'I missed out.'* Call-up for military service in Australia was based upon selection from the electoral register. Not every name was selected therefore, when questioned by an employer about the possibility of call-up. I was advised to say, *'I missed out,'* which was an accepted response.

The other plus to working in Australia, as opposed to the UK, was that there was no National Insurance requirement. When you applied for a job in Australia you didn't have to produce a NI number; the only thing employers cared about was whether they were likely to lose you due to the war in Vietnam.

In my new abode I shared a room with Rod whilst Billy took a room next door. And then something strange happened to me not long after we moved in. I woke up in the middle of the night to be confronted by a skull. It mirrored the size of my face from no more than twelve inches away, and stared straight at me through a gap in some curtains next to my bed. It was in the dead of night, but I was wide awake.

I screamed out, *'ROD! ROD! ROD!'* but couldn't make him hear me. He was fast asleep on the opposite side of the room. I half sat up in bed and continued screaming but couldn't make myself heard; it was as if I had laryngitis and had lost my voice. I wanted Rod to wake up and see the skull staring right in front of me. No matter how hard I tried I couldn't make myself heard; it was as though I was screaming as I was drowning. Rod remained oblivious to my spectral trauma and slumbered on. Eventually the skull dissolved back into the folds and disappeared behind the curtains.

Still recovering, but thinking about the skull, I half sat up in bed. I became lost in a fifteen-year-old memory of another nightmare I had when my mum walked out. I was four years old and awoke to see a nest of snakes weaving in and out of my bedroom curtains. Terrified, I screamed for my dad and went running into his bedroom. I was screaming, just like I had been now, screaming as though my throat had been cut. I pulled at my dad, frantically trying to wake him, as the snakes now writhed in and out of his pyjamas, slithering down his neck. When he awoke he took me downstairs, but they were there too, swirling in and out of the curtains in the front room. It was only when he opened the curtains that they slowly disappeared. I found it hard to believe that I couldn't differentiate between the impact both nightmares had on me. They had both made me scream, yet my screams were no louder than hoarse guttural sounds, emanating from deep down in my throat, as if my vocal chords had been severed. No matter how hard I tried I couldn't make myself heard. When Rod finally awoke I decided not to say anything to him.

Rod and Billy weren't as desperate for cash as I was, and so had the luxury of taking more time to find work they were happy to do. Rod soon found a driving job, and Billy found work in a warehouse. Life was sweet for a couple of weeks as we settled into working life in Australia. After payday we celebrated our new-found freedom on Friday night by going to The Waldorf nightclub.

This is where I met Cindy with her long, shining, chestnut-coloured hair that flopped around her face. It was her figure and abandonment on the dance floor that first attracted me to her. She wore tight, black flared trousers that complemented a narrow waist and highlighted an hourglass figure. Pert young breasts were tantalisingly hidden beneath a thin white satin blouse. There was an aura of innocence about her, a kind of purity. She had pale, unblemished skin and wide green eyes which looked directly at you. Initially, I was unnerved; I wondered if she could read what I was thinking. I imagined a voice in her head asking, *I've got nothing to hide. What about you?*

I learned that Cindy was just seventeen, but then I was only eighteen going on nineteen. It was a period when I was often preoccupied with sensual and sexual thoughts concerning members of the opposite sex. I put this down to youth and inexperience, a time when my testosterone was flying high and my libido was in orbit. It was a time of personal discovery for me. I was alone, left to my own devices and to make my own decisions. I discovered Cindy wasn't a showy girl. When she dressed up she didn't reveal too much of what lay beneath. And the more I got to know her the more I respected her. I felt comfortable in her company, something I hadn't experienced with other girls, apart from Jenny. I knew I wasn't *in love,* but that didn't mean I didn't want to spend the night with her, because I did. I knew when Cindy was with me, she *was* with me; I didn't need to impress her. I think I was overly insecure back then, but Cindy gave me confidence. She was the first girl I saw for any length of time, my first real girlfriend. I believed in her and completely trusted her.

When we left The Waldorf that night I knew I couldn't take Cindy back to my room as Rod would be there. I chose not to mention any carnal thoughts I had towards her because it was pointless. Instead, I acted out the role of the gallant escort; I walked her safely back to her parents' house in Tuart Hill. When we arrived Cindy said it was too late to invite me in, as she didn't want to risk waking up her parents or sisters. I played it cool. I'd half expected such an outcome and wasn't mad about meeting her family anyway. I reassured her it was *no* problem, and that I had to be up early for work the next day. We kissed, said goodnight and arranged to meet again. As I sauntered home I felt quite pleased with myself, as I hadn't come across as some sex-starved guy who only wanted to get my wicked way with her. I thought I behaved like a real gent, although circumstances had dictated it was more by accident than design. I reassessed my intentions with Cindy as a result of that evening and decided to take things slowly with her; I'd wait and see how our relationship developed.

Not long after that I got the sack from work. It was my own fault because I knew what I was doing; or to be honest, what I wasn't doing. I was never totally enamoured with window cleaning anyway, but on this particular February day it was well over 100 degrees Fahrenheit, and I felt hot, sweaty, tired and weary. I was working in tandem, or so I thought, with a Yugoslav immigrant. We'd been deployed to clean classroom windows along the whole side of a very large school. They were known as Jalousie or Louvre windows, which opened vertically and not horizontally, as was the norm in warmer climes. When you pulled a lever at the base of the window casing, a dozen glass slats opened with edges that faced you. They were more difficult to clean and more tiresome than those that opened horizontally. My arms began to ache with the up, down motion, and the awkwardness of having to wipe in-between the slats. I started to think about taking a break and decided to seek out the Yugoslav to discuss this. I looked in the classroom next door, but he wasn't there; nor was he in the next one, or the one next to that one. I couldn't find him in any of the classrooms down the side of the school where we were supposed to be cleaning. I decided to amend my cleaning schedule and only cleaned the windows in every other classroom, irrespective of whether they had been cleaned or not. It was obvious that a lot of windows hadn't been cleaned and equally understandable that complaints from the school followed. I was held responsible and was paid off, although I received a full week's wages for only two days' attendance that week.

Back at *the digs* I dropped lucky again in my search for work, when the other ex-orphan, Toby, mentioned Perth City Council had vacancies for labourers. He worked there, and so filled me in on where to go and how to apply.

It was getting towards the end of summer in Australia and, thankfully, the temperature dropped. I found it was a job I loved because it was outside in the sunshine and fresh air; although the pay wasn't that great.

For the first few weeks I was in a team of four: two skilled guys, myself and an older Polish chap named Tomasz. We were detailed to re-lay hundreds of uneven and broken paving slabs that ran along a public footpath outside a community park, as well as in front of some private properties. The tradesmen did the measuring, levelling and trowel work; Tomasz and I did the humping, concrete mixing and cleaning. We all got on well. Although the weather was now a lot cooler in Perth, it was still as hot as warm summer days back in the UK. I'd strip down to the waist everyday, trying to rekindle the now-faded tan I'd acquired during those heady days sunbathing in Singapore. My skin soon darkened up to a deep russet brown, which prompted Tomasz to comment on a number of occasions, *'You mutter no recognise you, when you go back home.'* My torso had grown darker each time he said it, but I'd just smile and let it go. I didn't want to get drawn into the story of how I hadn't seen my mother for over fifteen years. And then one day I asked Tomasz what had made him come to Australia, and all he could say was, *'Bad peeple in my Kawntree. Bad peeple in my Kawntree.'* It made me think that no matter where you are, or whatever your circumstances, there's always someone worse off than yourself.

Whilst working during the day for the council my diet consisted of a couple of custard tarts, a Granny Smith apple and a bottle of cold milk. I bought all this from a nearby shop when we stopped for a break. When I was returning from the store to where we were working one day, an old lady accosted me at the bottom of her drive. I wondered if she was Greek and in mourning, as she was dressed all in black from the filigree lace of her head scarf to the soles of her shoes. She waved her hand up and down at me as I approached, and so I stopped to see what she wanted. As she got closer I could see she had a bunch of grapes in her hand. She thrust these into my chest and held them there as she smiled up at me; she simultaneously nodded her head up and down, intimating I should take them. I wasn't sure if she spoke any English but all I could say was, '*Thank you, thank you.*' I felt pleased; it was such a kind gesture. Each day afterwards, as I passed her house making my way back to work from the shop, she'd be by the entrance to her drive with a bunch of succulent burgundy grapes for me. Although we never conversed, she continued to smile and nod her head at me every time she gifted me the grapes. And all I could do was return her smile, and repeat '*Thank you,*' again and again. Her kindness rekindled thoughts of my mother once more and made me wonder if there was something in me that perhaps had reminded her of a long-lost son.

Things soon changed back at the house where we were staying. Rod still had his driving job but had seen an advertisement that involved driving tractors. He said it was up country, which meant it was in the outback. He said it was more money and that he wanted somewhere quieter. He thought he'd have less chance of being caught and feel safer in a smaller community. When he left I thought Billy might opt to take Rod's place and share my room, but he had other plans. Someone he worked with said there was a room going spare next door to them and asked if he wanted it. It was a lot closer to the city centre, on the other side of Northbridge, which made it more convenient for him to travel to and from work.

It was whilst I was still in the double room, after Rod and Billy had gone, that I had a visit from Liz, the only female in the household. I heard a tap on my door one evening, and when I opened it there she stood with a bottle of wine. She sort of tumbled in, thrusting the wine into my hands.

'I'm sorry to disturb you, Joe – but I need to talk to you.' She sat on the edge of the bed and started sobbing. 'Things aren't working out for me, Joe.'

'I'll just pop to the kitchen and get a bottle opener,' I said, and left, pulling the door to. When I returned she was lying on my bed, fully dressed, thank God. I opened the bottle and poured some into a couple of cups and went over. She sat up to drink, still sniffling and dabbing her eyes with a tissue.

'Glenn and I have broke up. I'm going to go home, and I wondered if you wanted to come with me?' I'd heard the story from the orphans that Liz and her guy, Glenn, had broken up. They told me that Liz and Glenn, an American, had been hitch-hiking around Oz, but now they'd finished he'd decided to go back to the States. Liz told me her home was in Albany, a small town 260-odd miles south of Perth on the southern tip of WA. She said I'd easily find work down there as it was home to a huge whaling station. The ex-orphans also mentioned to me that Liz had a young child, which her parents were looking after whilst she went travelling. This was something Liz had conveniently failed to mention. I knew straight away what my answer to her invitation would be. I rationalised a few things in my head, which only reinforced my decision not to venture down to Albany with her. Firstly, I hardly knew her, and she hadn't been totally honest with me; secondly, I wasn't the slightest bit interested in slicing up whales, let alone ingesting the noxious stench of their blood and blubber. And, thirdly, and this was the overriding factor as far as I was concerned: I could prophesise an unhealthy outcome for yours truly. This was purely based on the welcome I was likely to receive down there from your average Australian male. I pictured myself, a not-particularly-muscular British teenager, arriving in a small hick Australian town, with an unmarried girl who had a child. I imagined the sort of reception I'd receive. Based on what I'd heard, and the scary encounter I had with Wills in Fremantle, it didn't didn't bear thinking about. I told Liz I needed time to think over her proposition. It was around this time that the landlord asked me if I wanted to move into Billy's room, now that both Rod and Billy had moved out. He said he had someone interested in the double room I still occupied. I accepted his offer and used this to explain to Liz that I'd now definitely decided to stay in Perth.

I was still seeing Cindy, and not long after I moved into my single room I invited her back there. We'd been to a nightclub and I was surprised when she accepted my offer to come back. I left her in my room whilst I made us some coffee, and when I returned was delighted to find she had got undressed and slipped between the sheets. Cindy was sitting up in bed with the covers pulled up to her neck; she took her coffee with one hand, whilst the other firmly clutched the counterpane under her chin. I stripped down to my boxer shorts and then slipped beneath the covers beside her. Cindy suggested we put the light out, which I did, and then we both slipped further down beneath the covers. We began kissing when I realised she still had her bra and pants on. I fondled her breasts over her bra as we kissed, until she suddenly sat up, unhooked the clasp behind and discarded it. I felt the warmth of her now-unfettered bosom. Unhindered, I slid closer to her, kissing and caressing those proud, pert breasts. As I edged closer I slipped my leg between hers. I moved a hand down until I felt knicker elastic. Before I could advance any further Cindy's hand clamped down over mine.

'No, Joe. I don't want you to.' I wondered if *No,* meant *Yes? I could be persuaded.* I had now moved across so that I was nearly on top of her. I still had my boxers on but knew if things progressed, as I hoped they would, I could have them off in a flash and set myself free. I was now in a state of growing excitement as my leg interlocked with hers.

'No, Joe,' she whispered in my ear. *'Please don't. Please don't enter me.'* She stopped me in my tracks.

'I want to stay with you, Joe – I really do. But can't we just put our arms around one another – hold one another – and go to sleep. I want to be beside you, Joe – but I don't want to do it, not yet.' And that's how my lusty light was

extinguished that night. We kissed, cuddled, put our arms around one another and fell asleep. Although we remained in touch after that, I cooled it with Cindy and didn't see her for a couple of weeks.

It was during this hiatus that I bumped into someone I didn't know I knew. I'd gone into Perth centre and dropped into a record shop and asked if they could play me *The White Album* by The Beatles. It was quite a common request from prospective record buyers back then, to ask if you could listen to records before you purchased them. It was a chance to listen to new records inside individual sound booths, without owning the record or having a record player. As I listened to the album a girl who worked in the shop came over to my booth and mouthed some words at me. I couldn't hear what she said initially; I lifted the earphones off my ears.

'*I know you,*' she said.

'*I don't think so,*' I said. '*You must be mistaken.*'

'*No. I do. You're off that ship. You're in the navy.*'

'*Shush...*' I said, looking around. I was dumbstruck. I quickly ushered her into the booth beside me.

'*How do you know that?*' I asked, still surveying the premises to see if anyone was within earshot. We were okay; it was safe to talk. ' *How do you know I'm in the Navy? And you do know the ship has sailed again – right?*' She was grinning and nodding at the same time.

'*Don't worry, I won't say anything.*'

'*So how do you know me?*'

'*We had a couple of dances at The Blue Meanies nightclub!*'

Oh, another night when I must have been half-cut, flashed through my mind. *'Look,'* she continued, *'I've only come over to ask if you fancy coming to a party on Saturday night.'* I thanked her and said I'd love to attend, mainly because I was worried that she knew about me and my circumstances, and I wanted to make sure I could trust her. When she went back to the counter she wrote out her name and the address where the party was being held. I discovered she was another recent English immigrant whose name was Linda. She shared a flat with another girl, Diane, and they were having a joint house-warming party. Linda pointed out that her address, where the party was being held, was in walking distance from where I lived, on the far side of Hyde Park.

The girls' flat was on the first floor of a detached house, accessed via a steel staircase attached to the gable end; it had probably been a fire escape before the property was converted into flats. On the night of the party I arrived about an hour after Linda said it would start. Things were *buzzing* when I got there; people were milling around, drifting in and out of rooms. There was low lighting in the hall and lounge, which was where I found myself after I arrived. I was quickly redirected to the kitchen to deposit my offering of a bottle of wine. Here the light was extreme; I was dazzled by the bright white lights when I entered and had to raise an arm to shield my eyes. As I became adjusted to the glare I noted fluorescent tubes in the ceiling, which seemed to exacerbate the whiteness of the appliances housed there.

There was the normal ensemble of white goods: a cooker, fridge, freezer, washing machine, as well as an old, large, rectangular porcelain white sink. If that wasn't enough whiteness, then every wall, from floor to ceiling, was covered with white tiles.

I managed to grab a tinny of Swan lager and was relieved to return to the more subdued party lighting that illuminated the rest of the flat. I followed the music which led me back to the lounge, where Sam Cooke was singing *You Send Me*. I expected a few Brits to be at the party because Linda was an English immigrant, but I was also hoping there'd be a few other girls there too. At the back of my mind was Cindy, but I was really looking for someone to reciprocate the physical need in me. Linda was on the other side of the room, sorting through some records by the record player, with (who turned out to be) her flatmate, Diane. She saw me and came over. She pecked me on the cheek and introduced me to Diane; they were both pleasant, friendly girls, but not my type; I wasn't attracted to either of them. Diane was taller than me and appeared quite thin, whilst Linda, with her bright, smiley face, was the opposite: short and quite stocky. Diane excused herself saying she had to go to the loo, whilst Linda asked if I was okay. Satisfied that I was, she went back to sorting out their records.

I helped myself to a couple of beers and hung around in the lounge listening to the music. After a while a guy entered the room and stood next to me by the open lounge door. We acknowledged each other with a nod and a smile until, moments later, I felt what seemed like a hail shower, or a handful of grit, hitting the outside of my trouser leg. I looked down and saw shards of glass on the carpet. He had a broken wine glass in his hand; it was obvious he'd smashed it against the edge of the door. As I turned and looked at him he said in a broad Scottish accent, *'They'se some Aussies out there calling our wee girls.'*

'Eh?' I asked, not properly catching what he said.

'They'se some Aussie guys stood outside the toylet – calling names at our lassies – as they go in and out of the toylet. Weez about to teach them a lesson.' And almost on cue a chant went up, *'Tweet tweet – up the fleet! Tweet tweet – up the fleet!'* This was accompanied by stamping feet, as if an army squad was on the march. The guy next to me did a right wheel and left the room. Then all I could hear was a lot of shouting and screaming, in tandem with the manic chant: *'Tweet Tweet – up the fleet!'* And, in what seemed a matter of seconds, a door was thrown open and the sound of feet thundered down the outside steps. I stayed put in the lounge. I'd learned not to get involved in things that don't concern you. Diane must have seen the commotion out there as she suddenly rushed in crying and screaming. Linda went over and comforted her. All the hubbub subsided, so I left the lounge and went to see what had gone on. No one was about; the place was now deserted. I closed the front door which had been left open and ventured into the kitchen. I couldn't believe what I saw. The bright light inside had definitely lost its glare as the white goods and tiles were now crimson, covered with blood. It was splattered everywhere. A course had run down the fridge and was still drip-dripping off the bottom of the door into a small puddle on the floor. I'd never seen so much blood. I genuinely thought that whoever had

been the subject of such an attack might not live to tell the tale. When I returned to the lounge Diane was still inconsolable. I made a token offer to Linda, asking her if there was anything I could do to help, yet I knew my priority was to get out of there. Linda told me she'd called the police and they were on the way. She knew I couldn't do anything and understood that I had to leave. I managed to get away before the cops arrived.

A WALK ON THE WILD SIDE

When I got back from work one day Billy was waiting for me at my *digs*. He had a proposition for me: did I want to move (again) into a shared room with him at his new abode? He was sleeping in a large room with two beds situated diagonally across from one another: *'Plenty of space,'* he said. I'd been feeling pretty lonely since he and Rod had moved out and, as Bill said, we could split the rent and make it cheaper for us both. I went with him to take a look.

The property was set back from the road on Newcastle Street, still in Northbridge, but not far from the crossroads with William Street, and much closer to the city centre. The long building was on two levels, with two front doors in the centre on the ground floor, offering independent entrances to flats on each side of the property. The first floor had a balcony which stretched the full length of the building; this was partitioned off in the middle segregating the two blocks. Billy's room was through the left door as you viewed it from the front. His room was upstairs and to the rear, so no balcony. He said there was another guy who shared our side of the house, 'an old fellah called Arfur,' who lived on the ground floor. Arthur was happy to sort out tea and toast for us at breakfast, before we went off to work. Billy said it was the only time they met up and that in our half of the building all the other rooms, except for the shared kitchen and bathroom, were used for storage by the landlord.

The front door on the right side led to rooms upstairs occupied by some Aussies; two of them, Pierre and John, had the back room, whilst the other two, Wesley and Patrick, had a room next to them but at the front with access to the balcony. It was true that the accommodation was more convenient, being a lot closer to the council yard where I reported to each morning, as well as the city centre. We felt we wouldn't be so isolated in the company of other young guys who all appeared to get along. We were all of similar age and, as Billy said, there was more of a social life here than where we'd previously lived.

I took up Billy's offer and moved in with him. Billy had an evening routine with Wesley and Patrick next door, where he'd pop into their gaff on his way home from work most evenings. It was a place to meet and unwind, and soon became part of my routine too. Pierre and John, from the room next door to Wes and Pat's, were often present and we'd all sit outside on the balcony listening to the radio, smoking and generally chewing the fat. We'd sit there as the traffic boom below subsided as the working world headed home; the bustle of life died down as if synchronised to the setting sun. As our conversation became less voluble, and the golden rays slipped down and over the Indian Ocean, we knew it was time for bed. We'd always wish each other good night and promise to meet up again, same time, same place, the next day.

Wes and Patrick were happy for us to come and go as we pleased and use their balcony space, which was a haven for Billy and myself. For two guys on the run we'd found a safe place to share our thoughts and dreams. And a great social scene developed there between the six of us, where there was always someone to pal up with if you fancied a night out.

It's true that *nothing lasts forever,* and it wasn't long before others began to descend on 193, Newcastle Street. Friends were invited, then friends of friends, family of friends, acquaintances, work colleagues. Word got out and the list was endless, until it seemed like the whole of Perth's younger generation must have dropped in at one time or another. I thought it got out of hand and I started to feel uncomfortable and nervous. I felt it was becoming too much; maybe I was oversensitive because of the situation Billy and I were in, but Wes and Patrick didn't seem to mind the escalating number of visitors; in fact I think they enjoyed it. We started to call their pad the Revolving Door (the RD), as it was not uncommon for people to arrive and leave at any hour of the day or night.

As there were six of us guys residing in close proximity, quite a few girlfriends and ex's turned up; although a lot depended upon the nature of the relationship at the time. Patrick's roommate, Wesley, was a wiry guy, and there wasn't much of him; but what there was was solid. At twenty-two he was the oldest amongst us at Newcastle Street, apart from Arthur, that is. Wes was a private person, and kept himself to himself, and we probably learned more about Wes from Patrick rather than from Wesley himself.

Patrick mentioned a girl called Janine, who worked with Wesley and visited him regularly on Thursday afternoons. Apparently the sole purpose for this Thursday, afternoon rendezvous was to get laid by Wesley. He rarely mentioned it, although everyone knew it was going on and that he'd be incommunicado then. I don't ever remember him going on a date with Janine, yet every Thursday afternoon without fail, Janine turned up to be bedded. Wesley must have been satisfying some need in her, but he never bragged about it. On the contrary, after indulging in his arrangement with Janine for several weeks, he confided to me that he was, literally, *'f...ing fed up.'* I thought, *I wish I was getting laid regularly;* although not with Janine.

Whenever I saw Janine (usually after work on Thursdays when I dropped in), she always had too much make-up on. Her face was hidden beneath a thick layer of cream or powder, or a mixture of both. I was never sure which, and I didn't like to stare directly at her. I always thought her make-up could have been trowelled on. She had a bright rouge circle on each cheek, which from a distance looked like two tomatoes. Her blue eyeshadow was similarly over-done, with heavy mascara applied to what someone said were false eyelashes. Frizzy, sticky-out, wild hair completed her look. I often wondered if there was a real Janine behind the mask or was it her intention to look like a dark-haired dizzy doll.

Other frequent visitors to the RD included Yvette, the girl who helped with our cases at the Swan Hotel on our first night on the run. It turned out she was Janine's sister. Patrick copped off with her at some point, although I later bumped into Yvette when she was in the process of shoplifting. I'd passed her in a department store and saw her walking quickly by an island counter, where she swiftly lifted some knickers or tights from the top and walked on with no intention stopping. This coincided with me simultaneously recognising her, and shouting out, 'Hi, Yvette.' She was taken by surprise and dropped whatever it was she was nicking on to the shop floor. Obviously shocked and embarrassed, she quickly stooped down, picked them up and returned them to the top of the counter. Needless to say she scurried off without stopping to have a chat. I mentioned this later to Patrick, but it took him a while before he realised she wasn't quite the girl he thought she was.

Little Chris (LC) was another regular visitor. He was a slightly built cockney lad who lived in Fremantle. He worked with John, the Newcastle Street resident who shared a room with Pierre, next to Wesley and Patrick's. John was a tall, quiet guy who wore specs, someone I referred to as *the collar and tie,* since he always drifted into the RD straight from work wearing one. He worked in an accounts office at a bespoke cabinet makers, where Little Chris was completing a cabinet-making apprenticeship. Although not overly tall, LC had short spiky hair that stuck up like a long crew cut and made him look taller. He was quite arty and had embarked upon a project at the RD inside Wes and Patrick's flat. He planned to paint a mural across the interior gable end wall, which was the bed-sitting cum living room. His plan was to have a complete black backdrop across the wall, which he'd recently finished, but then overlay this with a huge Roman gladiator at the reigns of a chariot. The charioteer, chariot and horses were to be gilded in gold. LC showed us all a picture of the scene, which he had cut from a glossy magazine. It looked unbelievable. Everyone agreed it would be stunning when finished, a unique addition to complement the bohemian décor and furnishings already in place.

LC introduced his girlfriend, Christine, to the RD and she soon became a regular attendee in her own right. At first they'd always arrive together, but then she began to turn up on her own. I'd always escort her around the block to meet her father if LC didn't show, since her dad would pick her up to take her home at 10pm. I was just glad he didn't drop into the RD to witness the laidback lifestyle of the residents. Unbeknown to me there was an occasion when Billy had allowed LC and Christine the use of his bed next door, and I happened to stumble in on them unannounced. Understandably Christine was as embarrassed as I was. I glimpsed over and saw her tug the sheet and roll over to hide her face from view. Afterwards, when Christine and I were in the same company, we couldn't look one another in the eye for a while. And I made doubly sure that I never mentioned my accidental intrusion whenever we conversed with one another.

Christine had a petite figure, finely balanced on muscular thighs. Her legs were well toned, something I put down to her being a ballet dancer with the West Australian Ballet company. She had an angelic face with a pert nose, and soft, perfectly formed kissable lips. I always wanted to kiss those lips but only managed it once, sometime later. She had what I thought was an endearing habit, when just before she was about to say something, she'd flutter her long eyelashes and stare directly at you with her large wide eyes. She later told me me it was an affliction and *not* affectation; she said she had a blinking disorder which was a *sort of nervous tic.* Her short dark hair and dress sense screamed mod; but to Australians then, most of the UK fashion scene meant nothing. In truth Christine, with her classical clean-cut features, always reminded me of Julie Driscoll, and each time I saw her I couldn't get the words from the hit single *Wheels on Fire* out of my head.

Sometime later both Patrick and Wes (independently) confided in me that Christine's relationship with LC had gone awry and that she quietly fancied me. Was I interested? I wasn't sure. I always thought LC and Christine made a great couple; I didn't want to come between them. That time I kissed her was when I chaperoned her round the corner to meet her dad for the final time; thankfully we were early and he didn't see us. I always rued the fact that we never actually got together, but it was too late for us by the time I learned that Christine had definitely split with LC. Fate had intervened, and the destiny of some who resided at 193 Newcastle Street was about to be mapped out. Christine had mentioned she was due to go on tour with her ballet company around the whole of Australia, and now she suddenly announced she would be leaving next week. It had been one of those moments in life when you meet someone and there exists a mutual attraction that draws you in; but then circumstances hold you back. I imagined how things might have been between us if we'd got together. I wish we'd been closer, more intimate. When she left I yearned for her and regretted we had never consummated our feelings for one another. I consoled myself with the thought that, *We were in the wrong place at the wrong time,* and, *It just wasn't meant to be.* I tried not to think about it as time passed, but it didn't diminish the regret I felt.

I was still working for the council when I met Brad, a South African guy from Durban. Brad visually stood out because his mop of hair was shocking white, unusual for a young guy in his early twenties. He reminded me of an albino kid we had at school; although Brad had no other albino features. I first met him when we were deployed to work together in a park, a place where he spent most of the day grooving and digging nature. During that first day he continuously eulogised about how green the grass was and, *'How blue is that sky, man? Look at the branches on that tree, man, how they weave and bend. Look how the sun's rays filter through the foliage. It's like those branches could wrap themselves around you, like a python, man – and give you a big squeeze.'*

To be fair that was the only time I saw him truly turned on at work, as most of the time he was in the real world. As time passed we got to know each other better, but as the days went by he became determined to get me to trip-out. Eventually he succeeded. Brad had an endless supply of small pills he called Dexies, which he said were as good as anything he'd taken before. He said they were comparable to acid (LSD), but unlike acid, there were no bad trips. I'd never dropped acid, but had heard some horrific stories about people who'd taken a tab and completely lost it. Some had blown their minds and lost all sense of reality; they'd jumped off high-rise buildings thinking they could fly. Others experienced trips so bad that they hadn't recovered and suffered from some form of psychosis. Brad assured me there was none of that with what he called, *'These beaut pills.'* The normal dose, he said, was ten pills, but if you really wanted to *zap out, man,* twenty would do the trick.

Eventually I was persuaded to sample the ten pill deal for my first Dexy trip. Brad informed me it usually took forty-five minutes to turn-on, although it could take an hour; a lot depended upon when and what you'd eaten. I took the tabs just before walking into the city centre. I went to see Linda in the record store where she worked, as I was keen to listen to The Beatles' new release, *Get Back;* but more importantly I wanted to quiz her about what happened after the bloodbath at her house-warming party. I wondered about those guys who were glassed at the hands of the Maryhill Fleet.

I listened to both sides of The Beatles' record as the shop was busy and I couldn't speak freely with Linda. I listened to the flip side which featured John Lennon singing *Don't Let Me Down;* this became one of my favourite Beatles tracks of all time. I then asked Linda to play Desmond Dekker's *The Israelites,* which, mainly through UK immigrant sales, had climbed the Australian charts. The Aussies in Perth seemed a little backdated to me and were mainly still into psychedelic music. Reggae and soul were virtually unheard of over there. I listened and waited for the shop to empty, before I managed to catch Linda alone to find out what happened to the guys at her party. She told me that two Aussies were badly injured; one nearly lost his hand. She advised me to stay away from her flat as the police had been frequent visitors since that night. Diane had provided them with all the names of those who attended the party. She mentioned Scott McDonald as the instigator of the violence that night. Linda knew him from the days when they'd emigrated on the same ship together (via the popular ten-pound passage scheme to Australia). She learned on that voyage he had a previous conviction for slashing someone's face in the street when, apparently, he didn't like the way the guy looked at him. I said I didn't know McDonald and had no plans to make his acquaintance. When I left Linda in the store I was confident that there was a subliminal understanding between us. Although there wasn't a romantic connection, I trusted her. I was confident she wouldn't betray me to the authorities. We looked at one another for a transitory moment and said a silent goodbye. We both realised we probably wouldn't see one another again.

The Dexies didn't hit me until I stepped out of the record store and back into the street. As I walked along the pavement I noticed how things started to slow down. I was, literally, *on the road* to getting high. I soon became somebody who felt like somebody else, somebody walking in slow motion. The whole world had slowed down. I was head and shoulders above the traffic and everyone else along the pavement. I looked down on them; I was Gulliver in Lilliput. I turned my head and saw I was level with the third floor of the old merchant buildings on the other side of the street. I asked myself: *Am I actually walking that slowly? Am I really taking such giant steps? Am I really that tall?* I looked down and noticed how long my legs looked, as I bounced along. I felt the pavement rise and fall as if I was walking on sponge. I'd lost my bearings and felt disorientated. I was on William Street but heading in the wrong direction, away from Newcastle Street and where I wanted to go. I wasn't sure I'd be able to find my way home; I became anxious and scared. I turned off into a side street and stumbled into someone getting out of a taxi. I scrambled my way passed them and into the back seat before they could shut the cab door.

'Please, mate. I'm sick. I've gotta get home. Newcastle Street, Northbridge.' I sounded breathless. I was determined to plead my case before the driver could say a word.

'You're lucky, mite. If I'd got another fare booked you'd be out on yer arse!'

'Thanks, mate – really appreciate it.' He stared at me through the rear-view mirror before he banged the cab into gear and we took off. I was thrown across the back seat into a half-lying position and was quite happy to stay like that, lying on my back and staring up at the sky through a side window. And that's when I saw him. God. He was high in the sky looking down. I'd never pictured Him before. I'd never imagined what He might look like; it was something that had never entered my head at any time in my life. I wasn't even sure He existed. I'd always believed in Jesus: someone who'd lived 2,000 years ago and who had provided the inhabitants of the world with a template for life, a template for everyone to refer to and follow, in order to harmonise and co-exist with one another in a wild, chaotic and lawless world. I'd never thought of God as a person, never visualised God in human form. But now I could see Him, and He appeared for all the world as if He personified the ultimate businessman. It was impossible to conjure up anyone who looked more distinguished or worldly-wise than He did. He was European with a bronzed look, possibly of Italian extraction. His, thick, wavy, steel-grey hair was slicked back, and He was immaculately dressed in a dark, navy suit. I assumed it was a suit, but my vision to the sky was restricted because of the tall buildings on either side of the street. I could only see the top half of Him, a bust, where he wore a dazzling white shirt and crimson silk tie underneath his jacket. He was smiling. He beamed down benevolently as He surveyed his creation from His heavenly vantage point. I got the impression He was satisfied with the work He'd done so far. He didn't speak but just observed. I didn't feel judged, although I got the impression if He'd said something to me it would have been along the lines of, *'You're OK. Just do your own thing.'*

That Dexie trip was the forerunner of others, which increasingly took on a beatific kick. A few of us had started to frequent charity shops and bought decent second-hand clothes, usually baggy trousers, sleeveless sweaters and straw trilbies or pork-pie hats. I'd developed, what was for me, a habit of wearing a mixture of fairly flamboyant clothes. Since my sole intention was to go out and get high, I called it my *tripping gear.* It mainly comprised of a ripped T-shirt, an old pair of faded Levis and an electric purple corduroy bomber jacket borrowed from Patrick. The *piéce de rèsistance* to this outfit was a pair of kangaroo-skin slippers, lined with fluffy white sheep's wool but with a sturdy plastic sole. The slippers were designed like bootees and covered my ankles. Although intended for indoor use, they served me well out on the streets during sunny days. The final accoutrement to my costume was a straw pork-pie hat, which I perched precariously on top of my head, probably because it was a size too small. However the *coup de grâce* was a small brush, about eighteen inches long, with a mixture of bright red and yellow bristles at one end. I called this *my wand,* and it became my constant companion during my drug-infused wanderings. Whenever we met someone or bumped into an acquaintance, I felt compelled to gently brush them with the bristles and declare, *'Here, let me put a good spell on you!'*

Once, when I was tripping out with Patrick and Rose, a woman accosted us as we emerged from a shop in London Court. She smiled, jangled a collecting tin in front of us and asked if we'd like to contribute to her charity. I'd just purchased a large watercolour print of the *Sermon on the Mount* by Claude Lorraine, which I had rolled up under my arm. I quickly unfurled it and asked her: *'How would you like to make a donation to **us**?'* I knew we had hardly any money between us, and although I didn't expect her to give us anything I wanted to deflect her away from the expectation that we'd be contributing to her collection. She beamed at the picture when she saw it, then studied our faces, then back at the picture again. And then, whilst she was still beaming, I brushed her with my wand and put a good spell on her. This time I said, '*God Bless You.*' She looked straight at me, as if confounded, and then scuttled away to pester someone else. I don't think she knew what to think of us. She probably thought we were mad, but in a good place; and in our surreal, dream-like world, we probably were.

During that same trip when we stepped outside of London Court, the mock-Tudor shopping alley in the centre of Perth, we found ourselves standing in front of Trinity Church. It is one of the oldest churches in Perth and has a beautiful facade. It knocked us out. The Romanesque style has a high rose window, twin towers and octagonal spires that tower over a large portal entrance. The throngs of people rushing hither and thither on the pavements, the boom of the traffic in the street, the stifling heat, all jarred with our heightened state of consciousness. We climbed up the steps to the church and went inside where, literally, it was *so cool*; the suffocating, claustrophobic city life immediately evaporated. The calm, slightly chilled silence inside the church collided with bright rays of sunlight that filtered through the stained-glass windows. These were filled with reds, yellows and blues, each a dazzling mosaic that featured an inspirational figure who proclaimed faith and protection. On the upper level, overhanging the congregational pews on the ground floor, were ornate viewing galleries supported by intricate cast-iron balustrades. We stood in awe, silently appreciating the distillation of time and peace. We absorbed the golden beauty of the interior we'd stumbled upon, and I believe it was the first time I truly understood the meaning of *glory*. My eyes followed streams of sunlight as they poured through the windows to the far end of the church; there they fell upon a crucifixion of Jesus nailed to a wall next to the altar. He appeared as if under a spotlight; His dappled features magnified his suffering with grief and pain etched across His face.

Adjacent to the effigy of the crucifixion were some giant organ pipes, half hidden behind a raised pulpit. I glided down the aisle between the pews towards the pipes. They were magnificent. I slowly reached out my hand and stroked them. These huge, silver-grey steel pipes were unblemished, as smooth as any marble I'd ever touched. As I caressed them I thought I heard a heavenly choir of angels singing, '*Hallelujah! Hallelujah! Hallelujah!*' I turned to find that Rose and Patrick were still in raptures over the kaleidoscopic vision of light that danced in front of their eyes from the stained-glass windows. I moved forward and stumbled into a lectern of solid wood. On top of the lectern was a huge bible that lay open with script in large print. I started to read it and as I did I began to shake. *Was this a miracle? Divine intervention?* The page facing me was *The Sermon on the Mount,* taken from *The Gospel of St Matthew.* I was compelled to speak out loud, to preach from the pulpit like a lay-preacher. I read from the page before me:

> 'Blessed are the poor... for theirs is the kingdom of heaven.
> Blessed are the meek, for they shall inherit the earth.
> Blessed are those who hunger and thirst... for they shall be satisfied.
> Blessed are the peacemakers... they shall be called sons of God.
> You are the light of the world...
> Let your light shine before men...'

I'd skipped through the text, editing passages as I read, for the benefit of my captive audience. Patrick and Rose had turned and remained silent and statuesque throughout, until it became obvious I'd finished. They then started whooping, threw in a few *"Amens,"* and rounded off their appreciation with some *"Hallelujahs".*

I'll never understand how my spell-casting, the purchasing of a print depicting *The Sermon on the Mount,* entering the church and finding a bible open on the exact page that put my picture into words, all conspired to collide that day. It was uncanny and an unbelievable coincidence. Maybe it was a minor miracle? Whatever it was, we were all blown away at how all those things unfolded, when we later reflected upon the happenings that took place that day.

Patrick had met Rose when he had visited the chemist where she worked. He'd been there a few times, before they struck up a conversation whilst he was waiting for a prescription. It turned out that Rose had moved to WA from Adelaide, as had Wesley and Patrick. After reminiscing about Adelaide, Rose admitted she hardly knew anyone in Perth, and so had a non-existent social life. Pat had felt sorry for her and so invited her to drop in and meet the gang at his and Wesley's pad in Newcastle Street. Pat was pleased she accepted his offer to come over and meet everyone. He was that sort of guy: full of kind gestures and good intentions, someone who'd go out of his way to help people.

I met Rose when she dropped in at the RD for the first time. She was wearing a kaftan, and her short blonde hairstyle was more mod than hippie. She'd kicked off her shoes and was wandering around barefoot, clutching a red rose in one hand and a cigarette in the other. When I asked her what her name was she came right up and stared into my face. She didn't answer me initially but instead held up the rose and fluttered it under my chin. It reminded me of those days when I was a small boy at school, and we played *tickly under there* (the chin) with buttercups, to see if you liked butter. I then noticed how dilated her pupils were and how pale her face was.

Her slightly rouged cherubic cheeks stood out and contrasted sharply with her dark heavily laden eyeshadow. She then said, *'Guess?'*, in answer to my question. I didn't need to, as I already knew who she was from Patrick.

'Let me think,' I pondered, and raised my forefinger to my lips. *'Hyacinth.'* I smiled. She didn't smile back. I was glad of the opportunity to speak with her since there was a certain mystique hidden behind her dark eyes. She intrigued me; there was something about her I couldn't put my finger on. Although I thought we had connected, I later learned from Pat that Rose was stoned and completely out of it when I first met her. He told me Rose was a regular drug user, mainly barbiturates, and that her main supplier was Jeremy, the chemist she worked for.

When Patrick, Rose and I tripped out that day in London Court, and visited Trinity Church, Rose ended up coming back to my room. Patrick had offered her some Dexies, which she'd accepted, but they were taken on top of whatever she had already taken from her chemist supplier. It was hardly surprising that she didn't feel too good when we arrived back in Newcastle Street. Rose said she felt tired and wanted to lie down. Patrick explained that he couldn't accommodate her as Wesley was home all day in their room. I knew Billy was at work and so offered her my bed to lie down in. We went upstairs and I helped her undress down to her panties and bra, before she settled down under the covers. She held out her hand to me and pulled me close so that I sat down on the edge of the bed. *'Please. Come inside and lie down beside me. It was so beautiful today in the church. Come on. Keep me warm.'* I bent down towards her and we kissed. I didn't need much persuading to get into bed and join her, and so quickly stripped down to my underpants and climbed in beside her. We continued kissing until Rose unclasped her bra and released those heavenly breasts. I couldn't help thinking, *I'm in here,* as I lowered my head and caressed those proud nipples with my lips and tongue. I moved my leg astride hers and moved down, kissing her belly, luxuriating in her warm, soft flesh. She cupped my shoulders in her hands and pushed me, then placed a hand on top of my head and forced my head down towards her groin. I grabbed her knicker elastic on both sides and yanked her knickers down to just above her knees. Rose then bent a leg at the knee and pulled her foot up and through her knickers, thus freeing herself and allowing me uninhibited access to her quim. I nuzzled into her with great alacrity. My nose, lips and tongue knew no bounds. Almost immediately I heard sighs, groans and gasps from above. As Rose became louder, and more ecstatic, I delved deeper, like a wild boar snuffling truffles from the forest floor. I soon decided to abandon my foraging and mount up, only to face disappointment below. I'd been duped. The fervour and excitement in my head was a figment of my imagination.

I'd be overexaggerating if I said I was half way towards a *lazy lob;* the truth was that I was as limp as a wet fish. I was embarrassed, but Rose laughed it off; she was pleased things could go no further. She'd taken hold of my forearms as a precaution, to keep me at bay, and confessed to me that she'd forgotten to take the pill the night before.

This coincided with my not having any protection either, and when she said the last thing she wanted was to have any unwanted surprises it lessened the impact of my disappointment. I became distracted and preoccupied with thoughts concerning my erectile dysfunction. I replayed the circumstances that led to my lack of libido and stored it in the back of my mind for future reference. I consoled myself, legitimately I thought, that it was the result of a druggy droop.

I didn't catch up with Rose again, and our relationship never actually progressed. Her attendance at the Revolving Door dropped off, until she stopped visiting altogether. It was much later on when I asked Patrick how Rose was, after he mentioned he'd been to the chemist where she worked. He said things weren't good. He said he'd visited the chemist on numerous occasions since I'd last seen her, and each time he'd managed to learn more about her circumstances. During one visit she'd confided to him that she couldn't do without her *little bennies,* and that she struggled to pay for her habit. She confessed she felt manacled to both her job and to Jeremy. On another occasion Patrick said she looked desperate, appeared nervous and kept glancing back over her shoulder to see if Jeremy was watching them when they were talking together. She admitted she'd stopped calling round to the RD because Jeremy didn't like her going there. Patrick described Rose as being *"caught in Jeremy's web"*. He said the last time he spoke with her she joked that she might have to marry Jeremy so that she could *"stay on board the benny train"*.

Patrick implored Rose to seek help and to make an appointment to see her GP, but he didn't think he was getting through to her. He said she had a vacant look about her, a distant languidness, which made it difficult for them to have a meaningful conversation. He said she'd lost her spark; her spirit was gone. He said it was as if she was permanently down after being stoned. Rose wasn't the person we'd known and loved. He said this was the last time he'd actually spoken to Rose. And although he'd been to the chemist since, Pat said now it was always Jeremy who came across and served him. Pat felt he was being scrutinised by the chemist, *under the microscope,* as Patrick put it. On one occasion he saw Rose at the back of the shop stealing glances towards him when Jeremy had his back turned towards her. Rose remained distant and didn't even bother to come over and say, *'Hello,'* to him. Pat said she was pale, looked thinner, and her wide eyes stared at him with no sign of acknowledgement. He added that the last time he'd visited the chemist, there had been no sign of Rose. I'd heard enough by now and wished I hadn't enquired about her. I didn't want to hear any more. I felt bad but knew there was nothing I could do to help Rose.

I was still in touch with Cindy and we'd go out on a date now and again. At the time I'd accepted that there wasn't going to be any full-on sex with her; but she was a good looking girl, lovely to be with, and any guy would be proud to be with her. Although nothing had been planned, I met her older twin sisters one night when we were out having a drink. Cindy suggested, spontaneously I thought, that we drop into The Waldorf nightclub for a dance. When we arrived she spotted her sisters sitting together at a table and so, quite naturally it seemed to me, dragged me over to meet them. They were only a couple of years older than Cindy but taller and heavier. They both had large Roman noses, which made them look harder. It made me wonder if the twins were from the same stock as Cindy, since she was petite, refined and delicate by comparison.

I went to the bar and only bought drinks for Cindy and myself, as the sisters already had drinks on the table. When I returned both sisters sat and stared at me. I imagined I was with Cinderella and her ugly sisters. We were introduced when we arrived and so I didn't feel the need to make polite conversation. Cindy was chatting away to them about the day she'd had at work, but I sensed them paying little attention to what she was saying as both sets of eyes bored into me. Their silent staring made me uncomfortable, and only confirmed my first impression: that I had an instant dislike for both of them. Cindy suddenly stopped talking in mid-sentence and asked:

'Hey! You guys must have met before? If not, you must have seen one another, surely?'

'I think I have seen him,' said one sister. *'Yeah. I'm sure I've seen him, too,'* said the other. All eyes were still on me, now waiting for a response. Cindy was smiling, looking from the sisters to me and back again. The sisters looked po-faced.

'No. I don't think I've had the pleasure.' I grinned. Both sisters looked askance at one another. I wondered if they'd seen through my pretence. I discovered one of them worked part-time as a waitress here at The Waldorf

(a popular weekend venue for the RD crowd). And that both of them worked full time at the same department store where I now worked. I hadn't been there long, and so it wasn't surprising that we hadn't met before. I now wondered why Cindy hadn't mentioned before that her sisters worked at the same place as I did, and then if tonight's meeting had been a set-up (by the sisters). They seemed to be in control, which only reinforced my belief that this meeting had been pre-arranged.

I was contemplating all of this when Cindy, as if reading my mind, squeezed my hand under the table. She then excused herself and went to the loo. As she left the table I half expected her two drongo sisters to follow; but no, they remained at the table. I looked up and they both still had their eyes firmly fixed on me. The one sitting directly opposite me suddenly rapped her knuckles hard on the table and pointed an index finger at my chest.

'Listen, mite. Oi'm telling you now. If you ever hurt Cindy – if you ever break her heart – I'm going to break you.'

'Yes. You'll be finished. It'll be the end for you,' added the other one.

'Do you understand?' said the first.

'We know who you are and where you're from,' hissed the second.

I looked from one to the other and said nothing. When Cindy returned I knew I wasn't going to tell her about the threat I'd received from her siblings. It was obvious Cindy must have said something to them about my status in Australia. The last thing I now wanted was to cause ill-feeling between any of us, let alone aggravate what I already felt was a mutual enmity between myself and her hag-like sisters.

Not long after my introduction to her sisters Cindy and I went out on a memorable date. We went to the pictures to see The Beatles' film, *Yellow Submarine,* and pretended to be celebrities attending a film premiere. We dressed up accordingly, with me wearing some recently purchased navy pinstripe strides and an immaculate white tailor-made jacket, which I borrowed from Pierre. It was something he'd acquired from one of his modelling assignments. Cindy replicated my black and white attire with a peplum tailored jacket and some hip-hugging black trousers. She lightly applied her make-up, which highlighted her soft unblemished skin, and her plaited hair accentuated her fine cheekbones. She had a wide-eyed innocence which made her look younger than she was, and when she arrived at the RD the response from everyone was, '*Wow!*' She looked fantastic and could have passed for a film star. I thought we both looked *pretty cool* when we stepped out that evening.

I didn't know it at the time, but that was one of the last dates I had with Cindy. I'd been thinking for sometime about how I could slowly distance myself from our relationship without hurting her feelings. I also didn't wish to provoke the wrath of her sisters. It was fortuitous that these ruminations coincided with a period when I was increasingly tripping out on my days off, which didn't leave much free time to see Cindy anyway.

It was during this spell that Little Chris and I had a memorable blast when we tripped out together. We went up to Hyde Park to soak up the beauty of nature and embrace all of the wildlife there. As soon as we arrived we turned on. We grooved around, played air guitars and sang some lyrics from *Itchycoo Park* by The Small Faces. Our audience included the famous West Australian black swan (which was the first time I'd ever seen one) and some ducks on the pond. But the highlight of that trip was a winged floating seed from a maple tree. We both looked up to the treetops simultaneously and let time stand still. We pranced around below in slo-mo, helplessly disorientated. A casual observer might have mistaken us for performing marionettes, as our arms and legs waved and dangled about freely, as if our movements were orchestrated by strings from someone high above the trees. We were still looking skywards when we both spotted this descending whirling maple leaf at the same time. This winged helicopter, as we used to call them, floated down between us, taking an age to reach our level from the uppermost branches of the tree. It spun and spun, around and around, whilst we pranced about in a circle below until it reached our level. We waved our arms and legs up and down as it continued on its slow downward spiral, until it finally fluttered to a halt and settled on the ground between us. The whole visual experience blew us away.

Although tripping out opened my eyes and made me more appreciative of nature and its beauty, I couldn't help but note how getting high coincided with a negative shift in my behaviour. Increasingly, when I came down after tripping out, I was really down. And the more Dexies I took, thinking I could escape the reality of my situation, the longer my downtime became. Initially, I thought that when I recovered from being down, everything would be as before and life would return to normal. It didn't immediately register with me how much more agitated and morose I became. I was blind to the consequences of tripping out more regularly, because I thought the length of time when I was stoned and out of it would far outweigh the depressive downtime I experienced. *How wrong could I be?* I discovered that turning on became counter-productive; I increasingly became short-tempered, frustrated and irritated with both myself and others. It was taking me longer to recover, than the euphoric spell I experienced when I was out of it. I realised that after tripping out normal service would never be resumed – and it was never likely to be if I carried on in the same vein. I was cascading down an emotional waterfall and could soon be drowning in a pool of depression.

I found it hard to be sociable with anyone. I began to retreat from the RD community earlier and earlier; everyone there seemed to be getting on my nerves. I'd retire next door to my bed alone. I'd lie awake and try to analyse what provoked my sullenness but couldn't put my finger on what it was making me unhappy. My thoughts would degenerate into speculation about how things might end up for me. I often wondered if I would ever get out of the RN. And if I did, when? My plan was to spend a couple of years on the run in Oz and then give myself up. It was never my intention to live permanently in Australia. I missed Manchester; I missed the walk down tree-lined Orchard Road in Northenden; I missed my adopted family of Auntie Marj, Tim, Susie, Chris and *Fudge* the dog. I wondered if I'd ever walk down that road to see them all again.

One evening, sometime later, I wandered round to the RD at Wes and Patrick's, only to discover things were definitely getting out of hand. Yes, there were always faces we knew and recognised there, people who habitually dropped in and we knew we could trust. But then there were always those friends of friends who we didn't know anything about. On this particular evening I thought the place was rammed with way too many visitors; I couldn't believe it. I kept thinking, *More and more people are dropping in; some we know, some we don't. Sooner or later Billy and I are going to get rumbled. We're drawing attention to ourselves living here; too many people are drifting in and out of the place. It's becoming too popular. We need to put a halt to it, or something will give and we'll get caught.*

It was then I spotted the two ex-orphans from where we'd lived before, Arnold and Toby. And they'd brought someone else along who I didn't recognise. I couldn't believe it, and I couldn't stand by and let this happen. I felt I had to make a stand. Paranoia kicked in and I let rip:

'What the f….k? What the f….k are they doing here?' I looked at Wes. '*This is getting too much… this place is becoming dangerous. There are too many people arriving here. It's like Clapham Junction!*' Wes said nothing and looked away. All the chattering around us quietened to a hush. I realised everyone present had heard my outburst and were now tuned in. I'd inadvertently drawn attention to myself, something I promised myself I'd never do. It had always been a priority of mine from day one: *Don't draw attention to yourself.* I realised I'd made a mistake as soon my mouth took off. I was the centre of attention, but I couldn't back down. I carried on, looking directly at the orphans and their tanned male companion. They were all sitting next to one another on the settee. The stranger amongst them had a walrus moustache and sun-bleached blonde, collar-length hair. *A typical Aussie,* I thought. He reminded me of one of those beefcakes Wills and I had bumped into in the pub in Freo, when the Abbo women had defended us.

'*And who's this?*' I blurted out, with the whole room listening. '*Who've you brought along now?*' The friend smiled at me.

'*It's Rod! It's Rod!*' the orphans shouted in unison.

'*What?*' I said. I didn't believe them and took a closer look. I didn't recognise him. He wasn't the Rod I remembered; he looked completely different. My stomach churned when I realised it *was* him. I'd over-reacted and realised I'd made a complete arse of myself.

'Oh, Rod, *I'm sorry. I'm so sorry, mate. I didn't recognise you. The hair, the suntan, the moustache. I'm so sorry, I really am.*' Rod just sat there and grinned. '*No worries,*' he said. *Just like a pukka Aussie,* I thought.

Although the orphans had helped me find work initially, which I remained eternally grateful for, I didn't feel guilty about having a rant at them. When we'd shared a house together I discovered how intrusive they were, always creeping about and wanting to know your business. Perhaps I was oversensitive then, given our circumstances, but I found I had little in common with them. I didn't particularly like them and often made excuses to avoid their company. Perhaps my judgement was prejudicial that evening, but I knew I'd made a mistake and apologised to the brothers and Rod. I was glad we buried any misunderstandings when we all shook hands.

Rod and I made our way out to the balcony where Billy joined us. It was quieter there and allowed us the freedom to talk more privately. Rod regaled us with anecdotes of his adventures in the outback. He enjoyed the tractor driving and working outdoors on a huge wheat farm, which was nearly five hundred miles east of Perth and over one hundred miles east of Kalgoorlie, a mining town. He said that was the place where he and some locals visited quite often to have a few beers and some female company. It was still a long drive from where they worked and so usually involved a weekend stopover. He admitted he could quite easily have stayed out there farming, but then, surprisingly, confided to us he was going to give himself up to the authorities. He said he'd phoned home recently and discovered his mother was very ill; she'd been diagnosed with terminal cancer and only had a few weeks to live. He said his mum had been hospitalised but was now back at home, where she wanted to see out her remaining days. He said he had no dad, but his younger sister was there, and a nurse dropped in daily to check on things and administer medication. He felt it was not only his duty to return home, but it was somewhere he wanted to be. He said he had no choice, something which

Billy and I completely understood. All three of us were the products of fragmented families.

We then discussed the likely disciplinary consequences Rod could face when he turned himself in to the RN. The fact that he'd given himself up would help his cause, particularly if he appeared as someone full of remorse and could convince them that going AWOL had been a terrible mistake. We even concocted the reason why he jumped ship: because of a girl. He'd fallen in love and couldn't bear to leave her. His love affair didn't last long and he realised, in hindsight, that he'd made a terrible mistake. He should apologise profusely for his actions, try and convince the RN that his future career was definitely with them. He should also make it clear, irrespective of his mother's critical condition, that he was on the verge of giving himself up anyway. He should point out that the sad news concerning his mother just happened to coincide with his decision to hand himself in. We played out a number of scenarios and excuses for his irrational behaviour. I felt sure Rod's compassionate circumstances would, ultimately, determine any punishment he would receive. My experiences of disciplinary procedures within the RN suggested Rod would only receive a suspended detention sentence. I thought he'd still be free, after he was sentenced, to request compassionate leave and be able to visit his mum.

Rod assured us that he wouldn't mention that he'd seen us recently, and we knew his word was as good as his bond. I thought afterwards how lucky we were that Rod had worked up country; it meant his whereabouts (and not ours) could be verified. Rod was a good hand, someone you could trust. When we said goodbye we wished him well, and I was sorry for the way things had turned out for him. That was the last time I saw Rod. I never heard of him again, but like to think that he received a suspended sentence and managed to spend time at home with his Mum before she passed on.

DINING, DANCING AND DYING

Although Wesley didn't take Janine out anywhere, he arranged a surprise night out for all of us guys who lived at 193 Newcastle Street. He retained a smattering of the Malay language, from the days when he'd lived there with his father who'd served in the military. Wes took us to a traditional Malay restaurant and managed to negotiate a special meal at a special price when we arrived: Maggi goreng noodles with prawns. Everyone enjoyed the meal and a good night was had by all. Wesley's reputation as a social events organiser was cemented that night, and we all agreed to make more of an effort to have a lads' night out once a month.

I was now tripping out regularly, without fully realising the subliminal consequences attached. When

I'd come down, and thought I'd recovered, I hadn't. I only thought I had. I found myself constantly thinking about the next weekend (or other days off) when I was free to blow my mind and turn on again. It was all I could think about. I became obsessed, living for the weekend in order to get high. It was an unreal place I could escape to and forget my current circumstances. I was desperate for that temporary release from invasive thoughts that continually plagued me, about, *What was I doing and where was I heading?* Those big questions about *what was I going to do with my life, and where would I end up,* constantly nagged at me.

I was now settled into my new job as a sales assistant in a large department store in the city. It was a vacancy John, Pierre's roommate, alerted me to when a good friend of his had left. It was in the shoe department, where there were two other employees. Cyril was the supervisor and Sid was an assistant like me. I'd decided to opt for indoor work, as the weather was now turning cooler. Again I was surprised at how easy it was to get a job in Oz, when no one asked about my employment history or for any references. For the third consecutive time I used the now familiar response that I'd *"missed out,"* when employers asked about Vietnam and whether I was due to be called up for national service. I couldn't believe it.

At work Cyril had a habit of swanning off and wasn't interested in his supervisory duties. He often left Sid and me to our own devices, and even abdicated the responsibility of my induction programme to Sid, who was barely twenty-one. Sid explained that apart from serving customers, I needed to know about stock control and storage, cashing up, tidying, tea and lunch breaks. I listened intently to everything he said, as I wanted to keep this job for as long as I could and not make any silly mistakes.

Sid told me that Cyril, who was in his fifties, had a fancy woman in lingerie, two floors up. If Sid wasn't around, Cyril would say to me: *Just popping upstairs – promised the wife I'd get her something.* Sid and I both knew where he was off to, but we never let on that we were well aware of his charade. We'd often keep watch and catch one of them returning from lunch before the other one, usually with a thirty-second interval between them. We were vigilant and made sure we were both busy when we spotted Cyril or his lady friend returning through the department-store doors. We didn't want him to know that we were well aware of his liaison. It was about this time that the store began advertising products over a loud-speaker system. A favourite was:

'Attention all customers – old and new – young and old!
We now have a new line in ladies' disposable underwear (and then music would start up and a choir of female contraltos would burst into song).
"*Wear them for a day, and then throw them away.*
Yes, wear them for a day, and then throw them away!'"

After the introduction of this little ditty, and when Sid and I had to ask each other where Cyril was, we'd always respond in a high-pitched voice, *'Oh, he's gone upstairs to fetch his paper knickers.'* It was a direct reference to him disappearing upstairs to meet his lingerie lady friend.

I got on okay with Sid, who, apart from showing me what the responsibilities of the job were, introduced me to a couple of dodgy practices. These enabled me to acquire some new shoes and a pair of kangaroo slippers. Another trick Sid alerted me to was one when the store had a sale on. Sales usually lasted a week or a fortnight and occurred quite regularly. Sid explained how you could make a few extra bucks during this busy period. A lot of cheap shoes and sandals arrived specifically for the sale, and were dumped on island counters situated in the middle of the store floor but adjacent to the shoe department. This allowed customers to approach their *never-to-be-repeated bargains* from all angles. There were occasions when there were more customers waiting to be served than there were staff available to serve them. And it was this that was crucial to Sid's money-making deception. He explained:

'When it's a particularly busy time, watch out for customers who give you the exact money for a pair of shoes or sandals. Often it will include a two-or five-dollar bill, or a combination of both. If they don't require change, screw the notes you've been given into the palm of one hand. And then immediately go to another customer and serve them. Don't go to the till. Transfer the proceeds from the previous customer into your pocket when no one is looking.'

It was a simple exercise and easy to execute. It also eliminated the necessity to visit the cash register and ring up a sale every time you served someone. I was grateful to Sid for this ploy and took advantage of it on more than one occasion. I enjoyed a few mouth-watering lunches on the strength of it, which ordinarily would have been beyond my budget.

I'd been in Oz for over three months now and felt my time there was beginning to drag. I knew I'd have to stay on the run for as long as possible if I was to have any chance of being thrown out of the RN. I was also aware that if I got caught, or gave myself up too soon, I wouldn't get the discharge I so desperately wanted. It was a fine line as to how long I needed to be AWOL. I kept telling myself, *Hang on for two years and then give yourself up.* At present I was trapped; I knew my life was on hold. I had no choice but to stick it out and accept that life on the run was the lesser of two evils. The alternative was unthinkable: to spend almost nine years anchored to a life in the RN.

The hot, dry climate in Australia stifled me; everything about the place began to grate on my nerves. And it may sound daft, but I missed the rain. I longed to see the luscious green fields and trees in the UK again, something I'd always taken for granted. Back in the UK I'd dreamed of warmer climes; now I was frustrated by them. I couldn't live the life I wanted to live because I wasn't free. But I knew any new life I planned wasn't going to be down under. I recalled the old saying, *No place like home,* and dwelt on what it actually meant; not a lot to me as someone from a broken home, although I believed it would be somewhere in the UK when I eventually settled down. *Home,* to me, transcended family. I thought *home* could be anywhere; I convinced myself I'd recognise it when I finally found it. I concluded that wherever my heart and soul felt at ease, wherever I felt comfortable, that's where I'd call *home.* I resigned myself to the fact that I just hadn't found that place yet, a place where I felt I belonged.

I had now become more consciously aware of how the slightest things irritated me. I started to clock my mood swings. And these became more frequent until I knew I couldn't carry on like this; life was becoming meaningless. Getting high was my only escape from the reality, but it was a double-edged sword. I was damned if I did and damned if I didn't. And I was short of answers. I was particularly down when Wesley announced his plan for another night out. He claimed it was, *'A secret outing – to take you all out of yourselves.'* I don't know why, but I wondered if Wesley had specifically organised this surprise night out for me, to cheer me up. Yet the voice in my head said, *Don't be daft – why would he?* Wesley's announcement provoked a lot of speculation amongst our gang in Newcastle Street and soon became a hot topic of conversation. Everyone wanted to know what Wes had in mind. Where did he plan to take us? Although our anticipation and expectations grew, as the date for our night out approached, Wesley remained silent as to the nature of the evening he had in mind.

When the appointed evening arrived we set off walking towards Perth city centre. Wes soon gave us a clue as to our intended destination: the Savoy Hotel in Hay Street. But he wouldn't say *why* we were going there, which only provoked further debate amongst us. Why would we visit one of the top hotels in Perth? Was another food night on the agenda; *was it another meal deal?* Wes was adamant: *'No! We are not going there to eat.'* Was there a special act or event on that night? Wes said nothing.

I then recalled a night with some of my messmates from the *Happy H* when we'd ended up at the Savoy. We'd gone upstairs and found a gorgeous bevy of girls who happened to be ladies of the night. There were about half a dozen of them, sitting on sofas, relaxing, enjoying what they said was their night off. And, as it happened, none of us did any business with them; but we'd chatted, socialised and enjoyed their company. *Wow,* I thought, *tonight's going to be some night!* I kept schtum and grinned at Wesley. *'I know where you're coming from, Wes – nice one!'* Wesley said nothing, but I wasn't sure if I detected a smug smile on his face after I said it. When we arrived at the Savoy and entered the expansive lobby, I headed straight for the wide open staircase to go upstairs.

'Hey!' shouted Wes. *'We're not heading that way,'* and he made his way around to the back of the stairs where the others had followed. They all turned and someone shouted, *'We're going down here.'* I retraced my steps and followed everyone down the back staircase that led to a basement room. The furnishings and layout inside were similar to the room I remembered from upstairs on my previous visit. As you entered, a snooker table was on the left and two identical sofas facing one another were on the right, with a small cocktail bar beyond. To get to the bar, as with the room upstairs, you had navigate between the legs and feet of anyone sitting on the settees. They were long three-seater designs where four people could just about squeeze in, if you didn't mind the physical contact of elbows and thighs of those sitting next to you.

Two young guys were playing snooker and four others were sitting directly opposite one another, two on each settee. When we entered the room all social activity froze as heads turned and stared in our direction. Any ongoing conversation was temporarily suspended as we weaved our way between the sofas towards the bar. I noticed one or two acknowledge Wesley as we threaded our way through. They sat there smiling up at us, as we plotted our way between them in single file. I noticed one of them stick his tongue out and waggle it lasciviously at Billy, who didn't notice this as he passed by in front of me. It made me feel uncomfortable and I wondered why we were here.

None of us were ever flush with money, and so whenever a crowd of us went out we'd often only buy our own drinks. Occasionally we'd buy in pairs or have a kitty and share a jug of lager, but on this occasion it was a buy your own night. Wesley arrived at the bar first and ordered his. We followed suit. I was the last to get served, and when I turned around there were only four of us left standing at the bar: Billy, Patrick, John *et moi*.

Wesley had squeezed himself onto one settee, and Pierre onto the other. The two guys playing pool had wrapped up their game and cosied up to the others; so there was now four facing four, all squashed together on the two settees. Wesley was sitting with one leg crossed over the other, and the foot of his upper leg was further wrapped around his lower leg. Personally, I found this sitting position uncomfortable and difficult to accomplish. I thought it was an odd way of sitting, and whenever I saw anyone sitting with their legs entangled like that, I imagined they were either practising contortionists or mad professors. I'd suddenly expect them to throw their hands wildly up in the air, start gesticulating, until finally they tied themselves up in a knot.

The sound of Wesley's voice floated across to us at the bar. It was impossible to decipher what he was actually saying, but I noticed a definite change in the pitch of his voice. I couldn't believe I was listening to the same Wesley I'd known for the past few months. The inflection and intonation of his voice rose and fell in an exaggerated way. He was sitting in an upright position with his chin thrust out and waving his hands in the air as he spoke. Effeminacy and affectation, both physically and orally, consumed him. Everyone sitting on the couches quickly followed suit; they all adopted a variation of tone to their voices. They mimicked the way Wesley spoke; some caught their breath and some sounded breathless. They were all camping it up.

I watched, fascinated. Each in turn adopted what they must have thought were female speech effects and mannerisms; although, personally, I'd never actually heard a woman sound like this or witnessed one act like this before. I found this sudden change in behaviour amusing, as they started to flick their hair back, touch up eyebrows with moistened fingertips, cross their legs back and forth in an exaggerated way, and hold their hands aloft to scrutinise fingernails. All of this behaviour reminded me of a drag act I'd seen; it crossed my mind that they'd missed their vocation. I thought if they possessed all the female paraphernalia of make-up, jewellery and long evening gowns, they could quite easily have made a living performing on the strip in Sydney's Kings Cross district.

Patrick, who was still at the bar with me, was wearing his long trench coat and commented, *'I'm keeping my coat on. And my arse is staying up against the bar.'*

Billy departed to the men's room as Wesley got up and came over to us. He whispered in my ear, *'Lester's quite taken with you. The one on the right that was sitting next to me.'*

'C'mon, Wesley – you know I'm not interested.'

'He's the one at this end. He's smiling up at you now.'

'I said, I'm not interested.'

'I'll tell him. But I know how disappointed he'll be.' And with that Wes turned around in a flourish, with his nose in the air, and almost tiptoed back to the settee. He squeezed back into his place next to Lester and whispered something in Lester's ear. Lester turned his head and pouted his lips in my direction. He then raised his hand and wagged his forefinger playfully, as if to say, *You naughty boy.* I thought, *He can think what he likes, but I'm not interested.* At that point I turned my back on those sitting and faced the bar. Patrick was still standing there with me with his coat on, and John was with us too, when Billy returned. He came bustling up to us, fresh from his visit to the men's room,

'Oi've just 'ad a lip-lock stuck on me. I was washing my 'ands, turned around to dry 'em, and then this geyser jumped me – and kissed me full on!' The three of us at the bar started sniggering, but we all, including Billy, stifled our amusement. We didn't want Wesley and his chums to think we were laughing at them. Wesley got up again and joined us at the bar.

'Lester's invited you all to a party at his house. He says, "Please come – it'll be fun."' Immediately I looked askance, questioning Wesley's unfortunate choice of words. 'No pun intended,' Wesley added quickly. And then he continued. 'But he does like the look of you, Joe – he's really smitten. He's even talking about love.' I thought, This is ridiculous, but said, 'Wes – I don't think so. I'm not that way inclined – sorry. And I'm going home when I've finished my drink.'

'What about you, Billy? Marty's got a crush on you.'

'No ta, mate – I'm shooting off, too.'

Patrick, myself, Billy and John all went home when we finished our drinks and left Wes and Pierre sitting on the sofas. Funny, but I'd never wondered about Wesley's sexuality before that night. And I would never have thought about it afterwards, if I hadn't witnessed his effeminate side during the course of that evening. He had never displayed such behaviour before and didn't display anything like it again during the rest of my time in Newcastle Street.

Not long after the disappointment of that lads' night out Pierre returned to the RD straight from a modelling assignment. He brought with him what I can only describe as a vision of pure delight. She was wearing an ivory-coloured silk dress with embroidered roses stitched all over the front. It was a hip-hugging, knee-length work of art that illuminated her curves beneath yet still left plenty for the imagination. When Pierre introduced her as Serena, she added that everyone called her Rena or Rini. I said I thought Serena or Serene sounded perfect, and wondered if she minded if I called her by one of those names. She said she didn't mind at all.

One of the girls at the RD that evening was so taken by Serena's dress that she shouted out, *'Give us a twirl!'* Serena duly obliged and then half-turned towards us. She stood still, momentarily, in a classic statuesque pose with one hand on her hip and her luxurious blonde hair falling across a pouting, sultry face. It was a flawless representation of an image I'd once seen of Marilyn Monroe. Everyone in the room applauded and a couple of wolf whistles rang out. I overheard Serena mention that the designer had allowed her to keep the dress.

From the very first moment that evening, when Pierre introduced her to everyone at the RD, she lifted my spirits and brought some sunshine back into my life. Yes, she was blonde; yes, she had a full-on figure; yes, she smiled a lot. And yes, I thought she was gorgeous. After that first meeting I saw Serena at the RD nearly every evening after work. She loved it there. I don't know how or why, or what it was between us, but we clicked. And, although I wondered what she saw in me, I couldn't help thinking that she was the best thing that had happened to me since I'd been in Australia.

Pierre had acquired some LP records, but no one had a record player, and so we relied upon Patrick's old transistor radio for music. The trouble with that was that John, a cricket addict, constantly tuned into matches or Aussie rules football commentaries. Both of these sports dominated the airwaves, and so it was difficult to find a station that played contemporary music, let alone our preference for soul or Motown dance music. But the main problem with the radio was the missing tuning dial; this meant we had to tune it in with a pair of pliers every time we wanted to listen to music.

It was on one of the nights when Serena was round that we tuned the radio in and caught Percy Sledge singing *When a Man Loves a Woman*. Serena held out her hand to me; I couldn't believe it.

'C'mon – let's dance,' she said. '*It's one of my favourite songs.*' It was an offer I couldn't refuse. I was nervous; I knew it was a slow soulful ballad that demanded a slow dance. My heart was racing as I stood up. We danced close together, against one another, and I struggled to control myself. I wanted to fold her in my arms and pull her closer, tighter to me. The urge to kiss her on the lips was irresistible; I had to fight hard to hold myself back. I forced my head to rule my heart. It was difficult but I reasoned, *Take your time; be gentle, patient; think about her and how she's feeling.* My brain was swimming; I knew I had to play it cool. I didn't want to behave like a love-struck schoolboy and act in a heated rush. I ended up placing my hands lightly on her hips; she reciprocated in kind by hanging hers loosely around my neck. Our bodies swayed rhythmically in time, from side to side. That dance with Serena reminded me of the sea, with us both gently riding the waves and drifting in together on the tide. As we smooched slowly, gently holding one another, the breeze from the balcony caught her hair and blew it away from her neck and across my face. I took the chance to let my lips lightly brush her neck. I closed my eyes and inhaled the sweet aroma of her delicate floral perfume and, just for a moment, I thought I was in heaven. For all of my frustrations and negative thoughts regarding my current situation, I couldn't help thinking that life doesn't get much better than this.

Afterwards Serena and I always had a dance each night. Yes, she danced with others, but it was they who asked her. I never once saw her ask any of the other guys if they'd like to dance. And yes, I was fascinated, maybe infatuated with her. I watched her dance with others and saw they always danced apart; there was always space between them. I guess I was smitten, as I couldn't help but look out for those things. I felt privileged to dance with Serena, to be that close to her. I felt comfortable in her arms, and I like to think she was in mine, because it soon became a habit for us both to end the evening with one last dance together.

After several nights in her company she whispered to me when we were dancing, *'You know I love it here. I love you guys – you're so cool.'* I wasn't sure about being cool, but then she said.

'You know we should go out one night together.'

'Who?' I asked, thinking she meant everybody.

'Me and you. Do it properly – have a dance – go to a club. What do you think?'

'Oh, Serena. You try and stop me!' She laughed. We didn't set a date that night, but I made a mental note to arrange something soon for us.

It was a few nights later, when Serena and I had finished dancing that she invited us all over to her place for a meal. She repeated how much she loved us all and wanted everyone to meet her mum. Discussions followed about what day was best? What we'd have to eat? How many could go? Serena said numbers didn't matter as her parents managed the immigration hostel in Perth. They catered for large numbers of immigrants who'd just arrived and who were still looking for accommodation. She said she'd already discussed the meal invitation with her mum and they'd decided a Friday night would be best. I suggested fish and chips, recalling fish on Fridays with the Catholic family I lived with in Manchester. All of the Brits amongst us had fond memories of the local chippy back home, and clamoured their approval. The resident Aussies were shouted down, and so it was agreed we'd introduce them to some traditional British tucker!

A couple of nights later at the RD, whilst trying to tune in the radio to find some dance music, the spindle snapped off in the jaws of the pliers. A few of us wanted to throw the damn thing over the balcony onto the street below, but common sense prevailed. The question then arose as to what were we going to do for music. Pierre's LP collection, some of which included *Tamla Motown*, now became the hot topic of conversation. We had the music; we just hadn't the means to play it.

Everyone was as keen as Pierre to listen to his own records, but for one reason or another no one had thought about buying a record player. Although it was too late to purchase one that evening, it was decided that all the Newcastle Street residents would chip in and buy one on payday. Until then we weren't sure what to do.

The dilemma with the radio had cropped up before when John was in control of it, listening to one of his matches. On that occasion we'd waited until the game was over; afterwards we alternated as to who had priority of listening to the radio for the evening. Pierre remembered a conversation he'd had with Serena when she'd confessed she had a portable record player. He now blurted out, *'You've got one, Serena. Why don't you go home and get it?'* I looked across at her and saw her screw up her face when she heard him. I knew she'd been asked before to go home and fetch it but had always resisted, and we'd managed to get by with listening to the radio. However on this occasion, with no alternative to play and listen to music, everyone (including yours truly) pleaded with her to pop home and fetch her record player. Although reluctant to go Serena finally relented.

She agreed to go on the proviso that someone went with her on her Vespa scooter. I wriggled out of this as I was only dressed in shorts, a T-shirt and flip-flops, and couldn't be bothered to go to my flat next door and change into some warmer clothing. Pierre, who knew her better than most anyway, through their modelling assignments, eventually agreed to accompany her. The evening was a lot cooler, and Pierre was one of only a few of us fully dressed; he only had to pick up a jacket from his room next door in the house.

After they set off the rest of us eagerly awaited their return; Serena estimated it would take her between three quarters of an hour to an hour. We sat around and waited; forty-five minutes passed and we sat around and waited. It got later, and later. An hour slowly turned into two; still there was no sign of Serena and Pierre. People started to drift off, until I finally decided to give up on them too.

The thought of getting up for work the next day finally overtook any desire to stay up and wait for them to return. As I returned to my room in the flat next door, where Billy was tucked up in bed, I couldn't help thinking about Serena and Pierre being together. My internal dialogue was relentless: *Trust Pierre, I bet he's cosying up to Serena's mum, soft-soaping her, getting his feet under the table. I should have made more of an effort to go and get changed. It should have been me who went with her.*

After our night out at the Savoy I wasn't 100% sure of Pierre's sexuality; but now I felt I'd missed a golden opportunity to get to know Serena and her family better. And what better way to do this than to meet, and talk, with her mum? The next morning as I walked to work it still bugged me to think of Pierre being with Serena for so long. I couldn't help but wonder, *What were they up to? Why were they away so long? Why didn't they come back?* My internal interrogation was relentless. *If they got back I wonder what time it was? Did they even come back? What happened? Has Serena fallen for Pierre? Are they a couple now?*

By the time I arrived at work that morning I was drained, a nervous wreck. I needed answers. My mind was in overdrive. I felt sick in my heart and my stomach turned. All I wanted to do when I arrived in the shoe department was turn around and go back to my room. Not knowing what had gone on between them became unbearable. It was that, that really got to me. The same questions kept repeating themselves inside my head: *Why didn't they show? And if they eventually returned to the RD, what had kept them?* I realised it would be a complete waste of time to immediately return to the RD as no one would be there; so I stayed at work. I thought if I kept busy it might quell the fears that filled my imagination concerning Serena and Pierre.

It was later that morning when serving a customer that John (Pierre's roommate) arrived unannounced in the shoe department. I was bending over, leaning towards a lady sitting in front of me and handing her a shoe when, oblivious to John's presence, I heard a voice behind me.

'Pierre's in hospital. And Serena's dead.' I stopped in my tracks. For a split second I wasn't sure what I'd heard, or who had said it?

'Oh my God,' the woman blurted out, and dropped the shoe. She held her hand to her mouth.

'What?' I cried. Surely, I'd misheard what someone had said. Did they say someone had died? Had I heard, *'Pierre's in hospital.'*? And so is it Serena who's dead? Had the wires in my brain short-circuited? I froze. Could I hear my heart banging, about to explode out of my chest, or did it skip a beat? And then John's dull monotone rang out again,

'Pierre's in hospital, and Serena's dead.'

'Oh, how terrible. My God, that's terrible,' cried the woman. I collapsed into a chair next to her. *'I'll leave the shoes for now, and come back again,'* she said, and got up and left.

'Sorry,' John said. *'I'm on my way to the hospital now.'* And then he, too, disappeared. I couldn't believe it. I was shell-shocked. Only a couple of days ago Serena and I were in each others' arms. And now nothing, silence. A

picture of her smiling face appeared in front of me; her reflection stayed focused behind my eyes. I shut them tight, thinking she would disappear, but she stayed there. And now I saw her face, unsmiling; she stared at me, her eyes tinged with sadness: dark, hooded, full of regret. I thought she looked as though she was trying to speak, mouthing words that couldn't be heard, like one of my nightmares. I couldn't believe what John had said. I sat there dazed, stunned. I took some deep breaths and put my head in my hands; tears welled up and my vision became blurred. Slowly the image of Serena's face faded, and she dissolved before I could work out what she was trying to say.

I was left sitting there feeling empty and alone, silently weeping inside. After a while Cyril spotted me and came over and asked me what was wrong. I dodged the truth by saying I had a terrible pain in my gut and felt too ill to work. He commented on my pallor and said I looked as though I'd seen a ghost. I nearly said, *I think I have,* but said nothing. He told me to go home and see a doctor if things didn't improve. I took his advice and headed off, trance – like, towards Newcastle Street with my head spinning and my eyes stinging. I was vaguely aware of cars and people rushing by, but the blurred reality of the world passed me by on that crazy journey home. By the time I reached my flat I'd come to the conclusion that there is nothing fair in life; nothing is certain. We are all born as victims, born blind into a world of preordained circumstances (of which we know nothing). No one has a clue about life and where it will lead them. And no one knows when or how it will end. All we know, if we survive the early years, is that it will end. Life and death are completely random; nothing can be taken for granted.

I was trembling by the time I reached Newcastle Street, shaking, as if I had a fever. I felt clammy yet, paradoxically, it was a warm, sunny day with a perfect blue sky. It was set up to be a day when nothing could or should go wrong, a day full of promise and optimism, a day for love and peace, a day when people should feel blessed. It wasn't a day to contemplate death. But, as I say, nothing in life is certain.

Feeling desolate, and devastated, I clambered up to my sparsely furnished room and lay on top of my bed. I spoke to my imaginary God and asked Him, *'Why? Why Serena? So young, so beautiful, so innocent? Why did it have to be her?'* And then, as if I was a member of the Plymouth Brethren, I wondered if it was me being punished. I asked, *'Was it me? Something I've done? Should I have gone with her? If I'd really loved her I should have gone with her.'* I couldn't make sense of it all. Finally, exhausted, I fell asleep. When Billy arrived back after work and woke me, it was dusk. He said he'd called in at the RD on his way home and saw I wasn't there.

We decided to return there, where everybody was in a state of shock. Wesley and Patrick both came over and the four of us had a communal hug; no one could believe or understand what happened.

I left the RD early that night, as I wanted to be alone in my room and grieve privately. I replayed the memories of the times I'd shared with Serena. Yes, we'd only known each other for a short time, but there had been some unforgettable moments in her arms. I recalled the time we danced cheek to cheek, so slowly, and let our thighs interlink. We'd squeezed up against one another. I remember thinking how privileged I was to linger in her essence. I now wondered what might have become of us. *What might have been?* I'd felt I was in love with her, but now I was left wondering what Serena thought about me. I was frightened to imagine that she might have felt the same about me – but it didn't stop me imagining.

I remembered how her face appeared in front of me after John relayed the news of her demise. She was there, alive inside my head, staring, with that haunting look in her eyes. I believe Serena had feelings for me, but I'll never know the true extent of those feelings now that she was gone. Any thoughts I had, real or imagined, would now have to remain unanswered. My eyes welled up with tears again as the reality of what happened returned. It was hard to admit to myself that, *Those days are over. They are lost and gone forever and will never be repeated.* I felt like I did when my mother left; I had to forget her, banish her from my thoughts and move on.

I wasn't sure I could do that. But it was with heartbreaking clarity that I realised Serena and I would never share another moment together.

Pierre came out of hospital after a couple of days. His recollection of events was that Serena had collided with a van at a crossroads; that's all he could remember. He said it was on the way to her home when the accident happened and so he never got to meet her mum after all. I couldn't believe how my mind had played tricks on me that night, and then the following morning on the way to work, and when I returned to my flat. I was amazed how I'd let my imagination run riot with crazy thoughts about Pierre and Serena being together.

I knew I wasn't going to attend Serena's funeral. I'd made a pact with myself a long time before I met Serena that I wasn't going to attend funerals. I learned to shut myself off from sad times; I didn't want to witness any more weeping and wailing than I had to. I'd shied away from the bad things that happen to other people in life. Ever since my mum walked out I learned it was best not to dwell on the desperate days and bad times that caused heartache. It was the only defence I knew. Yes, sometimes I felt callous; sometimes I felt cold inside. I learned and disciplined myself to walk away from the hard-luck stories of others; it was self-preservation. All I had now were my own personal memories of Serena: precious, private moments that I wanted to keep to myself.

BANGED UP

After Serena's death things happened quickly and took a turn for the worse. The six of us from Newcastle Street decided to go out on the night we should have been having fish and chips with Serena and her parents at their place. Johnny O'Keefe, an Australian rock 'n' roller, was appearing at The Waldorf nightclub that evening and so we decided to go there. To me the night was about forgetting that Serena was no longer with us, and you could argue it achieved its objective, but not in the way anyone would have wished or intended. I've often wondered since whether fate played a hand.

It would be easy to blame myself for the events that unfolded that night, but then you can always reflect upon the thoughts and actions of others, things that ultimately influence individual decisions and so, accordingly, determine how others act or react. There are too many *ifs* and *buts* that precede the *whys?* You could retrace your steps *ad infinitum* yet never find out which spark lit the fire. So why was Serena taken from us? The one certainty is that if Serena had still been with us we wouldn't have been at The Waldorf that night. So was it destiny or fate? *C'est la vie (ou de mort)* or *que sera, sera?*

Inside the nightclub we sat around a circular table. I sat there, in a place crammed with people, surrounded by friends, yet feeling lonely, depressed and isolated. I was a castaway, alone with my thoughts and memories of Serena. The guys knew how close Serena and I had been from our nights together at the RD. They understood my sullenness, the anger and hurt that consumed me. During that evening I drank and drank. I was full of self-pity and ignored my companions. I became oblivious to the music, dancing, and gaiety around me. I wondered why I'd come but then immediately reasoned: *Well, what else would I have done alone in my room all evening?*

As the night dragged on I fell asleep, slouched over the table, only to be jerked back into consciousness by some raucous laughter. I looked over and saw someone at a nearby table laughing and pointing towards us. The others at his table turned and stared, whilst this guy carried on with his inane laughter. He then started banging the top of their table with one hand, whilst pointing over towards us with the other. I tried to ignore him, but he kept on with his persistently loud laugh. I said to the others, *'If he doesn't shut up, I'm going over there to see what he's laughing at.'* I was self-conscious, and it felt like it was me who was the butt of his ridicule (for falling asleep). Billy and Patrick voiced their concerns: *'Leave it,'* said one. *'He's not worth it,'* added the other. I didn't wish to spoil the evening and cause trouble so heeded their advice and stayed put.

Unfortunately the whole scenario repeated itself when I dozed off in my chair again. I came to in similar circumstances, with the same guy laughing so loud he drowned out the singing of Johnny O'Keefe. I felt more sober this time, more in control. I headed over to his table with a fresh sense of bravado and confronted him and his mates. *'What's so funny?'* I shouted out as I approached. The guy got to his feet as I arrived, as did two or three of his mates; they stood up between us and so obscured my view of him.

'What the f--- are you laughing at? You want to f---ing shut up! We can't hear Johnny O'Keefe!' I shouted, and pointed towards the stage. Incredibly, as soon as they all got to their feet, they all immediately sat down again. I thought my salutary message had had the desired effect. *Well done,* I said to myself. *They've actually listened to what you've said.* I felt pleased with myself, as I'd shut the guy up without us coming to blows. What I'd failed to notice was that Wes, Patrick, Billy, John and Pierre had all followed me over to laughing boy's table. I couldn't have been as sober as I'd imagined because I was totally unaware of their presence.

A bouncer then appeared out of nowhere. He must have seen all of us desert our table and surround the other one occupied by four or five males. Instinct and experience must have alerted him that trouble was about to kick off. The bouncer came between us and them and asked what the problem was. To my amazement laughing boy jumped up and revealed a small dark ring, about the size of a penny, on his pristine white shirt. It stood out just above the belt buckle on his trousers, somewhere in the vicinity of his belly-button.

'You're joking!' I exclaimed. 'He's pricked himself with the pin on his belt.' And I genuinely thought that was what he'd done, that he'd accidentally stuck the buckle pin into his stomach whilst fastening his belt. It was only later that I realised how ridiculous that must have sounded; so much for the reliability of my internal barometer concerning sobriety. Thankfully the bouncer was as sober as any judge who donned the black cap. He saw beyond the smoke, haze and intoxication of the evening, and recognised the potential for an inflammatory situation where there was a strong possibility that violence might erupt. His thoughts of safety, control and possibly self-preservation took over, as he immediately ordered the lads that we'd approached to remain seated at their table. And then shouted at us, 'Get out. You'd better get out. Hurry up! This way!' and pointed towards the nearest exit. He ushered us off in single file, through the crowded nightclub, where another bouncer held a door open for us. We were chaperoned silently out into the street, where the cold night air hit us. I was tired and felt lost as we staggered back to Northbridge. It was strange how the silence and emptiness of the dark, deserted streets reflected our sombre mood; no one had anything to say. We were each internally locked into our own thoughts and emotions. To me it felt like the end of something; the end of an era? I didn't think anything would be the same again. What should have been a dream evening with Serena turned out to be a nightmare.

The headlines, emblazoned across newspaper stands on street corners the next day, were full of last night's events. Many read: '**Midnight Stabbing at Johnny O'Keefe Nightspot.**' Patrick relayed word from the RD that Wes had taken a knife off Pierre to stop *me* from using it? I couldn't understand this as I didn't recall any conversation about a knife that night. And it was only after I heard this that I learned Pierre carried a blade; it was something I wouldn't have used, and couldn't have used because I didn't know that one of us had a knife. In Manchester I'd known of a couple of people who'd been stabbed; at the time I made a conscious decision never to carry a blade. I held the view that if you carried a weapon then sooner or later you would be tempted to use it.

When I went to work on Monday morning Sid collared me as soon as I arrived. He quizzed me about the drama that unfolded at The Waldorf on Friday night. He was a big fan of Johnny O'Keefe and we both knew each of us was going to be there. I acted nonplussed to all of his questions. I said I wasn't aware of any disturbance; I told him I hadn't seen anything. His persistent questioning made me wonder if he'd seen us all being escorted out of the premises. Eventually I was convinced that Sid *had* missed all the commotion due to a toilet break; he just wondered if I'd seen what happened. He said he missed some of Johnny O'Keefe's set, which would have been about the time the bouncer appeared.

At around mid-morning that day Cyril asked me to deliver some expensive shoes to a friend who worked in a haberdashery shop a few blocks away. I was happy to oblige because it offered me some welcome relief from Sid and his incessant prattle about what had happened at The Waldorf. I milked the time I was away from the department store and took a leisurely stroll along the streets in the sunshine. I needed to clear my head, think things through. I was desperate for some *me* time to contemplate what the possible consequences of the other night might be. The severity of what happened had only just started to sink in. Up to now we'd heard nothing; I thought, naively, perhaps nothing would come of it. I lived in hope but couldn't help wondering what we could expect from the fallout of the stabbing. Now it was splashed all over the papers I guessed it was only a matter of time before the events of the other night came back to haunt us.

I still maintain that *stabbing* was too harsh a word for what happened that night. I was definitely befuddled with booze, but I can still see a small dark ring, not much bigger than a thumbnail, on the victim's shirt. It was more akin to being *pricked* with something the size of a meat skewer rather than being *stabbed* with a knife. I always imagine that someone who *STABS* makes a lunge; the assailant presses home with force and the resulting stab wound is much deeper, an action that is intentional and intended to cause serious injury. I know that night a knife was produced and contact was made, that people suddenly got to their feet and rapidly sat down again. And it was reported that the unfortunate recipient of the wound went to hospital and had a check-up; a dressing was applied, and then he was allowed home. Technically, they were stabbed, and it should never have happened, but to my knowledge there are no scales in relation to the severity of stabbings. In defence of the perpetrator, I don't think he ever had any real intent to inflict serious injury on his target. And if there had been a severity scale on stabbings, then I believe The Waldorf stabbing incident would have been recorded on the lowest band, if indeed it would have been classed as a *stabbing?*

On that Monday, after delivering the shoes for Cyril, I was feeling quite worried when I returned to my duties in the shoe department. My contemplations, whilst I was out and about, hadn't resolved anything but had rather added confusion to the situation we found ourselves in. It was later that day when Cyril took a call from the main office upstairs stating they wanted to see me. When I went up there I got a bollocking from the personnel department for not signing myself out when I left the premises. I wondered how they knew I'd been out of the building, but they did, and insisted I must sign out every time I leave the building during working hours.

They said that if I was involved in an accident whilst out of the store on their business, then it would invalidate any insurance cover. As soon I returned back down to the shoe department Cyril received another call from upstairs.

'*They want to see you, again,*' he said. '*They didn't say what it was about.*'

I now became more worried and wondered what they wanted. I couldn't think of anything specifically but had a bad feeling about this. I don't know why but I thought I might get the sack. I thought about any other misdemeanours I might have committed; but surely they would have mentioned these during my previous visit? I racked my brains trying to think of anything I'd done wrong; I couldn't think of anything other than arriving late for work a few times in the mornings. Maybe my clocking-in card had been monitored and they decided enough was enough; maybe they thought I was taking the piss?

I decided to give myself time to think before I arrived in the main office again. It was on the top floor, and if you didn't take the lift you had to climb four flights of stairs at the rear of the building: a cold, lifeless vacuum with a cast-iron stairway; the only sign of life was the echo of your footsteps as you went either up or down. I made a slow, laboured ascent. I convinced myself I'd been recalled upstairs for poor timekeeping. I thought about plausible excuses I could offer them; all I could think of was: *I've not been well lately.* I wasn't sure this would suffice. Perhaps there were other issues I wasn't aware of surrounding my work; but why wouldn't they have mentioned them a few minutes ago? And anyway, wouldn't Cyril have said something about my performance? It all felt a bit ominous; something didn't quite add up.

I entered the HR office and was greeted by two heavily set guys in sharp mohair suits. Both were sitting down; one was stretched back with his elbows out and hands behind his head. He was reclining on the back legs of his chair. He sat on the far side of a desk that faced the door. The other guy faced him and had his back to me; there was a vacant chair next to him. He was leaning forward and speaking quietly; as I entered their conversation dried up.

'Hello Joseph – or is it Joe?' said the blue suit behind the desk. He rolled forward, swept to his feet and held out his hand in one movement.

'Joe,' I replied and shook his hand. The one on my side of the desk was dressed in a stone-grey suit. He also also got up and we shook hands. He left his hand open and gestured. 'Take a seat,' he said. Who are these guys? I thought. They were both big, wore white shirts, with plain ties that matched their suits. They reminded me of cloned mobsters. Their short hair was dark and slicked-back. Both had bronze, chiselled features. My mind was racing. Had I upset someone? Have they been sent to put the frighteners on me?

'Now Joe,' said blue suit, 'where's your passport and ID card?' Straight away I knew the game was up. I'd lost or mislaid them. I thought I'd hidden them under the mattress at the first place we lived in when we jumped ship; but when I discovered they were missing I decided not to go back as it was too risky to try and retrieve them.

'Why? Have you found them?' I said.

'No,' they replied in unison. I smiled. I definitely knew I'd been caught; there wasn't any point in denying I was on the run from the Royal Navy. It transpired that these two guys were from the Central Investigation Bureau (CIB) in Perth WA, and the least of their worries was the fact that I'd gone AWOL from the RN. They wanted to know about Friday night at The Waldorf.

They said they had a reliable witness who could identify I was there that night. They took me into custody and wanted to know who else was there, how many of us were there, what their names were, what we did afterwards where we lived. The list was endless. They took me to Perth City lock-up, which was a huge building that resembled a large multi-storey car park from the outside – only one with windows. The primary purpose of the lock-up was to hold suspects, allowing the police more time to gather evidence before bringing any charges. The lock-up was an open, spacious holding cell, halfway up this monstrosity of a building, and took up the whole length of a floor on one side. On the opposite side, divided by a long corridor, were individual cells that housed two or three people. These cells had vertical prison bars from floor to ceiling so that the occupants could be viewed from the corridor without the need to unlock cell doors. And although each cell contained private facilities with a drawable curtain, privacy was still definitely at a premium.

When I entered the lock-up facility, which could probably hold a hundred or more, there were about thirty-five people in custody. My first impression of those under suspicion was that many of them fitted my idea of the stereotypical shady character. I noticed how many appeared sly and would steal glances at you. I'd sometimes catch them looking my way because they weren't quick enough to look away when I looked at them. They appeared furtive, nervous and agitated; such behaviour, in itself, attracted suspicion. I was uneasy in their presence and knew I needed to be on my guard. I was careful about who I approached, spoke to and who I sat next to. I spent most of my time wandering around, up and down the lock-up, steering clear of those who looked like bad news.

One guy I noticed stood out against all the rest. He was barefoot and dressed in frayed, stained white shorts, and a sleeveless, soiled blue check shirt; his ragged appearance complemented his long, blond unkempt hair and straggly straw beard. At first he reminded me of a castaway, *a Robinson Crusoe* character who could have spent months on a desert island. But later, after observing him continually pad up and down next to the huge windows that stretched the full length of the lock-up, and which afforded panoramic views of the world outside, he reminded me of a caged lion. He was restless; the dull thud of his feet pounded from one end of our cage to the other. I thought he would never rest until he was free to roam out in the wild again. All the time I was in there I didn't see him communicate with anyone; certainly no one tried to approach him. I wondered if this was because of his wild look or his reputation.

There were two English guys in there who I did speak to; both looked respectable in comparison to the others who were being held. They wore open-necked white shirts, dark trousers and polished shoes. I learned they were ex-Army. They said they were being held on suspicion of ram-raiding, something they were more than happy to admit to. They described their technique to me in some detail: how they'd reverse their vehicle into the plate glass window of a jeweller's store, keep the engine running, jump out, and whilst one held a sack open the other would grab as many rings and watches as he could. And then they accelerated away. They said it would take them about a minute from the time they crashed the car into the window. Both sounded quite proud of what they'd achieved; it didn't appear to bother them that they'd been caught. They were quite prepared to serve a stretch inside: *'It's the risk you take,'* one said. *'Part of the job,'* said the other, and held his arms out whilst simultaneously shrugging his shoulders up. He stared straight at me as if he could take on the world, and then rounded it off with, *'It's the price you pay. You know what I mean?'*

'Yeah.' I nodded and thought, *Well, you're a wanker, mate?* I couldn't understand anyone who accepted being locked up as part of life. Yes, everyone has freedom of choice; but why trade freedom, such as it is, to deny yourself the beauty that exists outside in the world?

The lock-up was a busy place; people came and went all the time. Throughout the day many were called out for interview by detectives; some returned and some didn't. The number of detainees rarely dropped as other suspects replaced those released. The turnover and busy nature of the place surprised me; but, unsurprisingly, most of the suspects in the lock-up actually looked suspect. It was strange, but the more I studied the faces and mannerisms of those in the lock-up, the more I felt they possessed an innate criminal tendency. I reasoned we're all animals and all born unequal. And for many crime *was* a career; it was a life they chose, even if they weren't born into it. I studied those in the lock-up more closely and whiled away a few hours playing who's who, trying to match faces to the crimes they might be suspected of. I thought every criminal on the crime spectrum was present: pickpockets, muggers, burglars, vagrants, rent-boys, smash-and-grab merchants, fraudsters, alcoholics; every low-life imaginable. And after I'd matched them all to some crime or other, I couldn't help thinking that the more you studied their faces, antics or foibles, in unguarded moments, they all could be as guilty as sin. I was probably totally wrong as appearances often deceive; but I found the mental exercise entertaining and it helped while away a few hours.

What surprised me was the absence of Abbos in the main lock-up; there wasn't one was amongst us where we could all mingle freely. The only Aborigines I saw inside were sleeping it off in individual cells. Their culture, like Native Americans in the Wild West, were alien to our western predilection for alcohol consumption. My mind flashed back to images I'd seen in and around Perth, where groups of Abbos huddled together, often sheltering in the shade under the low-hanging branches of trees. They were a common sight in most public parks around the city, where they could openly be seen swigging liquor, usually cheap wine or sherry straight from the bottle at anytime of the day.

I stayed overnight in the lock-up, sharing an individual cell with an eastern European. I didn't trust him; fortunately he didn't speak much English, and so there was little communication between us. I decided not to lie down on one of the beds in there but chose to sit on a mattress with my back against a wall and doze. I felt safer that way. I hardly slept, but I survived. I was glad to hear the morning herald its arrival: the buzz of the day shift as the whole place woke up again. I'd had a long, uncomfortable and disturbed night.

We were all herded back into the main lock-up area after a mug of tea and toast, and not long afterwards a guard called me out and escorted me down the corridor to an interview room. The two CIB dicks who had apprehended me at the department store were waiting there. One was standing and the other sitting behind a table. They beckoned me to sit in the vacant chair facing the guy sitting behind the table. I had my back to the door and couldn't see the other guy standing behind me. The one facing me said:

'Now Joe. We don't want any bullshit. We want to know who you were with at The Waldorf on Friday night. We want names.'

'I've already told you.'

'Tell us again.'

'There was Billy, Pat, Pierre, John and myself, five of us.'

The guy behind me whacked me across the back of my head with the heel of his hand.

'Don't lie, Joe. We have it on good authority that there were six of you that night. Six!'

'I don't know. I only remember the five of us. I was pissed. You don't understand. A girl we knew had died. We'd gone out to forget. I was upset. I wasn't myself.'

'Well, who carries a blade? Who had the knife?'

'I don't know. I didn't think anyone carried a knife.'

'Well, you do know people who carry knives, Joe; people who cut other people up.'

'What do you mean?'

'Well, you were at that party. You remember the one? The one where some of our fellow countrymen were bottled and slashed. You're a friend of Scott McDonald. He's a mate of yours, isn't he?'

'No. I don't know him.'

'Well you were at the same party as he was.'

'Yeah. I've seen him; but I don't know him, not personally.'

Another clout across the back of my head followed, which made me lurch forward.

'Stop f---ing us about! I'm getting tired of you not knowing anything! Playing dumb! Now who, amongst your little gang, carries a knife?' The guy behind me now grabbed my hair. I thought he was going to slam my face into the table. I'd had enough. I didn't have the bottle to take any more. I hadn't betrayed Wesley as I hadn't mentioned him; his name was what they wanted to make up the six names from the five I'd given them. From my statement at the very beginning I'd only admitted there were five of us present. I never changed my story. I religiously stuck to what I said, which was a hazy pretence of the events that unfolded that night. I now felt, to a certain extent, I was about to chicken out, but I'd had enough. It was time to give them something in an effort to get them off my back.

'I've since heard that Pierre carries a knife. I don't know. I've never seen him with one. It was just someone mentioned it.'

As soon as I said this he let go of my hair, throwing my head forward. I was just glad I was off the hook, at least temporarily. They now had another lead to work on.

I knew deep down that Pierre would crumble; he wouldn't be able to stomach the intimidation. I was confident that he'd tell them exactly what happened that night. The two cops exited the interview room and left me to be escorted back to the lock-up area. I was left to stew. I hoped my reasoning was right, that Pierre would buckle under the CIB's bullying tactics. I waited, praying Pierre would give the CIB what they wanted. Thankfully my prayers were answered. The next time the two dicks visited me I was released from custody, but before they handed me over to the Australian naval authorities they said:

'Before you disappear, Alcock, let me tell you something. If Queen and country didn't have need of you, we'd be throwing a few charges at you ourselves; like witholding information, perverting the course of justice, assisting an offender. You'd better thank your lucky stars you're serving in Her Majesty's service, otherwise you'd be serving time over here.'

I was allowed to pick up my things from the flat in Newcastle Street before being escorted to the cells at the Australian naval base, HMAS Leeuwin. Whilst packing I heard one of the dicks comment about the excessive amount of footwear lying around. I said nothing. Something else registered with me too: one of them mentioned there was a homo amongst us. I knew they'd been to the other rooms next door by then, and it reminded me of Wesley and his charade with his *friends* at the Savoy. After that night he'd shown me an ornament he had; he called it his prized possession. It was a six-inch bronze figurine of a monk with his head shrouded in a hood, but when you turned it around and viewed it from behind, it was transformed into the sculptured head of a circumcised penis. It had pride of place on Wesley's mantelpiece. I guessed the comment that the cops made meant they'd seen it and identified it as a symbol of homosexuality? I couldn't think of anything else.

At the time I couldn't work out why Wesley had taken the knife from Pierre that night. What was he thinking? Patrick told me he took it off Pierre so that I couldn't get hold of it; but that didn't make sense as I wasn't aware that Pierre carried a knife. And if Wes was trying to protect me, why? It was only much later that I discovered what prompted Wesley to act the way he did that night at The Waldorf.

HMAS Leeuwin was an Australian training centre for fifteen-year-old boys, similar to the boys' RN training centre at HMS Ganges in the UK. Leeuwin was situated close to Fremantle on the banks of the Swan River; it was an idyllic setting, but one which I saw very little of from the confines of my cell. I was being held there until arrangements were made to fly me from Perth to Singapore. My trial for desertion was to take place at HMS Terror, adjacent to the Sembawang dockyard in Singers.

When I arrived in Singapore I was placed in Terror cells, and had a medical check-up almost immediately. The MO was a female of about fifty who had me stripped down bollock naked. Her nutmeg-coloured, weather-worn face, from too much sun, couldn't hide her fine features; there was no doubt that in her day she must have been quite a looker. She knelt down, lifted my cock and inspected me down there. She wrapped her fingers around my member and held on to it for a little longer than necessary, I thought. I glanced down and caught her looking up at me. I'm sure I captured the glimmer of a smile on her face, but I immediately looked up and away. I knew I was clean and was determined not to get aroused. She gave me a gentle squeeze and then let go. I imagined she'd had a hell of a life, and it made me envious, *That's all I wanted, to be free to enjoy the best years of my life.*

The cells at Terror surrounded a square lawned area and were entered through a barred lock-up gate. The regulating office was housed next to the gate, and the cells followed some concrete paving around the grassed area. When I had to get my wash things and toothbrush from my holdall, under the supervision of the duty reg, he spied my kangaroo slippers. He offered to buy them off me, but there was no way I was going to let him have them. They were my only memento of the time I'd spent in Oz. The reg kept on and on; he pestered me no end about letting him have them, but I held out. I was adamant that I was going to take them home. I suppose he could have taken them if he wanted to, and no one would have been the wiser.

What I liked about this guy was that there was no ill-feeling between us, even though he wanted my slippers so badly and I refused to part with them. He reminded me of Steve, the reg back in the MCTC, because he was one of the few naval patrolmen I encountered who showed compassion. All regs had power over you, but he was part of a minority who didn't abuse it. He impressed me when he allowed me to have my cell door open every night, until the last possible moment before he went off watch. He didn't have to do this; but I was glad he did. It was a blessing to have ventilation percolate around the cell, which otherwise resembled the inside of a sauna when the door was slammed shut. Sweat could ooze from your body and leave your shirt wet, even when you were standing still or lying motionless, especially when banged up in that box. There were times when I could smell the heat and humidity of the tropics outside, when warm drops of sweat would sting and tingle the rim inside my nostrils whenever I inhaled a deep breath through my nose.

Apart from making life more bearable by having my cell door open, I was especially grateful one evening when I spied a huge Bombay Runner skim across the cell floor and take refuge under my bunk. I looked underneath to try and flush out this unwelcome visitor but I couldn't see it; my bunk, as in all cells, was bolted firmly to the floor. It was impossible to see the critter because it was concealed under the camouflage of darkness. Thankfully my cell door was still wide open, and so I ventured out in search of my humane gaoler. I found him in his office and asked if I could borrow a broom to extricate my uninvited cellmate. He was more than happy to oblige. This meant a lot to me as I'd always had an aversion to creepy-crawlies, and I certainly didn't want an infestation of giant cockroaches in my cell, let alone any under my bunk.

When I returned to my cell I flailed the broom under the bunk until the Bombay Runner suddenly made a dash for it from under the end of the bed. By the time I dropped the broom, picked up the faded green hardback bible from the bedside table and then dashed across to the wall next to the cell door, this giant black cockroach had scuttled up the wall to head height. I slammed the bible onto it, making a loud crunching noise, and then wiped it clean with some blanket at the foot of the bed. I felt relieved that I'd now be able to sleep peacefully in my bed. As I lay down my eyes once more fell upon the old bible next to me. *Yes,* I smiled again, *God does work in mysterious ways.* But I was most grateful to the reg as a custodian; his relaxed attitude towards my needs made all the difference. They were only small gestures on his part, but sometimes that's all you need when you're down; often an act of kindness, no matter how small, can give you a lift and restore your faith in humanity.

A few days later I had my warrant read out, and the result was much as I had expected. My ship, the *Happy H,* had long been back in Pompey, and since I'd already served sixty days in MCTC at Tanglin, Singapore, the naval authorities saw no point in sending me back there to serve another sentence. I was now sentenced to 90 days, detention inside RNDQ (Royal Naval Detention Quarters), Portsmouth.

BACK TO BLIGHTY

We flew from RAF Changi to Lyneham, Wiltshire a flight packed with young families either returning to Blighty from a holiday visit or from long-term overseas service. Me and my naval patrolman (NP) escort were handcuffed together and dressed in full naval rig; we were the only passengers in uniform. If that wasn't enough to attract the curiosity of other passengers, then our white-topped caps with HMS Terror emblazoned across the front, not to mention the NP's blinding white armband, belt and gaiters, certainly was. We stood out like a couple of naturists in a fashion parade. I thought my status as a prisoner gave a false impression to other passengers; I became increasingly uneasy and self-conscious.

When it was time to board we were shuffled to the front of the queue and so were first to settle into our seats.

As everyone else boarded a lot of them paused and stared at us, but every time I met someone's gaze they quickly turned away. I looked around and caught others further down the plane craning their necks, pointing and mouthing words. Maybe it was my imagination running riot again; but I sensed their unease and felt mine grow. I saw more nodding and pointing in our direction; comments were being made between passengers, as they took to their seats and stowed hand luggage overhead. I was anchored to the window seat and hemmed in by the NP; I felt claustrophobic. Some of the mums that passed us along the aisle ushered their children quickly past, shielding them by placing themselves between us and their kids. I started to feel like a pariah plagued with pestilence. *Why don't you put a bell around my neck?* I thought. I decided I was going to explain my situation, but I needed to choose my moment carefully. I waited until just before take-off, when the NP undid the handcuffs. I feigned to fasten my seatbelt as he fastened his, but as soon as he was secure in his seat I leapt to my feet.

'I'm not a criminal!' I shouted. *'I haven't done anything wrong! I just want a discharge!'* The NP fumbled with the buckle of his seatbelt. *'I made a mistake signing on, that's all! I'm not a criminal. I'm not guilty of anything. I'm innocent just like you!'*

The NP unbuckled himself and went to grab me by the shoulder, but as he stood up, I passed him on the way down. *'I'm only working my ticket!'* I shouted again.

'What's that all about? What do you think you're doing?' snarled the NP.

'*I'm fed up of people staring at me – thinking I'm a thief or a murderer.*'

'*You pull a stunt like that again and...*'

'*What?*' I said, smiling. '*Put me on a charge?*'

We refastened our seatbelts and settled back. I took some deep breaths and closed my eyes. I felt calmer; I'd had my say. My thoughts turned to all these kids on the plane; after all, my alcoholic dad had been in the RAF. I wondered what the future held for them. Where would they be when they were my age? I'd achieved nothing. I was on the run. *On the road to nowhere,* I thought. I guessed I'd have to jump ship again as soon as I was out of DQ's. When I opened my eyes and looked around no one stared at us now, not the mums, dads or kids.

My thoughts turned to my own mum and I wondered where she was. I fumbled for my wallet and took out a well, worn black and white photograph of her. It was of a raven haired beauty, about thirty years old, holding a baby (me) wrapped in a white blanket. *God, I'm 19 and I still miss my mum; yet I've missed her all my life,* I thought. I now took time out on the plane to assess my situation. I realised I was on my own, and all I could look forward to was three months in detention. It was time for me to move on and stop feeling sorry for myself. I thought about life and how some things are beyond your control – how shit happens to you. But then it isn't always like that; there are other things that *you* can make happen. There are times when you can take control of your life, plot your own destiny. A lot depends on what you want out of life. I knew I'd have to reassess as I went along; what would my options be when I got out of DQ's; and, again, what would my plans be, if and when I eventually got out of the Navy. I'd begun to realise that the only person who could change my lot in life was *me*. I felt more determined to do something about it.

The plane began to descend for refuelling at RAF Gan, an island outpost in the Indian Ocean. We were the last ones to disembark, but it was good to stretch my legs. I breathed in the warm balmy air as we sauntered across the tarmac. My escort was closer than my shadow, but he'd been okay since my outburst on the flight. Everyone from the plane headed for the Blue Lagoon Hotel; everyone, that is, except me and my shadow. I couldn't believe how the two of us headed straight for the guardroom. As we made our way there I could hear waves crashing into the shore; these became mingled with the rustling foliage of towering palm trees, continually shaken by the breeze drifting in off the Indian Ocean. I inhaled deeply, closed my eyes and held my breath. I felt free – just for a transitory moment.

The guardroom was a long, low, wooden building with a dimly lit veranda. Light filtered through underneath the front door as we approached, and the sound of our footsteps on the wooden boards drowned out the ocean breeze in the treetops. The RAF police inside the hut were all for banging me up for the duration of our stop.

'Hey, come on,' I protested. '*Where am I going to go to? We're on a little island, in the middle of the Indian Ocean, in the dead of night. I'm not going anywhere. Where can I go? And anyway, I want to go home. I want to do my time.*' They all looked at one another. The chore of paperwork and procedures, which they'd have to complete, intervened on my behalf. They decided to take the easy option, which meant they could return to their coffee, chatter and game of cards. This allowed me and my escort to head over to the Blue Lagoon Hotel for a breakfast at 2.30am.

We made another fuel stop in Cyprus before we reached the UK. The dry white heat there was stifling, a breathless experience where mirages quivered and shimmered up in a haze from the tarmac. The bleached grass next to the runway looked whiter than the sun. The pilot announced before we landed that it was 94 degrees Fahrenheit, and yet it was barely half past ten in the morning; unbearable.

As we descended into RAF Lyneham, Wiltshire, I was still hemmed into a window seat by my escort. As it happened I didn't mind, as I was privy to some glorious views of the English countryside. I savoured such moments, feasting my eyes over a green, green world. I focused on old oak trees, as if for the first time, and small copses, then patchwork fields of grass, barley and corn, patiently waiting for their golden moment. I saw every shade of green imaginable, with the odd brown ploughed field interwoven between. All of England's green and pleasant land was rolled out below, the landscape segregated by hedgerows and fences, and then further dissected by dark, narrow country lanes. I soaked it all up and locked it away in my mind's eye. To me this was freedom in its purest form, something for the mind to conjure up when dark days descended and beauty and light was banished from my world. Whatever else they take away from you, they can't erase the life you've lived and the memories you have.

As I gazed down again I was reminded of those immortal lines by Rupert Brooke: *'That there's some corner of a foreign field that's forever England.'* And probably for the first time I fully appreciated what the beauty of England meant to me. It was a far cry from our sizzling stop-over in Cyprus, and even further removed from the stark, barren interior of Australia. In spite of my current predicament I was, paradoxically, at peace with myself and the world. I realised I had finally arrived home; this was where I belonged – England was home.

We travelled down to Pompey from Brize Norton in an RN tilly van, and as the journey progressed I became increasingly subdued and isolated. Through the windows of the van I observed ordinary folk going about their daily business. I envied them their freedom. It was only when we approached the outskirts of Pompey that thoughts about life inside RNDQ's hit me. Rumours had abounded amongst lower-deck ratings on the *Happy H*, about how spartan life was inside DQ's. Many claimed you needed to be a real hard case to survive; this wasn't strictly true. I learned such gossip was often propagated by guys who'd never been inside DQ's themselves. By the time we arrived at the main gates on Anchor Road, I felt as prepared for detention as I'd ever be. And I was about to find out for myself what life was really like inside the walls of the infamous Pompey RNDQ's.

The rules and regulations inside were no different to any other detention centre, in that they had to be obeyed and strictly adhered to. If they weren't followed then you'd be placed on another charge and receive additional punishment; this usually meant loss of remission. The regime inside Pompey DQ's was vastly different to my experience inside MCTC, Singapore. In Pompey monotony, boredom and mindless activities were the order of the day; PE and rifle drill took place in the morning, only to be repeated in the afternoon. This was the routine each and every day except for half of Saturdays and Sundays. Unlike MCTC there were no lectures, no stripping down and cleaning of weapons, no route or endurance marches; all of which had offered more variety during the day and helped time pass more quickly. The marches at Tanglin MCTC had the benefit of taking us all beyond the perimeters of the detention centre; they allowed us to reacquaint ourselves, albeit briefly, with the outside world. In contrast all the exercise routines in RNDQ's were carried out on a small parade ground. This was surrounded by thirty-foot high red-brick walls with large shards of glass concreted onto the very top course of bricks. Since no visitors were allowed inside DQ's I wondered if the wall was a dual-purpose construction. I thought it could just as easily have been built to prevent outsiders from getting in as much as to prevent prisoners from getting out, so cut off were we from the outside world.

Although physical fitness was an asset for survival in Pompey DQ's, there was no merit in the myth that you had to be a hard case to survive physically. Mental strength and emotional resilience were of far more value to those destined to spend time inside there, particularly if you wanted to preserve your sanity. I'm sure the regime in DQ's was designed to either break you or render you completely submissive. Personally, I thought of it as an achievement if you managed to serve 90 days inside there without cracking up, or being totally brainwashed. Everyone who served a long sentence in there had their own way of dealing with it, but obviously the longer the sentence, the greater the psychological impact it had on individuals.

In 1970 a hard-hitting TV documentary series called *World in Action* went inside RNDQ's, Portsmouth (the programme, I believe, was actually televised in 1971). The report suggested that at the time it was one of the hardest prisons in the UK.

*

The staff inside DQ's had to be addressed as *"Staff"*. These custodians were either ex-gunnery instructors or ex-royal marines, and old enough to be grandfathers to most of us. Many of these guys were winding down the clock on long service careers that must have spanned more than 30 years. And as far as I could see they appeared to be answerable to no-one.

The rules, daily routines and regime inside Pompey DQ's were as follows: no prisoner was allowed to speak, or converse, with anyone. If you were addressed by a member of staff, then you had to ask them for permission to speak or reply. Everywhere you went you went at the double; except in church. Each day began at 0530 hours with the order: *'Stand by your doors!'*

Cell doors would then be unlocked and thrown open, followed by the command, *'Two steps forward – march!'*

A crashing crescendo of military boots stamping on steel landings could be heard across two floors, as cell occupants came to attention outside their cell. Once everyone had been accounted for, the shout, 'All present and correct, Staff,' could be heard bouncing off walls and echoing through the building by the duty screws on each landing.

Everyone inside then *slopped-out* and returned to their cell to wash and shave. You returned to your cell for breakfast: a bowl of insipid porridge that had the consistency of goo, and a mug of tea. This meal was repeated each weekday, except on Sunday, when you might be surprised to find a sausage, rasher of bacon, or an egg. Other (repetitive) meals included: vegetable soup, boiled potatoes and an occasional sausage; it was always watered down rice pudding afterwards. Fish on Fridays was observed, probably for religious reasons, although this was barely half of a half of tasteless boiled fillet, camouflaged under a watery white sauce and accompanied with a dollop of mashed potato.

After breakfast you made sure your cell was spotless, cleaning the cell floor as well as a shiny stainless-steel piss-pot. Spare kit, too, had to be folded, squared off and laid neatly on your bed ready for inspection. Heaven forbid if anything was out of place, or if dust was found in any nook or cranny, since there was nothing your instructor enjoyed more than putting you on a charge.

Every weekday followed the same routine after breakfast. There would be PE: running around and jumping over a gymnasium horse-box. This was combined with exercises over a reduced assault course, which was contained inside a small parade ground about the size of a tennis court. These exercises were followed by rifle drill that was carried out at the double. After a five or ten-minute breather everything was repeated again. Lunch then intervened, with each meal eaten inside your cell. After meals there was time spent doing ropework. In the afternoon the whole routine of PT, assault course and rifle drill was repeated again. Afterwards the remainder of the day was spent in your cell doing more ropework. The irony for me was that my ropework was for a mat destined for the *Happy H,* or so my instructor informed me. On Saturdays time was reserved for dhobying kit and bedding, and taking a weekly shower. When you were locked in your cell and not doing ropework, or cleaning, you could select one book from a limited selection to read each week.

On Sundays everyone went to church, but for most of us it was not because of any religious conviction but rather to break up the monotony of life inside. After Sunday service a member of staff would stand on a raised dais on the ground floor, whilst we all assembled in front of him, and he'd then recite selected items of news to us from a Sunday tabloid. They would be snippets he found interesting, irrespective of whether or not we wanted to hear what he had to say. It was disappointing, but certainly preferable to the alternative of being banged up alone in your cell. We didn't have access to any newspapers ourselves; there was no radio to listen to, or TV to watch. Very occasionally the instructor in charge of your class would engage in conversation and mention some current event that had made the news in the outside world. This usually happened during stand easy, when we were out on the parade ground and isolated from others. The Sunday paper sermon was the only official news we received, since there were no visitors allowed inside DQ's.

The *World in Action* programme, mentioned earlier, had included interviews with defence ministers and other Members of Parliament, who, in spite of their seniority within government, had been unable to get through the DQ main gates to see what life was like inside. And when a minister did finally manage to gain access, after months of negotiation, all the inmates were confined to their cells; detainees were denied the privilege to describe what everyday conditions were like inside. The minister said the purpose of *his* visit was to look at the fabric of the buiding, to see if it was fit for purpose. He wasn't interested in the well-being of the prisoners. The truth was that we were all completely cut off from the outside world; the only source of verbal communication rested with the DQ staff the naval authorities employed. Even when questioned during the *World in Action* programme the recent Defence Secretary Dr David Owen was not fully aware of what was going on inside RNDQ's during his watch. Although he initiated some reforms, he couldn't say how many, if any, prisoners had been in solitary confinement, or how many had attempted suicide. He conceded, however, that our meals were inadequate and below the recommended daily calorific value.

Personally, I felt my time in RNDQ's was wasted time. I viewed it as a loss, a reduction of my lifespan on earth. I might as well have been dead, since I didn't exist as far as the outside world was concerned. I couldn't believe that a social revolution of peace and love was taking place in the UK during the 1960's, whilst another world of pre-Victorian deprivation co-existed inside RNDQ's.

*

On my second day in DQ's I got picked up for having a dirty piss-pot and put on a charge; technically, the charge was bullshit. My piss-pot wasn't dirty. This portable toilet gleamed inside and out and sparkled like light bouncing off crystal. The screws reckoned you should be able to use the reflection of the stainless-steel base as a mirror for shaving, and you probably could. But each cell had its own A4 size hands-free metal mirror screwed into a wall. My piss-pot was pristine and the only detectable dirt, which I was picked up on, lay inside the bottom of a very thin rim around the top of the pot. The base of the rim didn't shine because it was so narrow I couldn't get any of my fingers inside to rub and polish it. Try as I may, and my hands were by no means large, I couldn't reach the bottom of that narrow rim. And so on the following (third) day I was put on another charge for still having a dirty rim in my piss-pot; it was the second consecutive charge for the same offence. The net result was ten days' loss remissiom, five days for each offence. I was at a loss as to what to do, as my fingers hadn't shrunk and I still couldn't reach the bottom of the rim to clean it.

I nicknamed the screw in charge of our class, Smiler, as I never saw anything that resembled an agreeable expression on his face during all the time I spent in there.

However, on my third day I detected a vestige of human spirit in him, something that I never saw repeated again during the rest of my sentence. He offered me some salutary advice in relation to the cleanliness of my piss-pot, and so avoided the possibility of him charging me again for the same offence on the third consecutive day:

'Alcock. Get your dessert spoon, wrap your duster around the handle and dip it into some boot polish and pumice powder. Work the handle down into the rim of your piss pot, grind and rub it, and keep working it in. Got it?' I nodded. *'Well, bloody well do it! Or you'll be on another charge in the morning.'* When he exited my cell I stood there dumbstruck. I'd heard what he'd said but found it hard to believe. What was all this bullshit about? Perhaps I was too young and naïve then; was it really a lesson about how to use your initiative? I didn't think so. Why would anyone expect you to clean and polish a stainless-steel piss-pot with a metallic spoon handle? God knows. It reminded me of other crazy punishments I'd heard of when I was at HMS Osprey, where guys were made to scrub aircraft hangar floors with a toothbrush! I decided that this was just another mind-bending task to break your resolve, to teach you never to question an order. *You're not paid to think,* was common parlance aimed at the lower ranks. I took Smiler's advice and worked the grime out of the rim and so managed to pass muster the next day.

One Sunday morning, when we were having our weekly news bulletin read out to us, I noticed a picture of George Best on one of the pages. As a Manchester United fan I instinctively shouted out, and managed to get away with it:

'*What's George up to now?*' The duty screw surprisingly dropped his guard, studied the page and obliged. He informed us that George now had a new girlfriend, one more in a long line of beauties, but this time it was a Miss World. I smiled, as it brought back memories of City fans chanting from the Kippax at Maine Road. I was watching City take on United when George tried to beat one player too many and lost the ball. City fans were quick to goad him about his private life. It was just after Eva, his fiancé then, left him and went back home to Denmark. The quick wit and humour of guys on the terraces, albeit in poor taste, never failed to amaze me. All around the ground voices sang out:

> '*This old man, he played three*
> *Georgie Best has got VD*
> *With a knick-knack Paddywack*
> *Give the dog a bone*
> *That's why Eva f---ed off home.*'

I was in 53 Class along with some others – there were about a dozen of us. Each class in DQ's had a number that corresponded to a consecutive week in the year, but we, in 53 Class, were the exception. 53 Class was earmarked for repeat offenders, who had all previously served time in one type of detention facility or another. It was a misconception amongst rookies, experiencing detention for the first time, that we were hardened inmates. But they showed us a deferential respect, something we accepted as a privilege and wore as some kind of badge of honour – although this was totally unwarranted.

One breathless, blistering hot afternoon towards the end of June, I once again fell foul of Smiler's tyranny, this time with other members of 53 Class. We were having a stand easy break for a few minutes and stood in two rows of six. Smiler took it upon himself to confide in us just prior to our second period of rifle drill that day. I was at the front facing him when he bowed his head and held it there for a few moments in silence. I thought he was checking out my boots and gaiters for cleanliness, which made me nervously peak down and check them out too. I needn't have worried, for when he spoke my boots were not the focus of his attention.

'I have some terrible news to report to you,' he said at last. 'Terrible news.'

And without looking up, he added, 'Judy Garland has died.'

'Who?' I exclaimed. His head shot up and he fixed me with his eyes. I'd have been dead if looks could kill.

'Who the f---'s she?' someone else shouted from behind.

'Who said that? Who said that?' snarled Smiler, as he leant forward looking beyond me on both sides, left and right. He tried to identify the culprit from the facial expressions of those standing behind. I was lucky to be let off the hook.

'She was only the greatest actress that ever lived. A wonderful actress; there's never been anyone like her. You'll never see the like of her again. So own up! Who shouted out?' Silence prevailed. He wandered slowly around us on the front row to study the faces of those lined up behind. No one made a sound. I guess no one smiled, or smirked, as Smiler failed to identify who had spoken out of turn. After it became obvious that no one was going to own up for their outburst Smiler returned to the front of our class.

It was immediately after his announcement about Judy Garland that Smiler had us doubling around the parade ground and performing rifle drill exercises under that blinding, scorching sun. The rifles were old Lee Enfield 303s, with the breechbolt, hammer and firing mechanism removed. To describe the exercises as rifle drill was a gross overstatement, since there were only two basic commands you had to follow. As with marching, or doubling, every command was synchronised to be carried out on the beat of your left boot hitting the ground. During these exercises we had to hold the rifle out with our arms fully stretched, one hand holding the butt and the other the barrel. After the command, *'Carry on,'* the rifle would have to be pulled back into the chest and then out again, always in time with the left foot hitting the deck. Our arms were always fully extended when we held the rifle out in front of us, as well as when we had to lift it skywards and hold it high above our heads. The only other command *(surprise, surprise)* was, *'Hold!'* And this was perfectly timed to coincide with you holding the rifle out when it was furthest from your body. So there we were doubling around, holding out our rifles with outstretched arms, going round and round in endless circles. The length of time following the order to, *'Hold,'* was left entirely at the discretion of the instructor. It was he who decided how long we had to hold out the rifle at arm's length, before he relieved the agony by ordering us to, *'Carry on.'* This always brought temporary relief, but on this particular day it didn't take long before my aching arms and leaden legs began to dominate my mindset.

It was apparent Smiler, *the sick bastard,* was going to make us pay for our ignorance about JG. It was one of the hottest days that summer, and Smiler showed no mercy as he continually commanded us to, *'Hold.'* And each time he intentionally, and incrementally it seemed, delayed the instruction to, *'Carry on.'* So there we were doubling around with our arms outstretched forever increasing periods. I'm sure he became lost in his own world that day, oblivious to the torture he was putting us through. I studied him, standing motionless in the middle of our circle, as we doubled around. Sputum, like foam, erupted from the corners of his mouth. He had a glazed maniacal stare that reminded me of the automaton Army instructor in MCTC, Tanglin: the guy who took great pleasure in telling us how a grenade could inflict untold damage on the enemy when it was thrown into a confined space. They were two for a pair: crazed, hypnotised and totally brainwashed.

I continued to double around and around, inside that small, sun-trapped excuse for a parade ground for as long as I could. Sweat was pouring out of me; salt stung my eyes, and my vision became blurred. I couldn't wipe my eyes without letting go of one end of my rifle, so there was no relief. My Number Eight shirt was damp and became heavy as it clinged to my torso. I closed my eyes and prayed for the order to, *'Carry on.'* And then I hit the point of no return; I couldn't take any more. My strength sapped. I might as well have been holding a dumbbell in each outstretched hand instead of sharing the weight of a rifle. My legs turned to jelly as I plodded on until everything exploded inside my head. A voice said, *This is ridiculous; it's futile. F...k it!* I'd had enough, and seized the barrel of my 303 with both hands and broke ranks. I started spinning round and round, much as a discus thrower might in a competition; I wheeled in ever-increasing circles, faster and faster, until I hurled the rifle up towards the top of the perimeter wall. Unfortunately it never made it over the top but clattered high up against it and then bounced back down, severing the wooden butt from the steel barrel as it hit the ground. By the time my rifle had crash-landed, Smiler had pulled out a whistle from the breast pocket in his jacket and was blowing into it as if his life depended upon it. I thought his cheeks, as red and round as any Pink Lady apple, might burst, he was blowing that hard. I think he thought I was going to attack him, but that was never my intention. I simply decided to jack it all in. I needed a break from all the inane, mindless games that were frying my brain on such a blistering hot day.

I was in front of the skipper the next day and placed on a charge for disobeying an order. He sentenced me to three days' solitary confinement, and I was duly marched off to my new accommodation: a cell situated at the far end of the main block on the ground floor. It was well away from the other inmates who were housed over two landings above. The end cell, as it was affectionately known, was not dissimilar to other cells, but unlike them it was stripped of all furnishings. When I first entered I thought it was longer and wider than my other cell but later decided it was the emptiness that supported such an illusion. The outside wall, opposite the cell door as you entered, contained a small arched window high up and close to the ceiling. There was nothing in the room to stand on and so it was impossible to gaze out and view the world outside; however, I could see a slice of sky passing by if I stood on the floor and gazed up at a certain angle.

My sole companions in solitary were a white plastic piss-pot with a few sheets of toilet roll, a white plastic mug with some drinking water and an old, average-sized hardback bible. The end cell was devoid of a bed and bedding, and there wasn't a chair to sit on. I'd either sit on the hard concrete floor and use the equally cold wall as a backrest, or perch myself on my upturned potty. The bible, I found, was too small for both of my buttocks to sit on comfortably. The rule in solitary was that I could drink as much water as I liked, which was a lot less than I had imagined. I put this down to the fact that I was busy doing nothing all day long. Each day my meals were hand-delivered and consisted of four slices of dry white bread: two slices in the morning and two in the afternoon around tea-time. Basically I was on a bread and water diet in solitary confinement, and this lasted for three days. After three days on this diet you were allowed to consume standard DQ fare for the next three days. If you were still being held in solitary after that, then bread and water returned for another three days… and so it alternated…

The duty screw unlocked the door on my first afternoon in there and announced: *'Here you are, Alcock. Here's your bread sandwich.'* Soon after the door was unlocked again and I was called to attention when the medical officer (MO) attended. Although he asked if I was okay, he also informed me that the Skipper would call on his daily rounds in the morning and ask if I had any requests or complaints. He suggested that if I was unhappy with anything, and wanted to escape the mental stress of solitary confinement, then I should request to carry on normal duties; he said this was a way out of solitary and I'd be returned to the fold to serve out the rest of my time. Having only just arrived in solitary I didn't pay too much attention to his advice. I was determined to stick it out in the end cell for as long as possible.

Later that evening one of the screws unlocked the cell door and barked, *'C'mon Alcock, get out here and collect your bedding.'* When I stepped outside the cell I couldn't see anything. I looked around, but there was nothing in the corridor or adjacent to my cell that resembled bedding: no pillows, no blankets, no mattress. All I could see was a long, wide piece of solid wood, the shape and size of an internal door. It was leaning up against a nearby wall and it never crossed my mind that this had anything to do with my bedding.

'Well, *come on then, lad. Get a move on.'*

'What *d'yer mean, Staff? There's no bedding here.'*

'Yer *bed,'* the screw said, pointing to the object that looked like an old door. *'Get yer bed in. Stop hanging about!'*

'But *where are the blankets, Staff? Where's my mattress?'*

'C'mon, *don't piss about. This isn't Aggy Weston's. Get yer bed inside.'* I struggled with the heavy door. *'Now do*

you want any water?' he asked. *'Yes,'* I said automatically;
I really didn't need any as my mug was half full. I just
wanted the freedom to stretch my legs and so swallowed
what I had left in the mug. It was an opportunity to escape
the confines of the cell, and so I sauntered down to an
alcove halfway down the corridor where the wash basins
and taps were housed.

When I returned to the cell and was locked up again,
I noticed a raised block of wood was attached to one end
of my (door) bed; it was as wide as the bed itself, and
presumably was there to replicate a pillow. *Nice one,* I
thought, and rapped it with my knuckles, *a wooden pillow.*
I tried lying on this door for a bed every which way: on
my front, back and sideways. No matter which position
I tried to lie down, it was impossible to get comfortable.
And it was cold, much colder in that cell at night. I had no
covers, and all I was dressed in was a Number 8 working
shirt, trousers and plimsolls with no laces. During that
first night I found out how impossible it was to sleep at
all. I sat there on my wooden bed, which made a change
from the cold, hard floor, but it offered nothing in the way
of comfort.

As daylight gradually faded into night, so the
temperature inside the cell dropped further. I sat there
trying to doze but only became colder and colder. With
no blankets or covers, I couldn't stay still for very long. The
only way I could keep warm was to move around the cell,
and so I devised a routine where I'd alternate between rest
and exercise. At first, during the early part of the evening,
I'd sit on my wooden bed with my back against a wall; then,

as I got colder, I'd do some exercises and pace up and down the cell. This pacing up and down soon evolved into going for a walk. I measured the cell by stepping out around the perimeter walls and doing some crude calculations. I reckoned it was about six yards long by four wide, a rough approximation that needed to be doubled. I guessed that if I walked around it 90 times, hugging the walls, then I'd have walked about a mile. Every time I went for a walk I set myself a goal of two miles, and so the minimum I wanted to achieve was 180 circuits of my cell.

I adopted some exercises which I interspersed with my walks. At first I'd lie down on the wooden bed and do some sit-ups and press-ups, before getting up and going for a walk. When I got up from the bed a second time I'd jump up and down, stretching my arms and legs out in the shape of a star, an exercise I remember doing in PE as a kid at school. I performed this medley of exercises until I felt warm or got tired. Usually a period of rest would follow until I was cold again, and then I'd repeat the whole process again. I continued with this haphazard routine throughout the night. And every hour I heard the chimes of a nearby church clock ringing out: one, two, three, four and five. At five I knew it was time to listen out for the sound of movement above. I'd replay the scene in my head when all the cell doors would be unlocked, and the guys stamped out of their cells to the command of, *'Two steps forward – march!'* They'd crash their boots out onto the steel balcony, in preparation to slop out at 0530 hours.

Later, when the captain arrived on his rounds he asked, as the MO had predicted, if I had, *'Any requests or complaints.'* I let it pass. I reflected, *I've only been in solitary for a dog watch,* and I believed I was built of sterner stuff. I was sure I could stick out my stretch of solitary confinement for longer than one day. It was during that first full day that I discovered I could catnap on my potty, or occasionally on the cell floor. Time was up when my backside became paralysed with numbness.

The highlight of the day was when a shaft of sunlight beamed through the small high window and lit up the floor of the cell for about half an hour. I'd stand there and warm myself, soaking up those precious warm rays of light until they passed over: moments to cherish in solitary, since there was nothing to do in the end cell. I put catching any sunlight in the day high up on my priority list. Even on sunless days I'd stand there and watch clouds race across the sky, and on cold, clear nights I'd try and see the stars.

My ego was telling me that I was in control, saying, '*You can do this; there's nothing to it.'* But then, after a second long, cold, torturous and sleepless night, which involved wandering aimlessly around the cell once more, I couldn't wait for the skipper to appear in the morning at my cell door. When he finally arrived I answered, '*Yes, sir. I'd like to carry on normal duties.'* He duly granted my request and suspended the two remaining days of solitary I hadn't served. I returned to the fold but knew if I was sentenced to solitary confinement again, I'd have the two suspended days tagged on to the end of any new sentence.

Time dragged on and we were well into July when Smiler passed on some more news that was, literally, out of this world.

'*Men have landed on the moon! You wouldn't believe it. It was fantastic. To see men walking on the moon.*' We, in 53 Class, were nonplussed; it didn't mean anything. I thought, *The world knows more about the surface of the moon than they do about the regime and the living conditions we're subjected to inside RNDQ's.*

Not long after this, sometime in August, I received a letter. I'd written to Patrick in Perth, WA, when I was on remand at HMS Terror in Singapore. I informed him of my RN fate and that I'd be serving time in RNDQ, Portsmouth, and forwarded him that address. I now received a reply from him. Smiler handed me the already opened letter; it was something the screws liked to do. They read your mail, whether you were the sender or the recipient.

> *193, Newcastle Street*
> *Perth, WA.*
> *Thurs 24th July*

Hey, Joe!

(This brought a smile to my face, as it reminded me of those days back in *the RD,* when everyone greeted me with, '*Hey Joe,*' after the 1967 Jimi Hendrix record.)

> *I was surprised to see your letter, as I didn't think you were the letter-writing type. Please excuse my writing and spelling as I don't write letters as a rule. I finally have to tell you, man, of how I tripped out on forty – yes, forty – of those beaut pills, man. It*

was a real cool scene and did I go places. I took them with Little Chris who also tripped out. We took them about 7pm and walked around the streets until we turned on and then went back to my pad where Brad and Steph were waiting. Steph had brought over her stereo record player and Brad played his copy of Sergeant Pepper for us. I really zapped out when I heard George playing the sitar. I then realised the Indians are years ahead of us as far as finding peace of mind is concerned. It was a real experience. Then Jenny arrived and I tried to f--- her but I was so high I was impotent. By then it was midnight and she went home whilst Chris and I went up to Hyde Park. We walked around and freaked out with the ducks and reflections on the lake. It was 2am when we got back. I'd been high for 6 hours.

Sue and Jackie then arrived with some others from the Firecracker and I tried to con Sue as she had broken off with Billy. She left after about an hour just as I was starting to come down. Since then I've been on a really cool groove – so peaceful.

I'm now working for the council in the parks and gardens really close to nature. I'm also a vegetarian on a real health beat. Brad flew to Durban the Friday after I received your letter. I've had to play a real cool scene as the COPS have been round to search the place for drugs and they make about 4 visits a week. Old man Arthur has been to the landlord to complain that it's too quiet. He misses being able to complain *to me about the noise. Jenny has been calling every Wednesday and Sunday and I have been giving her a good f---ing, just what she needs (and so do I). Wes is still in jail on remand and goes to court once a week and gets put off for another week. Bad luck me not having $1,000 to bail him out. I'm sending Cindy's address on a note she wrote me. We went up to the National Park and I turned Cindy on with some of those beaut pills. She was fantastic – walking around digging all of NATURE giving off good vibes to a groovy sunset. But she is still the same easy going person as before. She was really wrapped up in the trip and says she appreciates nature more than ever. I really like her and hope you don't mind.*

Pierre is out of jail and him and John are as mental as ever but that's just natural for those two nuts. Billy was picked up on Sunday but broke out of LEEUWIN jail on the following Tuesday. They have been looking for him but still can't catch him. I saw him in town today but he is keeping away from my pad and going north. Val (LC's sister) said it was sad seeing you go and walk out to the plane and then fly off – but as we always said, man, life is sad. I have broken off with her as she was caught nicking stuff with YVETTE. Since then we've had Christine leave her record player here and I've bought DYLAN's new LP NASHVILLE SKYLINE – it has some really gas sounds on like LAY LADY LAY and I THREW IT ALL AWAY. Now for the big surprise! I might be stowing away to Durban in August on the SOUTHERN CROSS so

I can zapp out on some really good grass with Brad and his turned on CHICKS. Anyway must close now so write soon before I go. CHRIS, Little CHRIS, PAUL, ARTHUR, VAL, STEPH and WES send their love and regards, and I hope you get out of the mob OK. HAPPY TURNINGS ON. I would send you some of those beaut pills but the screws would take them and get high. Anyway best of luck and please behave. cheers, Patrick.

I read Cindy's note with her address on it – she wrote '*God Bless You, Joe – I truly mean it, Cindy x.*' And then underneath had added:

I'm sorry about my sister Gwen.
I still haven't forgiven her.

I thought about what she meant by that. And then it dawned on me. Of course it was Gwen: the sister who worked at the same department store as I had, and the one who also had a part-time job at The Waldorf. She must have been the reliable witness who told the cops about me. She would have seen me with the others when we all trooped out of the nightclub on the night of the stabbing.

I went back to Patrick's letter. I had to read it again… and again. I was replaying those times in Perth WA, when I turned on. I became agitated. I'd heard about flashbacks, but had never believed they could happen; I'd never experienced one. But now I realised that this must be what was happening to me. I read Pat's letter for a fourth and fifth time, and knew it was turning me on. I became euphoric and had that buzzing feeling. I tripped out in my cell. I started to groove up and down the full length of the cell beside my bunk. I dropped my right shoulder and swung my right arm demonstrably as I went up and down. I snapped my fingers as I grooved, like some flash dude. I was giddy with delight; I sensed freedom. A voice inside my head screamed, *I've had enough of this shit… I'm not doing it any more. I've had enough… no more shit.* I took off my boots, conscious of how they'd rubbed my toes. I grabbed my plastic bowl full of water and poured the cold water contents into them, until they were topped up. I reasoned it would be impossible to wear my boots because they're now full of water. I laughed thinking, *No more rifle drill.* I'd put an end to that part of DQ life as I believed the water would ruin my boots. I put my white pumps on, which were lighter and more comfortable. I got hold of my sailor's cap and gouged a hole in the white plastic top with my spoon handle and ripped it all off. I then donned the hat upside down: something we'd done on HMS Victorious after watching the Bonnie and Clyde film. When you stripped the white plastic off the top of a sailor's hat we discovered it resembled a trilby, or pork pie hat, when you put it on upside down. At the time, we did it to give us a mod look.

I was still in a heightened frenzy after lunch, when it was time for our cell doors to be unlocked and for us to step outside. I'd put my white front on under my Number 8 shirt; this was now unbuttoned and hanging loose outside my trousers. I rolled the sleeves of my shirt up, and had my ridiculous-looking trilby hat perched on top of my head. When the command to, '*Step outside... March!*' came, I jumped out with everyone else, who followed proper procedure and stamped to attention. Unlike the rest though, I stepped out and continued lifting my legs up and down, as if marking time, and simultaneously swung my arms back and forth. I was still in a groove. I crouched lower, as if performing some impromptu reggae jive. As soon as all the other guys on my landing clocked me they just went wild; they started hooting, cheering and shouting. The whole place erupted, which only served to alert the screws to my inappropriate dress and manic behaviour. When they apprehended me all I heard was laughter and jeering. The screws escorted me down the iron cantilever stairway and back into the confines of the solitary cell on the ground floor. All I kept thinking to myself was, *Well, I can't wear my boots again, they're full of water.* And at the time I wasn't bothered about being banged up in solitary again; at least my antics had brought some light relief to the rest of the guys inside.

When I was hauled up in front of the skipper the next day for *disobeying an order*, he asked if I had anything to say. I again pleaded with him that all I'd done was make a mistake when I *signed on*. I asked if he could recommend to the powers that be that they discharge me ASAP. Needless to say my pleas for freedom were ignored again. I was powerless, and knew deep down there was nothing more I could do other than keep on fighting, fighting for my freedom and to never give in. I was determined that once I got out of Pompey DQ's, I'd have to go on the run again; I'd have to keep up the momentum. The skipper again sentenced me to three days' solitary confinement but this time added the two additional suspended days on from my earlier sentence.

Life inside solitary confinement was the same as before; nothing had changed. This time I went in there more determined to see out the whole of my five-day sentence. The daylight hours remained warm and were ideal for cat-napping and reading the bible. I read St John's gospel:

'I am the voice of one crying in the wilderness.'

But the nights seemed longer, lonelier and colder than before. It was on the second day, whilst taking my morning constitutional, that I noticed a crack in some plaster on one of the battleship-grey walls. I dug my nails in and with a little leverage managed to claw a small piece out; it had the consistency of chalk underneath. I tried writing and so scratched it on the cardinal red flooring of the cell; it stood out like lipstick on a mirror. I pondered on what I could write with my newly acquired writing utensil. I thought some words rather than a picture, as my artistic skills left a lot to be desired. I'd been reading an Ogden Nash book that week and found a number of his poems amusing; but I wanted to convey something more than humour. I wanted to say something to these ancient custodians of ours, a message that reflected the changing times. In the end I hit on some lyrics from a song by The Rooftop Singers:

Walk right in, sit right down
Daddy let your mind roll on.

I thought it also said, *I'm not beaten yet;* and would sound quite hip to the older generation. I scratched the words in large letters at 45 degrees to the cell door, so that when anyone entered it would be impossible for them not to see what I'd written. My next visitor happened to be Nasty, the ex-marine PTI. He was a short barrel of a man, who certainly reinforced the tell-tale sign of ageing men: his waist measurement far exceeded his inside leg measurement, and by the look of him this had probably happened some time ago. He was my waiter that day, and when he unlocked the cell door with my bread sandwich I was sitting on the floor with my back against the wall. My message caught his eye straight away and he stooped down and read it aloud.

'*Huh!*' he grunted.

'*Come on in,*' I said. '*There's plenty of room for you in here. Take a load off, why don't you? Relax, man.*' Nasty's face froze with malevolence. He threw the bread at me and stood there staring at me for a moment, looking for all the world as if he was going to kick out at me. For a moment I wondered, *What's going through his head?* but thankfully he kept a lid on it, turned and left the cell, slamming the door behind him. I felt relieved and couldn't help thinking how different our generations were; we were born into two different worlds – each totally alien to one another.

Time, on my third day in solitary confinement, appeared to drag more than on any other day. And at tea-time on this third day I was sitting down eating my dry bread sandwich, when the keys in my cell door clunked, clicked and turned. It was Nasty who entered and shouted, 'On your feet, Alcock! The MO's here.'

I looked up at him, pointed to my mouth, indicating I couldn't speak until I'd finished chewing and swallowing my mouthful of bread. I made him wait before I said, *'Tell him I'm having my tea.'*

'On your feet, Alcock! The MO's here!' Nasty seemed to lift himself up and down on the balls of his feet as he said this.

'Tell him I'm having my tea. I'll see him when I've finished.'

'I said, get on your feet, Alcock, the MO is waiting outside to see you.'

And with that he aimed his boot and kicked me somewhere in the region of my hip bone.

'Yeah, well. Tell him I'm busy having my tea.' I looked up and could almost see the blood bubbling under his skin; his cheeks grew redder and his face puffed up as though he was about to explode. He stood over me, flabbergasted, apoplectic. I thought he was about to scream something, but only silence accompanied his contorted facial expression. He then did a smart about turn, marched a couple of steps to the cell door and addressed the MO, who was waiting patiently. I heard him say,

'The rating says he is having his tea, sir. He won't get up.'

'Excuse me?'

'The rating says he's having his tea, sir. He refuses to get up and stand to attention.' It was the MO who now entered the cell. *'Alcock – can I say something?'* Still sitting, and having my tea, I looked up at him. He bent slightly over me and spoke quietly.

'You do realise, Alcock, you won't get out of here. You do know that, don't you?'

I stopped chewing and said, *'What do you mean?'*

'Let me explain, Alcock. There are only two ways out of

here. You either do as you're told, and carry on with normal duties, or you end up in Netley. The decision is entirely yours.' I knew Netley, which was near to Southampton, had been the site of a major military hospital since Queen Victoria's day. It was now an operating psychiatric block that served both the Army and Navy. In the RN, Netley was commonly referred to as the Nut House, and appalling stories had circulated about how life inside there was hell. It was claimed electric shock therapy was used, and drugs were administered that could make you continually vomit. Apparently such remedial practices were believed to dramatically alter the behaviour of patients, particularly those with drug and alcohol issues. It was also thought such treatment could *cure* homosexuality, something that was still prohibited in the Armed Forces.

The next day after another aimless, uncomfortable and disturbed night, I weighed up the MO's advice. I decided to request to carry on normal duties when the skipper next appeared on his rounds. He granted me permission to carry on and suspended my outstanding two days of solitary confinement again. It was to be the last time I visited solitary, since no more charges were brought against me during the remainder of my time in RNDQ's.

Before I left DQ's there was an incident that involved Mcreadie, a long-legged lanky lad and a member of 53 Class. We were exercising on the parade ground under the merciless supervision of Nasty, the short, squat and rotund ex-PTI. A small queue had gathered waiting to jump over the horse box, which was a piece of equipment used daily as part of the assault course. Nasty always positioned himself close to the end of the apparatus with his arms outstretched, giving the appearance that he was concerned for our safety. I always doubted whether he would have been much use to anyone if they happened to mistime their vault or landing. On this occasion, when it was Mcreadie's turn to take his run-up towards the horse-box, he began his run languidly enough, and lolloped along until he got to within about ten yards of the box. Suddenly, he then burst into a sprint and took off as if his arse was on fire; he flew full pelt at the horsebox and leapt over it like some super-human gymnast. As he reached the end of the box where Nasty stood, he kicked his legs straight out and caught Nasty with a flying right foot square in the midriff. Nasty, either through complacency or inattentiveness, hadn't registered Mcreadie's change of pace when he attacked the box, and after Mcreadie's foot hit him collapsed like a sack of spuds. *'Take that, you bastard!'* Mcreadie shouted as Nasty clutched his gut and doubled over before hitting the deck. We all watched as he was left rolling around at Mcreadie's feet still clutching his stomach. We all doubled over ourselves; but we were in hysterics. Nasty tried to charge Mcreadie with assault, but he couldn't prove he'd kicked him deliberately. And there were no witnesses present willing to verify what happened, similarly, no one heard Mcreadie's outburst aimed at the instructor.

It wasn't long after this that Mcreadie slit his wrists in his cell. Slop out, first thing in the morning, was when we all doubled down to the ground floor, emptied our piss-pots and collected our razors to return to our cells for a shave. The alarm was raised when Mcreadie didn't return to the ground floor with his razor. When it was discovered what he'd done there was a huge commotion; screws were running everywhere. Eventually an ambulance arrived and he was carted off to hospital, only for him to be returned to DQ's within a few hours.

Within a month Mcreadie had completed his sentence and left us, but before I completed my sentence he was back inside for another stretch in 53 Class. He'd only been free for a couple of weeks, but he was now back with us serving a longer sentence than the one he'd just completed. He looked gaunt, tired and emotionally shattered. His dejected demeanour was there for all to see and was one of the saddest sights I'd seen. This time he wandered through the daily routines in a daze. His dark, hooded eyes reflected sleeplessness. His broken demeanour made me wonder if he cried himself to sleep at night. And I wondered whether he'd be able to carry on.

The MO's words about Netley returned and how the only alternative to serving out your sentence in DQ's was psychiatric treatment. After I finished my time I often wondered what became of Mcreadie. His demise was not dissimilar to that of Young George (YG), the braggart from Osprey who cracked up on the *Happy H*, and who remained fresh in my mind. I wondered how the RN could standby and watch, even be complicit in, the dismantling of the human spirit within young men. God only knows.

The skipper came to see me in my cell before I completed my sentence; Smiler was in attendance.

'I've got you a lovely draft,' the captain said. 'HMS Ganges. You'll love it.'

No I won't, I thought.

'You'll be Ship's company. I'm sure you'll find it most agreeable, Alcock. I'm sure you won't have any problems there. It's a lovely part of the country. And I'm sure it's somewhere where you'll be able to settle down.'

I didn't want to go over old ground and so kept quiet. *I don't want another draft,* I was thinking to myself. *You've not listened to a word I've said. I don't want to be in the Navy. I want to be free.* Smiler was with him. He chirped up:

'I'm not sure ALL COCK has any balls, sir. He appears quite partial to love-ins and sleep-ins, sir. He doesn't like work-ins.' I thought that was quite witty for Smiler, although I'd heard the all cock and no balls comments ad infinitum. I now knew it was him who'd read my letter from Patrick and the turnings on in Oz.

When I finally left RNDQ's I was taken straight to HMS Ganges, which was a shore base near Harwich in Suffolk. I hadn't been home, to the family I lived with in Manchester, for eighteen months now, and so after a couple of days I put in a request for a weekend leave pass. It was turned down on the grounds that there were too many others taking leave at that time. I waited a few days and then put another request in; again I was refused. It was now towards the end of September when I put a third chit in for a weekend leave pass. Again I was turned down; however this time I was offered a couple of days' leave, which would have to be taken in the middle of the week.

'What's the point?' I argued. 'Everyone's at work. I won't see anyone. I haven't been home now for eighteen months.'

'That's your fault. Take it or leave it,' came the stark

reply. I knew I'd be foolish to turn down this offer. It was evident that a weekend pass that covered a weekend, when everyone was likely to be at home, was never going to be offered to me. And it didn't take me long to realise that I wasn't flavour of the month at HMS Ganges; no one, as far as I could see, was going to offer me any support, or go out of their way to help me. If anything, I began to feel ostracised; so much for the prophecy of the RNDQ skipper, that I'd love it at HMS Ganges. I took the offer of a mid-week leave pass and eventually arrived back home in Manchester. I'd already decided I wasn't going to go back on the date when my leave expired. I planned to extend my middle of the week leave pass well into the following week, and thought I'd invent some illness that had prevented me from catching the liberty boat back to Ganges on time.

The ship's regulating office must have notified the police, because during the following week a constable called round at my address. I was lucky that everyone was out when I answered the door. I admitted to the PC that, technically, I was AWOL, but I explained that I'd been in contact with someone infected with measles. I said I believed this was highly infectious, and I had no desire to pass this on to the ship's company. I also said I'd tried, unsuccessfully, to contact the regs at Ganges to explain my situation. I assured him I would try and contact them again but this time would make sure I got through to them. I also confirmed that I planned to return to the ship in a few days' time anyway, as I felt much better. The constable appeared to be appeased, although he did say if the police had to call round again I'd be taken me into custody and handed over to the RN authorities.

When I returned to HMS Ganges the chief regulating officer put me on a charge for desertion. I informed him that he couldn't do that as I wasn't a deserter. There was silence in the reg office. I felt quite pleased with myself, quoting the Queen's Book of Regulations to all the regulation staff who obviously weren't aware of their own rules concerning desertion.

'*Desertion is when a man deserts his post or place of duty with the intent of never returning.*' (Or words to that effect.) '*I returned on board of my own free will; therefore I cannot be a deserter,*' I said.

'*Piss off back to your mess, Alcock,*' replied the jaunty. '*We'll come and fetch you when we want you.*'

When I returned to my mess some guys were playing cards. I thought I might be able to join them, so stood there silently watching and waiting until an appropriate moment presented itself to ask if I could join in. At that point the chief steward burst into the mess:

'*Come on, Alcock. Get your Number Twos on – you're on duty in the wardroom.*'

'*No I'm not. I'm off watch, Chief. I'm starboard watch.*'

'*No you're not; you're on duty watch.*'

'*No I'm not,*' I emphasised. '*Port watch is on duty today.*'

'*Since you went AWOL, and with all your f…ing about, I've changed the watch system. And believe me, Alcock, you're ON duty watch.*'

It was a stitch-up. I knew I should be off watch. I'd calculated which watch I'd be on to coincide with my return. I knew I wouldn't want to be on duty as soon as I arrived back on board. *The bastards,* I thought. I was now convinced they had it in for me. I went to my locker next to my bunk and got changed. Since I'd complied with his order and was getting changed, the heat was temporarily off me; everyone's attention was elsewhere. I grabbed my cigarettes and lighter and made off to the heads. No sooner had I sat down on the toilet seat in trap one (of four) and lit a cigarette, when I heard the chief's voice booming out around the mess.

'*Where is he? Where's Alcock? Find him, someone. Quickly. Look outside. Surround the building. Quick. Don't let him get away.*' I couldn't help laughing to myself inside the cubicle. As if I was going to do a runner; where would I go? All I wanted was a quiet smoke before I was banged up again. Yes; I decided I wasn't going to go on duty, whether the chief had changed the duty watch system or not. And after a few drags on my cigarette someone arrived to check out the heads and banged on my locked door. '*Don't panic,*' I said. '*I'm not going anywhere. I'm just having a smoke. I'll be out shortly.*'

I was put in a cell by the main gates and informed that the original charge of desertion had been changed to long absence; an additional charge of wilful disobedience from the CPO steward for not going on duty as he ordered was also added. The next day I was required to see a medical officer, a two-and-a-half ringer (lieutenant commander) in the sick bay. I guessed, if I was to be put away again before sentence was passed, then the RN had to check me over to see if I was physically fit. I wasn't sure what to expect when I arrived at the sick bay, but once I stepped inside I found an oasis of peace and tranquility. I couldn't believe it: soft music played, featuring waves lapping onto a shore accompanied by tropical birdsong. I sat waiting for my appointment and dreamed I was a million miles away; I closed my eyes and could have been transported back to Gan in the Indian Ocean.

An assistant indicated the MO's office and that he was ready to see me. I knocked on his door before entering and heard, *'Please come in,'* and then, *'have a seat.'* The MO was shuffling papers on his desk and had a pen poised in hand. *'Alcock, is it?'* He looked like he was ticking, or checking something. I responded.

'Yes, sir.'

'And your service number?'

'P100159, sir.'

'Good. We don't want to examine the wrong one, do we? Tell me, Alcock, how do you feel?'

I had been weighing things up and could tell the MO didn't have an axe to grind. He showed no animosity towards me, not like the rest of the ship's company I'd recently encountered. I was pleasantly surprised by his demeanour and manner. And this, together with the welcoming and caring ambience inside the medical centre, had a calming effect on me. I felt both relaxed and comfortable. I saw him as an officer I could trust, someone who addressed me as an equal and didn't talk down to me. I sensed I'd been given a great opportunity to tell someone who had humanitarian ideals exactly how I felt. The recent experiences which I'd witnessed at close quarters, concerning the demise of Mcreadie and YG, meant I could let this guy know how close *I was* to a mental breakdown. Personally, I didn't think I was that close; but who knew what psychological trauma it might cause if I was to receive back-to-back 90-day sentences inside RNDQ? I'd seen the symptoms that destroyed both Mcreadie and Young George and decided to give it my all. I wasn't going to hold back and let our philanthropic friend get a word in edgeways. I realised this was a last-gasp opportunity for me to make a bid for my freedom. I let rip:

'Do you think I'm a criminal? Do I look like a criminal? Have I done anything wrong? Have I committed a crime? What have I done wrong? I haven't done anything wrong – not in the eyes of the law. I made a mistake – that's all! I made a grave mistake. I signed on. I shouldn't have signed on. That's the only mistake I made. Do I deserve to be locked away – to be punished – to be in solitary confinement – to be put on bread and water – no I don't! And I'm not going to do it anymore – I've had enough. They can stick it – I'm not doing it any more. I've asked and asked if I can be discharged – I want a return to civvy street – but they won't listen. I'm not cut out for the services – the Navy. I made a mistake – that's all I did! A monumental mistake!'

The diatribe continued; on and on I went. And he didn't manage to ask another question during the whole of my rant. *'Do you think it's right? Tell me if you think that's right. What have I done to deserve this? Nothing. Nothing. That's what. I haven't done a bloody thing – except make a mistake.'*

The MO asked me to strip off, which I did, and he then gave me a physical examination. All through his procedure I kept up my protestations of innocence. He didn't utter another word, until he said, *'Put your clothes back on.'* I don't think he said anything else before I was escorted back to the cells. As I left I glanced back at him sitting down at his desk lost in thought; he looked straight at me and then began writing as I closed his office door.

I was found guilty of both charges: long absence and wilful disobedience, and had my warrant read out two days later in front of some of the ship's company. It was customary practice to have witnesses attend when sentencing was passed on ratings who had committed serious offences. I couldn't believe it when the commander read out:

'Services no longer required. The rating will serve 42 days in MCTC Colchester, and then be released from Her Majesty's Service.'

To say I was ecstatic is an understatement; I was delirious. I struggled to stand up straight. My legs went weak and I nearly fell over. Although I managed to stand to attention (of sorts), I wobbled when my knees buckled. I was grinning from ear to ear; the euphoria I felt was overwhelming. My head spun; I was dizzy with delight. My raw emotion was there for everyone to see, something that didn't go unnoticed by the jaunty. He later commented back at the Regulating Office: *'If you weren't off to Colchester, Alcock, I'd have you on one or two more charges. Insubordination for one; never mind absent from place of bloody duty.'*

MCTC Colchester was the only detention centre I served time in without losing any remission. I only served 28 days because I kept my nose clean and earned a third off my sentence. I was determined to get back to civvy street and reclaim my freedom as soon as possible; there was no point in misbehaving.

The MCTC itself was spartan; we were all herded into old World War Two, possibly WWI, corrugated steel arc-shaped Nissen huts. They resembled tubular tunnels, with an archaic stove burner in the middle that had long out served its purpose. It was freezing cold at night, and yet it was only October. One day, whilst serving my sentence there, I remember some officials were about to visit. We were instructed to clean up a walkway beneath some telephone wires around an office block, a place where stress-free birds perched and relieved themselves from up above. I couldn't believe it. Another example of service bullshit; or in this case *birdshit*? There we were, down on our hands and knees, scrubbing shit off paving slabs. *What's going on?* I thought. *Surely whoever's visiting has seen birdshit before; they must realise it is a natural bodily function. What's so terrible about nature and seeing it in all its glory?*

I knew I wouldn't have to put up with this crap for much longer, and so I kept my head down and put some effort into the task. I didn't want to make any more waves. I was handed two letters just before I walked free from MCTC Colchester, which I stuffed into my coat inside pocket. I forgot all about them until I took my coat off on the train travelling back home to Manchester. When I was handed them I hadn't noticed they'd been forwarded twice before: from HMS Ganges to the MCTC, but prior to that from RNDQ, Portsmouth, to Ganges. They were both from Australia, and the first I opened and read was from Cindy. It was short and to the point. She wrote:

Hey, Joe I hope this finds you well. I don't know how to say this but Patrick has died. We were tripping out at South Perth Zoo, when he suddenly decided to clamber over a fence and say 'hello' to the polar bears. They killed him. It was horrible. Sorry to be the bringer of bad news but I thought you should know. Look after yourself, Joe, God Bless, Cindy.

I was stunned. I sat there and read it over and over again. Crazy thoughts flashed through my mind about freedom and peace. And then about drugs and Patrick, and how he'd searched for peace of mind. And now, I guess, he'd found it; although I knew it wasn't in the way he would have wanted. I then thought about my own drug-taking, and how I used to turn on to escape reality. How I tried to transcend the world and my troubled life. I knew I'd tried to search for something that was never there. But the reality for me was that now I *was* free. I'd survived these last three years, which at times had seemed like the nine years I'd originally signed on for. But now it was time to start again.

The second letter I opened was from Wes and sent from Fremantle Prison. It read:

Hey Joe, I just want you to know that you still stand with me as before. I don't blame you for anything, so don't worry. I've always had very strong feelings for you, you must know that. I do hope we can stay in touch? I guess my stretch inside will be longer than yours but I hope you eventually manage to get out of the Navy? Please write to me – and who knows, we may meet up again in the future! I do hope so. Love you bud, Wes.

I looked at the dates of both letters and realised that Wes must have written his when Patrick was still alive. I wondered how I had survived when others had died and suffered. It now dawned on me that Wesley thought a lot more of me than I realised, not that it would have made any difference from my perspective. But he must have had some misguided belief that he needed to protect me, hence disarming Pierre, and acting the way he did in the Waldorf. I knew I wouldn't be writing back to Wes or Cindy. I'd already decided to put that part of my life behind me. I realised how lucky I'd been, and recognised how precious life and freedom was. I still had a lot of living to do but knew that I needed to take care. I promised myself on the train home that day that I wasn't going to let anyone lock me up again. And yes, I was now on a journey home to Manchester, but I hoped it was the beginning of a much longer journey – one that would carry me through the rest of my life.

Twelve years later the author had gained a degree and post-graduate diploma. He became a careers officer in the hope that he could inform young people about the 'choices' in their lives and careers – and not make the rash decision he made as a clueless adolescent.

GLOSSARY FOR ROYAL NAVAL SLANG/TERMINOLOGY

Aggie Weston's – Royal naval rests, offering baths lodgings and other facilities.

Airy Fairies – Derogatory name for Fleet Air Arm personnel.

Andrew (The) – The Royal Navy.

Bag off – Sexual intercourse.

Banyan – Beach party with food and beer.

Blue Liners – Naval-issue cigarettes with a blue line across the packet.

Bombay Runner – Very large cockroach.

Bootneck – A royal marine.

Bunrun – The officers mess/wardroom.

Civvies – Civilian clothes; out of uniform.

Crabs – Pubic lice.

Dhoby(ing) – Wash(ing) clothes/uniform.

Dog watch – A derogatory term for sailors who have only been in service for a very short time. Literally, there are two dog watches each lasting a couple of hours.

Flats – Passageways/corridors on the deck of a ship between two hatches.

Four ringer – The rank of a captain.

Gash bin/spitoon – Rubbish bin.

Heads – Toilet.

Jaunty – Master at arms, in charge of regulators – naval police.

Killick – A leading hand; one rank above an able rate but below a petty officer.

Lazy lob – Partial erection.

Liberty boat – A small vessel to take Jack ashore.

Matelot – a sailor.

Nine O'Clockers – A snack at 2100 hours/supper.

Oggin – The sea.

Oppo – Short for opposite number, a (mess) mate.

On the run – Going AWOL;,deserting ship.

Party – Sailor's girl (friend).

Pig – Impolite term for an officer.

Pompey – Portsmouth.

Rabbits – Presents/souveniers.

Regulators/Regs – Naval police.

Scran – Food.

Singers – Singapore.

Stoker – Engine-room mechanic.

Two and a half ringer – Lieutenant commander.